Cats'
Most Wanted™

Also by Alexandra Powe Allred

Dogs' Most Wanted™: The Top 10 Book of Historic Hounds, Professional Pooches, and Canine Oddities

Teaching Basic Obedience: Train the Owner, Train the Dog

Cats'
Most Wanted™

The Top 10 Book of
Mysterious Mousers, Talented
Tabbies, and Feline Oddities

Alexandra Powe Allred

Potomac Books
Washington, D.C.

Please note: The medical advice in this book is not intended to replace what your cat's veterinarian tells you. All health-related problems require professional intervention, and you should see your cat's veterinarian before following any recommendation from this book. Any application of the recommendations is at your discretion, and neither the author nor the publisher assumes any responsibility or liability therefor.

Library of Congress Cataloging-in-Publication Data

Allred, Alexandra Powe, 1965–
    Cats' most wanted : the top 10 book of mysterious mousers, talented tabbies, and feline oddities /
    Alexandra Powe Allred.—1st ed.
        p. cm.
    Includes bibliographical references and index.
    ISBN 1–57488–858–7 (pbk. : alk. paper)
    1. Cats.   2. Cats—Miscellanea.   3. Cat breeds.   I. Title.
SF442.A48   2005
636.8—dc22   2005002261

Printed in the United States on acid-free paper that meets the American National Standards Institute Z39–48 Standard.

Potomac Books, Inc.
22841 Quicksilver Drive
Dulles, Virginia 20166

First Edition

10   9   8   7   6   5   4   3   2   1

Contents

Preface

In September 1988 Evie Swarts of the Society for the Prevention of Cruelty to Animals (SPCA) received a report that a cat had been bound to a tree and set on fire. Swarts went to the rescue, finding Burnie, a three-year-old black cat. After a long, painful recovery, Burnie went on to star in the educational program "Breaking the Cycle of Violence," which teaches compassion, empathy, and justice for animals.

Burnie is just one of many abused animals, and her plight reminds us of the often-troubled history of the cat. How this animal could be so loved and so despised is a mystery. The behavior of cats has always been consistent—they've been faithful companions, strong hunters, and entertaining and engaging friends. In exchange, humans have been anything but consistent. Our ancestors both worshipped and persecuted cats. Today, we love cats. We have cat movies, books, and magazines. Yet we hunt them. We hate them. We neglect and ignore them.

I've been guilty, in part, of the latter. When my sister and I were kids, we used to visit my grandparents, who owned a Siamese named Suda. Suda did not like kids, and as we ran around the house, she would attack us. On one particularly horrifying occasion, Suda hid on top of a bookshelf and lay in wait. Ambush! As I ran around the corner, she pounced on my head, clawing at my scalp. For years I was a bonafide cat hater. Then, not so very long ago, I was presented with a gift—a starving, dehydrated kitten who had unwittingly traveled in the engine compartment of a car in the middle of summer in Texas. I had a choice between allowing the pathetic little guy to come home with me or go to the shelter; and though I already had a vast array of animals, I couldn't let him go to the shelter.

Now I own two cats. One purrs; one chirps. One cuddles; one rubs. One actively seeks attention while the other likes to be sought out. When they sleep, one always wraps an arm around the other. One walks my daughter to the bus every morning while the other hangs out by my garage, waiting for me to come home. Having always been a dog person, now I find myself wondering how I ever managed to get through life without a kitty cat as well. They are so hugely entertaining and sweet and loving that I felt the need to share the wonders of cats.

C. Kay McElroy

King of the jungle and victim of the exotic pets import business.

Along this journey I have met many cat-loving friends, but perhaps the most amazing one is a woman who continuously reminds me about the important role we play in the lives of cats. As you will read in the chapter "The Real Cat Woman," C. Kay McElroy has dedicated her life to saving domestic, feral, and exotic cats who have lost their rightful places in our society. And when I say "rightful place," I mean it. These animals aren't just here for our enjoyment; they have as much a right to life as we do. This is where C. Kay McElroy comes in. She has helped to pass legislation in her state, Mississippi, to ensure the protection and safety of exotic animals. But Mississippi is just one state in a very large country in a very large world—and animal protection is an international issue. It is my hope that this book, and the amazing cats and people within it, will help educate the world about the rightful place our animals have on this planet— even my old nemesis, Suda.

A word from C. Kay McElroy:

During the past seventeen years, I have learned about exotic animal auctions, unscrupulous exotic animal breeders, canned hunting ranches, profit-minded charlatans disguising themselves as conservationists, and very prestigious universities that backdoor their poor, diseased, mistreated laboratory research animals into the black market. There are no rules regulating owning and treatment of exotic animals even as there are more than seventy websites from which one can purchase any exotic animal that one desires to own. The big egos who patronize these sites want to "tame the wild beast" but cannot, and they end up mistreating and/or killing their animals. Did you know that there are approximately 180 accredited zoos that house about 250 tigers, but there are more than 7,000 pet tigers in the United States? There are more tigers living in cages than there are tigers living free in the world. I have seen firsthand lions and tigers housed in cages in basements and cement holes in the ground. I attended my first exotic auction in Missouri in 1987 and am still haunted by the memories of the six-week-old hippo separated from his mother, crying his heart out, and the baby monkey taken from his mother in front of the auction crowd, sold to a woman for $200. Since my first rescue in 1987, I have saved more than two hundred animals, including lions, tigers, leopards, bobcats, cougars, and domestic cats and dogs. This is not even the tiniest tip of the iceberg, but I will continue until my last breath to try to educate people about our precious gift—the animal.

C. Kay McElroy
Cedarhill Animal Sanctuary, Inc.
144 Sanctuary Loop
Caledonia, MS 39740
www.cedrhill.org
ckmcelroy@aol.com

I
Long Live the Cat

Cat Myths

Mystery has always shrouded the feline. The cat is a powerful, agile hunter moving silently through the night, stalking its prey; or a calculating thinker that has incredible patience when setting its trap, yet is impatient with unwanted acts of affection from humans. The cat is a creature of great beauty, defying gravity with athletic feats and supreme acts of grace. From the ancient Egyptians to the Shakespearian era and into modern times legends of the cat have grown into extraordinary myths.

The belief that cats have nine lives and that black cats are bad luck are the undisputed champions of cat myths, which are discussed in the "Bewitching Cats" and "Cats and Superstition" chapters. While there are literally dozens, the following are the most common myths thought by many to be true.

1. CATS ALWAYS LAND ON THEIR FEET

Because of this myth, cats have been the subjects of far too many childish adolescent experiments in which little Timmy dropped Ruffles from the shed roof (or worse). While kittens are born with a self-righting reflex called the vestibular apparatus, they aren't always able to land on their feet. The distance of a jump or fall could be too great or too short for the cat to turn itself around. This myth, which often leads to injury, is one the American Veterinarian Association would like to see go away.

2. TAKE YOUR BREATH AWAY

Careful if you have a newborn in the house. Cats will sneak into the baby's room at night and suck out his or her breath. This myth began during the eighteenth century when cats were once again accepted into the household but were still viewed by many with great suspicion. Whether cats simply smelled sweet milk on the lips of sleeping babes or sought warmth in the crib (something they still do today), survivors of the witch-hunt generations believed cats were dangerous around newborns—a myth that became common *knowledge.*

3. THE CAT'S PURR

"Cats purr only when they are happy." The reality is cats also purr when they are sick, hurt, and in some cases, even when they are dying. Don't trust the purr to mean that everything is all right.

4. DON'T FEED THE BARN CAT

"A good mouser is a hungry mouser." This myth has endured since the Black Plague, when cats were desperately needed to hunt and kill flea-ridden vermin that spread disease and death throughout Europe. The truth is cats will always hunt. Just as all little boys love trucks (there are exceptions as some cats aren't interested in hunting at all, and some boys like Barbie dolls, but that's another book), cats will always enjoy the hunt. In fact, feeding a cat will ensure keeping it around the house or barn to fight the unwanted vermin.

5. CATS AND ALLERGIES

Everyone knows that cat hair is the number one cause of allergies among pet owners, right? Wrong. It's not the hair; it is the cat's saliva on the fur that causes an allergic reaction

Author's collection

One-time stray Benson defies myths about feeding barn cats as she clears the family barn of mice, rats, snakes, insects, and frogs.

among pet lovers. The allergen becomes part of dander (flakes of skin and saliva), which comes off the body during petting and even when the cat is walking through the house.

6. CATS NEED MILK

Mother's milk is the best, but after twelve weeks or so, kittens no longer require milk. Mother Nature and mother cats seem to agree and usually wean the babies naturally. Still, humans have always loved the notion of giving cow milk to kittens. Because cats and kittens used to be so important to the farm, it was a common sight to see cats fighting over spilled milk in the cow-milking station in the barn. Indeed, the notion—if cats wanted the milk so badly, they must really need it—was a good one, and farmers were all too eager to offer a little extra milk to the cats to keep them in the barn. However, the cats did not and do not need the milk. In fact, cow's milk can wreak havoc upon a young cat's digestive system, causing all kinds of gastric disturbances.

7.   CATS NEED GREENS FOR UPSET TUMMIES

Which came first, the chicken or the egg? The upset tummy or the need to chew plants? Cat owners see their precious kitties chewing on green leaves only later to discover piles of leafy vomit. The assumption has always been that cats eat plants to settle their stomachs. Not so, says feline specialist Philip Shanker, DVM, at The Cat Hospital in Campbell, California. According to Shanker, cats eat plants . . . because they can. What might start out as playful batting of the leaves or just plain boredom often ends with the destruction of a favorite houseplant. (See "Most Common Behavioral Problems" for advice on how to discourage this behavior.)

8.   CAT SCRATCH

"You can train your cat not to scratch." Yeah right! Asking a cat not to scratch is like asking a bird not to fly. While you might be able to discourage scratching against your hand or furniture, the action of scratching is very important to cats. Scratching allows cats to flex muscles, leave their scent (which is both a comfort and a survival instinct), and claim their territory. Even cats that have been declawed (a painful procedure that is *highly* discouraged) will still go through the motions of scratching.

9.   CALICOES ARE FEMALE

This myth is based in truth. Almost all calicos are female. According to the College of Veterinary Medicine at the University of Missouri, a recent study revealed that about one out of every three thousand calicoes is male.

10.   CATS ARE LONERS

While cats are independent animals, they are also highly social creatures that enjoy the company of others. Strays will often form large colonies, just as the big cats do, to live and hunt as a large tribe.

The First Cats

Cats do not appear in early cave drawings or rock art because they were not a source of danger or game to prehistoric peoples, but thanks to the discoveries of paleontologists, we know something about ancient cats.

1. THE CREODONTS

The creodonts, the earliest carnivores, bore very little resemblance to today's cat. Slow-witted (as were their prey), with a long body and short limbs, this mammal appeared roughly 60 to 50 million years ago during the Paleocene era. They had powerful jaws with forty-four teeth, thirty-three molars, three incisors, one fang, and seven grinding teeth—perfect for tearing and ripping. They soon evolved into a variety of hunting cats, some as large as the lion. By the Eocene era, the creodonts were virtually extinct, making room for the more powerful and efficient hunters.

2. THE MIACIDS

This mammal had fewer teeth (only forty), including four cheek teeth called carnassials, used for shearing flesh. The miacid was far larger, more powerful, and more thoughtful than the creodont. The miacid trapped its prey and is thought to be the forerunner of today's carnivorous animals, including the feline, but this species did not survive long and evolved into two different creatures.

3. THE HOPLOPHONEUS

The most distinct difference between the hoplophoneus and the dinicitis, the second descendant of the miacid, was the structure of their mouths and jaws. In the hoplophoneus, the upper canines were significantly longer—as they were in the saber-toothed tiger. Otherwise known as the smilodon, the hoplophoneus had a thick, shaggy coat and a large body. It was an active hunter, covering great land mass in its quest for food. The smilodon disappeared more than twelve thousand years ago, whereas its relative, the dinicitis, thrived.

4. THE DINICITIS

The dinicitis, the first of the "stabbing cats," appeared in the Oligocene era, some 40 million years ago. Although it was a plantigrade—a mammal that places all the foot bones down while walking, something today's cat does not do—it had the first cat look. Its sleek body, powerful legs, and long tail made it a hunter to be taken seriously. Like the modern cats, it had three eyelids, but unlike today's felines, it had a very small brain. Not until the pseudaelurus did the earth see the "cat" of modern times.

5. PSEUDAELURUS

Also part of the stabbing cat family, this mammal emerged during the Miocene era, some 20 to 10 million years ago. The pseudaelurus is argued to be the first true big cat, as we know it today, walking on the tips of its toes (digitigrade) like the modern cat. Similar in size to the tiger and with large extra teeth, this cat was highly efficient in stalking and hunting its prey. Today, only one species, known as acinonyx (or the cheetah), exists that came from the modern genera of the pseudaelurus. And, amazingly, very little has changed between the cheetah and its primitive relatives.

6. *FELIS LUNENSIS*

Similar to the modern smaller wildcat, the *Felis lunensis* arrived on the scene during the Pliocene era 12 million years ago. While this cat didn't have the super-sized teeth of the saber-toothed cats, the *Felis lunensis* was still a problem for humans as a competitor of the hunters for birds and small game.

7. THE FELIDAE

In the beginning of the Pleistocene era, large cats such as the lion, giant cheetah, and lynx roamed the forests of Asia, China, and Europe. Archeologists have discovered ruins that suggest China was home to the giant tiger; Europe, to the cave lions and leopards; and gradually, North America, to the giant jaguar. Included in the Felidae family is the smaller-featured feline species that includes the manul and Martelli's wildcat.

8. THE FOREST WILDCATS

By the end of the second Ice Age, three different variations of the wildcat had emerged. Some 600,000 years ago, the cats spread across Europe, Asia, and Africa. The first, the forest wildcat (*Felis silvestris*) appeared throughout Europe and Russia and continues to dwell in forests there today. They are highly antisocial and fierce, similar in looks to the North American bobcat.

q. THE AFRICAN WILDCATS

Like the forest wildcat, the African wildcat (*Felis silvestris libyca*) is nocturnal and, as a result, rarely seen by humans. Its places of origin are North Africa, Israel, Crete, Sicily, and Sardinia. The African wildcat lives on almost any kind of terrain—forest or savannah, rocky or sandy plains—but has typically chosen to remain close to human settlements. Unlike the forest wildcat, this cat can be tamed.

10. **THE ASIATIC WILDCATS**

A natural cave dweller, the Asiatic desert cat (*Felis silvestris ornata*) first appeared in what is today Iran, Pakistan, India, and Asiatic Russia, and continues to live there in present times. Sightings of the Asiatic desert cat are more frequent than that of its European and African cousins, and like the African wildcat, it can be tamed, suggesting the possibility for long-term relationships between cats and humans. In fact, archeological digs in ancient caves reveal the bones of these wildcats. Did ancient man live alongside these early cats? Or were the cats an early food source? Much of the history of early cats is left for speculation, unlike the well-known and sometimes torrid history of the domestication of felines.

From Campsite to Bedside

Just as the wolf began to hang around campfires for scraps of meat and eventually became part of a working relationship with humans, evidence suggests that wildcats began to move closer to human villages in search of food and gradually became domesticated. While the cat probably never sought human companionship for the sake of petting and cuddling, people did serve a purpose, and as long as we were of use to the wildcat, we could expect their company. This has been the modus operandi of the cat since the beginning and has not been changed by domestication.

1. THE CAMPFIRE BUDDY

As humans began to establish settlements, they began to accrue a variety of animals. The domestication of dogs, goats, cows, and certain fowl began long before the domestication of the wildcat. These other animals served as food sources or, in the case of the dog, as hunter/protectors. Wildcats, on the other hand, were noted as effective vermin hunters, who could tidy up the campfire area. Humans created the perfect food sources for rodents—trash and scraps—and in effect, the ideal hunting ground for wildcats. While people and cats did not initially bond, they were so useful to each other at first that they tolerated and accepted the other's presence.

2. THE TEAM PLAYER

As early humans turned from their nomadic ways to farming, they began to amass food supplies. The Mesopotamians and Egyptians learned they could trade and sell grain for power and prestige. But no sooner did they begin this enterprise than there arose a spoiler—the rodent, which stole from their granaries. Desperate to rid themselves of mice and rats, people encouraged cats to live among them, going so far as to provide the felines with shelter, food, and drink in exchange for their skill as efficient mousers.

3. THE GOD

Cats with tabby-like markings similar to the African wildcat established themselves as the guardians of grain. They became so valuable to early Egyptians that they were soon regarded as gods. Bastet, the goddess of fertility and maternity, had the body of a woman and the head of a domesticated cat. She was revered as a representative of the cat's ability to care for people. Supremely successful hunters, cats proved to be powerful, agile, cunning, and when necessary, lethal. Their cool, aloof behavior no doubt created their aura of greatness, and they were considered sacred.

4. THE HOUSEHOLD COMPANION

In April 2004 the archeological team led by Jean-Denis Vigne of the National Museum of Natural History in Paris made an astonishing discovery at a burial site at Shillourokambos, a Stone Age village in Cyprus. An eight-month-old cat's skeleton was found beneath a layer of dirt that was roughly 9,500 years old. Buried next to the body of a thirty-year-old person, it is believed the cat was a pet. This discovery contradicts previous beliefs that cats were domesticated around 4,000 B.C. It was previously believed that cats were a part of most Egyptian households at that time, but this new finding puts the feline in Cyprus as well. Paleobiologist Blaire Van Valkenburgh of the University of California-Los Angeles says, "The burial site strongly suggests at least some cats were tamed at the time. Cyprus is an island. People clearly brought them there for some reason."

A cat figuring was also found at the site, one even older than the bodies of the cat and human, suggesting a "spiritual" reverence for cats. It was considered a great fortune to own and keep a strong feline.

We know that Egyptians believed a cat could bring good luck to the family. When a house cat died, the owners went into mourning. They had the cat embalmed, placed in a wooden coffin, and interred at the Great Temple of Bastet at Bubastis. Only after a proper period of grieving did the family introduce a new cat into the home.

5. **THE COMMODITY**

Grain was not the only thing traded by early humans. Cats were quickly swept into the prosperous business, traveling around the world. Initially, cats were used by sailors who were constantly besieged by rodents aboard ship. A good mouser was worth its weight in gold and was treated with as much respect (or more) among the shipmates as was the captain. The crew understood that their health and livelihoods depended on the strong hunter. While even the dog—man's best friend—was forced to wait for scraps after mealtime, the cat was welcome company in the ship's mess. A cat on board, given full run of the ship, was considered good luck— an excellent way to sail.

6. **THE IMMIGRANT**

From the trade ships, early cats sailed the world. Although Egyptians forbade the export of cats (they wanted to keep this great animal for themselves), the more entrepreneurial Phoenician traders smuggled domesticated cats out of Egypt. Before long, Roman, Babylonian, and Phoenician sailors were sailing to Europe, China, India, and Japan with felines on board. A long-standing joke among cat lovers is how manipulative even the early cat was, using humans to transport them around the world! Well before the birth of Christ, tabbies were fully domesticated in Italy and other parts of Europe.

7. THE EVOLVING FELINE

As cats continued to be transported around the world, the African, European, and Asiatic wildcats began crossbreeding. The short-hairs (presumably of African and European stock) bred with the long-haired descendants of cats from Iran, Afghanistan, and Central Asia, creating new breeds with different physical and behavioral characteristics. These gradual genetic changes laid the groundwork for today's wide and grand variety of cat breeds.

8. THE VICTIMS

Forget Darwin's survival of the fittest. Early cats went through a test of existence that had nothing to do with strength or agility and everything to do with terrible luck. As cats and humans entered the Middle Ages, the Catholic Church began to feel threatened by pagans, including the cat worshippers. Pagan cults were deemed evil, in cahoots with the devil. Highly suspicious of cats, who were often credited with supernatural powers, the Catholic Church ordered that any and all felines should be killed. During this awful period in history, cats were burned, sacrificed, tortured, and murdered in the name of God.

9. THE RESCUERS

By the A.D. 1300, the Catholic Church had another problem to contend with. Millions were dying from the Black Plague, a disease transported by rodents and fleas. With more than one third of the population of Europe dead or dying, the value of the cat outweighed any proclamations the Catholic Church could make. While the Church still deemed the cat evil, people began to embrace felines once again. A natural-born mouser, the cat seemed to be the only way to combat the plague. Yet, so many cats had been destroyed in earlier years, the ratio of rodents to cats made the task of killing all rodents seem impossible. Ironically, dogs had also suffered greatly in previous years, also deemed unsavory by the Church. Together, cats and dogs (namely, the smaller hunting "rat" breeds) battled back against the vermin. By the A.D. 1600, cats and dogs were fully back in favor with humans.

10. THE INTRODUCTION OF BREEDS

Disgusted by the "long ages of neglect, ill-treatment and absolute cruelty" that cats suffered at the hands of humans, British author/artist and noted cat-lover Harrison Weir created the first British cat show in South London in 1871. Although there was a cat show as early as 1598 in Winchester, England, there is no record of how the cats were judged or by what criteria. But at Weir's first show, a written log of physical and behavioral characteristics for domesticated cats was created, initiating the recognition of breeds and the establishment of standards for evaluating them.

Cats in Religion

Throughout the millennia, cats have played a role in religion—from being pagan gods to inspiring parables and fabled lessons in the world's major religions. Although there is no mention of cats in the Christian Bible, felines have long been favored friends of popes, saints, and prophets. In fact, in the book *God's Broker: The Life of John Paul II as Told in His Own Words* by Antoni Gronowicz, Pope John Paul II tells of a dream he had while he was a cardinal. Homeless and half-starved, a mother cat and her six kittens went from building to building, in search of food and shelter from the rain. At every turn, the cats were rudely turned away, and in his dream, the then-cardinal tried in vain to get the people to give shelter and care to the cats. His cries were not heard, but eventually, he awoke from this dream. In the book, the author notes the tremendous sadness on the Pope's face as he recalls the poor cats.

1. ADAM AND EVE

According to ancient Hebrew lore, Adam had a wife, before the infamous Eve, who was named Lilith. A fiery female, Lilith refused to submit to Adam and was banished from the Garden of Eden. While Adam took another wife—and had a whole new set of problems—Lilith roamed the earth as a demon. Sephardic Jews hold the belief that Lilith changed into a large black cat named El Broosha, who searched for newborn babies and, when able to be alone with them, sucked their blood. This horrid tale is the basis for folklore and many scary late-night stories around the campfire.

2. **BUDDHA KITTY**

In Southeast Asia, one Buddhist sect believes that those individuals who reach a higher plane of spirituality are blessed in the afterlife to enter the body of a cat and live life as a cat until that cat dies. Upon the death of the cat, the person's soul enters Paradise. The extraordinary relationship between humans and cats within this Buddhist sect may be seen in their artwork, which shows cats at the feet of certain statues of Buddha. In other Buddhist lore, cats are viewed as good luck and their presence is reason for grand celebrations. For example, in 1925 when King Prajadhipok of Siam (today's Thailand) was coronated, a cat was present to serve as a representative of the former king, Rama VI.

3. **ISLAM AND THE FELINE FRIEND**

Unlike the dog, cats are held in great favor in Islam. Not only Muhammad's teachings but also his personal preferences were regarded as gospel as Islam spread eastward through Asia and Africa after the great prophet's death in A.D. 632. Muhammad had great affection for a cat named Muezza. He took Muezza with him everywhere and loved the cat deeply. Muhammad, it is said, would wash himself in water from which he had seen Muezza drink and is rumored to have cut off the sleeves of his treasured robes rather than disturb his sleeping cat snuggled against the fabrics. When the cat awoke, it bowed to Muhammad, who stroked Muezza three times. Muhammad's cat was given a permanent place in Islamic Paradise, and to this day, cats are allowed inside mosques.

4. **THE CHARTREUX**

The first legend of the Chartreux holds that cats were brought to the Carthusian monastery, the Grande Chartreuse, in southeastern France by knights returning from the Crusades. The cats were a gift to the monks of the monastery that was founded in 1084. In a second legend Carthusian monks traveling to the Cape of Good Hope in South Africa in the seventeenth century discovered this breed and were so enamored with the feline's personality that they brought a pair back to the monastery. Doglike in nature, the Chartreux will protect its owner against danger and will retrieve. However these cats may have come to France and the Grande Chartreuse, they still reside with the monks today and are held in the highest regard.

5. **NOAH'S ARK**

The Manx is cloaked in mystery and surrounded by legends about its tail—or lack thereof. As one story goes, in the early Middle Ages, Viking warriors stole the cats' tails to decorate their helmets. To deprive the Vikings of this prize, European queens began biting the tails off of young kittens. Predating the Viking story is a tale from the Celts that holds that anyone who trod on the tail of a cat would be bitten by a viper. To prevent the good Celts from this possible danger, cats were henceforth born without tails. But perhaps the most beloved Manx legend is from the biblical story of Noah.

The cats, so the story goes, were the last to board Noah's Ark. Because of their independent spirit, they were not at all interested in hurrying aboard. But as the rain began to pour, the anxious Noah slammed the heavy door to the ark, thus catching the tail of the Manx.

Noah's Ark is also the setting for another cat legend. In this story, Noah is faced with the trouble of rats, which doubled and, then, tripled in number soon after he closed the ark door. Noah went to the lions to ask if they could help solve his pest problem, but the lions told him that they would not be able to maneuver around quickly enough to trap the small, active vermin. With great intentions and all his heart, one lion searched for a solution for Noah. In the midst of his efforts, he sneezed and from his nose came the powerful likeness of the lion in the form of two small cats, who promptly put an end to Noah's rat problem.

6. THE VATICAN'S OWN

The Prophet Muhammad was not the only religious figure to be smitten with cats. A large, black-stripped cat named Micetto was a favorite of Pope Leo XII (1760–1829). Born inside the Vatican, Micetto visited the Pope constantly (and, it has been said, the Pope also visited the cat) until the two were inseparable. Like Muhammed, the Pope was unable to resist Micetto as he rested in the folds of the Pope's elegant white robes, an honor for the cat alone.

7. ST. AGATHA

St. Agatha (d. 251), also known as Santo Gato (St. Cat), lived in regions of the Pyrenees Mountains in southwestern France. On her feast day, February 5, she is believed to appear in the form of an angry cat to seek revenge and punish women who have angered her.

8. RELIGIOUS SLEEVES

From the sleeves of Muhammad and Pope Leo XII's great robes came stories of feline friendship and devotion. And these two are not alone. Legend holds that the Italian St. Francis of Assisi (1181–1226) was saved from a plague of mice when a cat miraculously sprang from the sleeve of his robe.

9. ST. GREGORY THE GREAT

This saint, with no worldly possessions of his own, carried with him only his companion, a cat. It is said that the cat gave the great saint inner peace and strength in times of strife and turmoil. When St. Gregory (540–604) sat meditating for hours and hours, his cat was always with him.

10. ST. IVES

St. Ives (1253–1303), known as the patron saint of lawyers, also believed that the companionship of a cat brought serenity and calmness. He often appeared in portraits standing with cats, but was also depicted as a cat himself.

Bewitching Cats

C ats, witchcraft, and the devil have been depicted as a unified team since medieval times. While cats proved themselves to be worthy hunters and companions, a great cloud of superstition was cast over the fair feline. As Edward Topsell once wrote, "The familiars of witches do most ordinarily appear in the shape of cats. . . . This beast is dangerous in body and soul." In uncertain times, mythology and religion played against cats, and made them the scapegoat for pain and suffering. As you will read, while the cat ultimately survived genocide, many superstitions live on.

1. THE PROCLAMATION
In the late fifteenth century, Pope Innocent VIII ordered that all cats be destroyed. The pope adamantly despised magicians and witchcraft, as well as the Freya cult—a cat-worshipping (among other things) sect—and was suspicious of any man, woman, or cat connected with these things. By virtue of being a cat, the medieval feline was between a rock and a hard place. Cats, along with suspected witches, were burned to death.

2. NINE LIVES
During the Middle Ages, many believed that a witch could change into the form of a cat and back again, up to nine

times. Because it was also believed that cats could foretell disasters such as floods, famine, and fires, the thought of witches slipping back and forth between cat and human forms was all the more awful. They—both witches and cats— held untold powers that were both entrancing and terrifying.

3. DEVIL CAT

During the reign of Elizabeth I, witch trials had reached great popularity. In fact, in a twenty-year span, more than 150 witch trials were conducted in the county of Essex, England, alone. In 1566 a mother and her two daughters were put on trial along with their cat, a white spotted feline named Satan. It was so stated that the mother, Agnes Waterhouse, communicated to the devil through her cat Satan. Both Satan and Waterhouse were executed. As concern grew that the spirit of the bedeviled could escape into another soul, suspected witches (and their cats) were burned to ensure eternal damnation.

4. THE MASK OF EVIL

During the witch trials, many became concerned that the (predominantly) women brought before the court might suddenly spring into action, turning into cats and unleashing total havoc upon innocents. The worried began to wear masks on the back of their heads—because cats attack from behind—to fool the devil himself and remain unharmed. Colorful, decorative masks became commonplace in the courtroom.

5. A SPATE OF CONFESSIONS

By the late sixteenth century and early seventeenth century, as panic rose, a surprising number of cat-loving citizens stepped forward to confess their witch-crafting ways. Whether they truly believed they were witches or, more likely, were coerced to come clean, these individuals told the court of their devilish relationships with their cats. In Windsor, England, in 1579, a woman confessed to feeding a demon in the form of a cat with bread, water, and her own blood. Others confessed to using their cats to deliver curses, diseases, or bad luck to unsuspecting villagers. Suddenly, cats were responsible for anything and everything gone awry.

6. BLACK CAT

Sadly, the most frequently named bad-guy cat during the witch trials was the black cat, which became a symbol of mystery and wickedness. As the trials received more and more attention, images of elderly women and black cats were the common set. Bastet, the pagan cat goddess who represented the evilness and danger of cats to the Catholic Church, was frequently depicted as a woman with the face of a female black cat.

7. THE DEMON CATS OF SWEDEN

In Mora, Sweden, in 1699, three hundred children stood accused of using demon cats to steal butter, cheese, and bacon from local villagers. Fifteen children were killed for their crimes, and for the rest of that horrible year, thirty-six children were whipped before the doors of the church could be opened on every Sunday.

8. BLOOD SUCKING CATS

During the sixteenth and seventeenth centuries, many people believed that cats could turn dead bodies into vampires. In the legend of Hecate, cats could bite, then inject blood into the deceased, turning them into vampires. Until Bram Stoker's *Dracula* in 1897, most believed that vampires came in the form of either cats or wolves.

9. SALEM'S CAT

As the witch trials in Europe came to an end, trials began with a fervor in the New World. More than twenty women were executed in 1692, along with an undetermined number of felines. Because early settlers had a much different relationship with cats than Europeans, cats did not suffer quite so much in the colonies. It has been argued that the cats that crossed the Atlantic on the Mayflower had proven valuable, keeping the food supply free of rodents. Still, many of the superstitions regarding cats held in America today are the direct result of the Salem witch trials.

10.   **ALL HALLOW'S EVE**

Today, although we are enlightened and loving toward our friend the cat, damaging cat stereotypes still abound. As an example, it is the common policy for pet stores and animal shelters to pull black kittens and cats from viewing during the weeks preceding Halloween. Sadly, whether for actual witchcraft rituals, disgusting practical stunts, or shock effect, black cats are often harmed during "black cat" festivals at this time of year.

Cats in Ancient Times

B ecause of the importance the feline held in early civilization, it is no surprise that the cat features heavily in ancient mythology. The powerful, fearless hunter represented
good fortune, life, death, and revenge.

1. THE MOTHER OF ALL CATS

During the second century A.D., the great philosopher Plu-
tarch wrote that the Egyptian cat always gave birth to just
one kitten in her first pregnancy. She would have two kittens
in her second pregnancy, adding one kitten to each pregnancy until she reached the number seven. This, he con-
cluded, made an average of twenty-eight kittens per mother
cat—the exact number of days on the lunar calendar—
adding testament to the important role cats played in Egyptian life. The cycle of the cat was equal to the cycle of life.

2. THE LOVING GODDESS

Perhaps the best-known goddess of the feline world is Bastet.
Once worshipped as a lion-headed woman, during the first
millennium B.C., she began to be depicted as a lissom domesticated cat. In some regions, people believed that Bastet
was the daughter of the creator god, Atum; others worshipped Bastet as the daughter of Ra. Regardless of her par-

entage, the significance of Bastet lies in how she was worshipped—as the goddess of childbirth and maternal love.

3. THE POWERFUL CAT

Sekhmet, the sister of Bastet, was a feline goddess believed to have helped wipe out plagues and famine—but not without a price. As is typical of a cat's manner of hunting and killing, Sekhmet's victims were tortured and toyed with until she was ready to withdraw her claws. But when she allowed her subjects some rest, she was as beloved as Bastet. A daughter of Ra, Sekhmet was sent to Eqypt when the sun god feared humans were plotting against him. Encouraged to punish the ungrateful humans, the goddess slaughtered everyone in sight, until the land was red with blood. After several days of killing, Sekhmet had developed a taste for blood, and Ra decided she needed to be stopped. The sun god devised a scheme, in which he fooled the goddess with a mixture of beer and red ochre. Sekhmet lapped up the concoction, thinking it was blood, and was forever cured of her craving. Forgiven for her killings, she remained a symbol of prowess.

4. CAT FIGHT

The Egyptians' cat worship was legendary in the ancient world. Their loyalty to their feline friends was so intense, it is said, that their love and devotion was sometimes used against them. In a 525 B.C. battle between Persia and Egypt, a Persian commander invented a new tactic for combating the strong Egyptian forces. As legend has it, the Persian officer placed cats along the front line of his military. The Egyptians refused to do battle for fear of hurting or killing any cats, and their army was destroyed.

5. THE MIDDLE SISTER

While Bastet ruled Lower Egypt and Sekhmet ruled Upper Egypt, the lion goddess Pakhet (the tearer or she who snatches) held Middle Egypt. Like Sekhmet, Pakhet was feared for her ferocity. Sometimes human, sometimes cat, she punished who and when she saw fit. When Pakhet took human form, she kept the company of cats. For this reason, a woman and her cat were always a welcomed couple in the home of an Egyptian.

6.   THE LEGEND OF HECATE

As legend has it, the Greek goddess Hecate used cats to conjure up the spirits of the dead. As the goddess of magic and a graveyard haunt, she employed a woman who had been turned into a cat, Galenthias, to raid tombs. While this story was recognized as only legend, it was a popular tale throughout Europe, espousing the cat's reputation among the living dead.

7.   OF GODS AND CATS

The Babylonian gods of silver, gold, and wood were always depicted with cats sitting on their shoulders because cats were believed to have mystical powers. Among these powers were an extraordinary ability to hunt, see in the dark, and maneuver among both the living and dead without harm.

8.   RA AND ARTEMIS

While cats held great power on the ground, battling vermin for the Egyptians, much Egyptian mythology places cats in the heavens. Ra, the sun god, it was said, turned himself into a cat every night to fight the evil serpent Apopis. A solar eclipse was considered a sign of Ra's defeat.

Ancient Egyptians believed that Artemis, the moon goddess, turned herself into a cat and hid in the moon so that the dragon-headed monster Typhon couldn't find her and chase her into Egypt. Cats were seen as mysterious creatures of the night, able to hide as well as they could hunt.

9.   PERUVIAN DEMONS

While much of ancient mythology comes from the Greeks and Egyptians, not all cat stories heralded from that part of the world. In the Quechua tribe of Peru, a mythological cat demon named Ccoa was believed to destroy crops with hail and lightening when she was displeased.

10.   GOLDEN FLOWERS

Also known as Kinkwa-neko, these mythological creatures of Japan came in the form of red cats—greatly feared animals that possessed magical powers and could transform themselves into beautiful women. In Japanese lore, Golden Flowers in either form could not be fully trusted.

Cats and Superstitions

S ince the first cat made a bed among humans, many superstitions about the animal have arisen. During mythological times, people believed cats could determine one's lifeline, one's love life, and the weather. Cats could even sour milk and bring good harvests. Many of those early superstitions have lived on through the centuries.

1. BLACK CAT CROSSES YOUR PATH

What could be worse than a black cat crossing your path? Since medieval times, the black cat has been associated with the devil and witches (agents of the devil). To have a black cat cross one's path was very scary business indeed for it was a sure sign that the devil was nearby. Throughout continental Europe and the Americas, when a black cat crossed your path, custom was to quickly retrace your steps, backwards, without turning your back to the cat, so that any chance of meeting with the devil would be avoided. The British, in contrast, believed that to see a black cat, an agent of the devil, in person was a sure sign of being spared.

Today, the superstitious among us no longer believe that black cats are the devil's agents but that they represent bad luck—a silly sentiment rooted in the witch-burning, hysteria-ridden era of our past.

2. CAT IN THE WALL

Cats have not always fared well in Britain, where people once believed that if a cat was holed up inside the construction of a new house—within the walls—good luck would be brought to the homeowners. From the seventeenth to the nineteenth century, the body of a cat within walls or under the front porch of a new home promised good health, good luck, and good fortune. The Black Plague may be responsible for this superstition, thanks to the many cats that effectively killed disease-spreading vermin, wiping out disease and restoring hope to English villagers. Why wouldn't you want a cat in your wall?

3. CATS AND WOMEN

Girls of marrying age who raised and cared for young kittens would never marry, and women who had loved cats as young girls would die as old maids—or so the saying went. In America, it was believed that if a family in the Ozarks kept black cats around the house, their daughters would be old maids. The fear was that a cat's persona was so powerful that women could and would become consumed with love for the feline, forgetting all else. Today, the female-feline connection continues—the vast majority of cat owners are women.

4. A FORK IN THE ROAD

As French lore has it, the black cat can be very lucky indeed. If a black cat is tied at a five-way intersection, the cat will run toward a hidden treasure when released. While most Europeans believed a black cat coming toward you was a sure sign of bad luck, a black cat running away promised good fortune.

5. WEATHER CATS

Many superstitions revolve around weather-forecasting felines. Perhaps this is because ancient cultures associated the cat with fertility or because cats are frequently associated with witches and the ability to perform acts of disaster in the form of violent storms or plagues. In continental Europe, a cat that cleans itself with great fervor is thought to be predicting rain, while in England such an act promises drought. Throughout the world, the twitch of a cat's tail and the way a feline plays, sleeps, or walks may also be a determinant of weather.

6. LUCKY IN CATS, LUCKY IN LOVE

The kind of cat you find—or the kind of cat that finds you—may predict your future. In Britain, white hair on a black cat can mean good fortune in love or wealth, and in continental Europe, a cat given as a gift will bring good fortune, while a cat purchased will be a pet only. In China, should a light colored cat come to your home, you will have good luck. If the cat chooses to stay, good fortune is sure to follow in the form of love or health. In most lucky-charmed cat superstitions, it is the cat that chooses luck's recipient.

7. CATS OF JAPAN

Throughout Japan's history, the relationship between cats and people has been quite agreeable. Unlike in most of the world, the image of the cat in Japan has been relatively positive. Although some early stories describe cats as demons, most Japanese artistic depictions of felines have been done with great sensitivity and love. Japanese sailors believed cats aboard ship brought good luck and could foretell the weather. Three-colored cats—that is, white, red, and black cats—could predict and warn crew members of upcoming storms. Today, sailors from Japan have more cats on board their ships than any other sailors have.

8. WARTS AWAY

For centuries it has been believed that the mere rub of a cat's tail could cure anything from illness to warts. Again perhaps because of early association with witchcraft or ancient connection to maternal love and fertility, superstitions say cats hold certain healing powers. A male tortoiseshell's tail, it is believed, can help remove warts if rubbed against the skin in May. And the rub of a tomcat's tail can similarly remove a sty in the eye.

9. EVERY GOOD HINDU

A popular Hindu belief dictates that a good Hindu must feed at least one cat in a lifetime.

10. THE HEAD OF A CAT

In the Philippines, it is believed that cats sometimes eat the meat of a coconut because long ago the coconut was a cat's head.

Felines and Proverbs

1. A cat is a lion in a jungle of small bushes.

    —Indian proverb

2. The cat has nine lives: three for playing, three for straying, three for staying.

    —English proverb

3. The rat stops still when the eyes of the cat shine.

    —Madagascan proverb

4. Happy owner, happy cat. Indifferent owner, reclusive cat.

    —Chinese proverb

5. A lame cat is better than a swift horse when rats infest the palace.

    —Asian proverb

6. Old cats means young mice.

    —Italian proverb

7. Beware of people who dislike cats.

    —Irish proverb

8.   Handsome cats and fat dung heaps are the sign of a good farmer.

—French proverb

9.   If you play with a cat, you must not mind her scratch.

—Yiddish proverb

10.   Wherever the mice laugh at the cat, there you will find a hole.

—Portuguese proverb

Head-to-Tail Feline Facts

For centuries, scientists have referred to the cat as the perfect animal, and in recent years, zoologists have described felines as the perfect masterpiece of construction. For its relatively small size, the feline is powerful, agile, and graceful with a machinelike precision in the development of nerves and muscles. From their amazing ability to defy gravity to their keen since of balance and hunting skills, cats are truly animals that inspire awe. Below are the top ten facts of feline evolutionary development.

1. CAT'S EYE

Contrary to popular belief, the mighty feline hunters cannot see in the dark. But their superior eyesight does allow them to see in dim light, detecting things humans cannot. In the daylight, the iris of the cat's eye reduces to a mere slit, protecting the inner eye from bright light. At darkness, however, the iris muscles expand, allowing more light to pass through the retina at the back of the eye. A reflective layer in the eye called *tapetum lucidum* produces the glowing eyes we see when a cat is caught in car headlights and allows cats to move through the night, doing what they were designed to do—hunt.

2. THE SCENT MAP

Even the most innocent cat gestures are rooted in ancestral hunting skills. The typical housecat often scratches its chin on the edge of the sofa or coffee table to, one assumes, relieve an itch. In truth, the cat is marking territory. By rubbing its head or flank against furniture, trees, or even people and animals, it leaves its mark, and in taking in other smells, the cat learns about the outside world. By creating a scent map in this way, the hunter learns how to identify different scents.

3. CAT'S WHISKERS

Whiskers are one of the cat's most useful tools, allowing it to literally feel its way through the dark. Studies, including those conducted by four-year-olds with scissors, have shown that once whiskers are cut, cats become very disoriented and agitated. An average of twenty-four deeply embedded whiskers divided equally on either side of the face act as sensory detectors for the cat, providing information about its surroundings. Cats also use their whiskers to gather information once they have captured prey and are too close to look at it.

4. THE SABRE-TOOTHED TIGER

Unlike humans, cats do not possess teeth for grinding. The main function of a cat's teeth is slicing and dicing. The classic cat kill—for both the large and small cats—is breaking the neck of the prey by inserting its fangs into the space between two adjacent cervical vertebrae and forcing the bones apart. Feline hunters are quick and efficient in this action. Scientists believe that the size and the spacing of a small cat's fangs are designed to match the skeletal structure of the standard house rodent—the mere dental structure of the cat makes it the perfect mouse-killing machine. A large cat's teeth are similarly sized and spaced in comparison to their typical prey on the savanna.

5. SOUNDS OF MUSIC

The rustling of little mouse feet might never be detected by the human ear, but to the cat, it is musical. Built like tiny satellite dishes, cat's ears allow them to hear sounds two octaves higher that what humans can detect. Extraordinary hearing is one of the greatest gifts to the hunting cat, that relies on sounds, waiting patiently in the brush (or behind the sofa) for its prey to appear. Why does your house cat respond so intensely to the sound of crinkling paper? It interprets the sound as mice rustling in their burrows. A natural born killer, the cat is constantly honed to sounds we cannot hear and ready to pounce.

6. CAT PRINT

The cat's foot is comprised of soft, spongy pads with tufts of hair between the toes to muffle sounds so that a hunting feline can effectively sneak up on its prey. For this reason, the cat has received the unfair reputation as being sneaky (even evil) when it is truly the ultimate stalking machine. Cats have digitigrade feet, meaning they walk on their toes with claws retracted. Walking this way, they are not only in sprint position, ready for a chase (and pounce) at any moment, but they are also sure not to leave any footprint for anyone or anything to follow. Many experts believe the cheetah, the only member of the cat family unable to retract them, may owe its speed to its claws.

7. CAT HAIRS

Unlike the dog, which through breeding manipulations by humans, developed specific traits such as herding, the cat is a product of natural selection. As a result, cats have a spectacular variety of coat colors and patterns. The coloration of the wildcats is relevant to their habitat. Sandy-colored cats come from the desert or semidesert regions; dark gray or brown-spotted cats originate in densely forested regions; and striped cats are from the jungles or prairies. The domesticated cat's coat is the perfect camouflage for its own back-yard garden. Even as kittens, felines will actively select a hiding or play area that most disguises their own coats. The instinct to be hidden is innate.

8.   FEET FIRST

Undoubtedly, the cat is an amazing hunting machine. But of all its attributes, the cat's ability to land on its feet after falling from the most precarious positions is the most astounding. This skill, called the self-righting or righting reflex, comes from the vestibular apparatus, which is particularly well developed in cats. Located in the inner ear, this organ transmits information to the brain about the positioning of the cat's head in relation to the ground. The instant a message is received, the cat squares its head to the ground and the rest of the body aligns itself with the head. In a fraction of a second, the cat is able to turn itself to the perfect landing position.

9.   CAT'S TAIL

As you will later read in the chapter "Cat Tails," the cat tail is very expressive in regards to a cat's mood. Cats communicate with other animals and their owners with their tails. As the efficient hunter, the cat also uses its tail as a counter-weight, so that it can peer over a ledge or a narrow passage without losing its balance. Their tails also guides cats as they change direction during a high-speed chase. Using the cheetah as an example, the tail is a vital tool in the chase and capture of prey. As the cheetah makes sharp changes in direction, its powerful tail snaps back and forth, keeping the cat from losing its balance and on track behind the fleeing prey. Finally, in the self-righting action, the tail is used to maintain balance and enable a cat to land on its feet.

10.   JUMPING CAT FLASH

Remarkably, cats can jump up to six times their own height with the aid of their powerful hind legs. Although they appear to jump, and climb, simply for the love of jumping, and

Author's collection

The cat's amazing balancing act.

climbing, cats, from the first wildcats to today's house cats, have instinctively tried to watch the world from the highest possible post. Using a high vantage point, they can spy possible vermin and stay out of harm's way, avoiding predators such as coyotes or dogs. But what goes up doesn't always come down—easily. Thanks to the design of their claws and feet, a downward climb can be difficult for a cat. To avoid a difficult climb, cats have always been good judges of how far up to go. Only when they are inexperienced or in a panic to escape another animal will they forget themselves and climb too high. Cats do get stuck in trees—that's not just in the movies—but if left alone, cats will eventually get hungry and find a way down. (If you find yourself watching a cat climb down a tree, you might want to turn the other way. Cats are not particularly graceful on the way down, and you may embarrass the cat by watching.)

Benson is rescued after enduring twenty-two hours of
sleet and rain. Yes, firemen still do this!

The Hunter: Your Cat's Ancestral Traits

The need to hunt is just as prevalent in the lives of domesticated cats today as it was for the wildcats centuries ago. The notion that farm cats should not be fed is a myth. In fact, if the cat is fed, it is more likely to reside on the farm and be the effective mouser it was hoped to be. Cats are, by nature, nocturnal, predatory, and territorial—all the makings of the perfect hunting machine. Whether a feral, barn, or house cat, the instinct to hunt during the night is alive and kicking. Here are the top ten links between the lynx and your purring tabby.

1. MOTHER KNOWS BEST

While the mother cat still has newborns in her nest, she will kill her prey before bringing it back to her babies because they are too young to watch and learn and because there is always the risk the still-live prey could hurt her young. Once the kittens are a little older, the mother cat will bring home live prey so they can watch how it is killed, and eventually, the kittens will go along with their mother to watch her ambush and kill dinner. In the wild, kittens are expected to fend for and feed themselves by the age of four to six months. Domesticated cats, while under less pressure to educate their offspring, still encourage kittens at four to six months to make mock kills on inanimate objects. Even the apparently innocent rough and tumble play of kittens is not without purpose. They are learning how to use their claws, pounce, bite, and jump on each other.

2. LOCATION, LOCATION, LOCATION

Until the kitten is about twenty to thirty days old, the nest must be secure, snug, and out of the reach of other carnivores. But once the kittens' teeth begin to break through their gums and they are ready to eat the solid foods their mother brings home, she will move them to a new nest, near a better food source. Whether in the wild or domesticated, mother cats instinctually make this move with all the kittens. Nests may also be abandoned because of prying humans or wild animals stalking about.

3. WILD HUNTS

Cats in the wild eat their kills quickly because of the threat of scavengers encroaching on their meal. In fact, big cats will often eat as much as they can stomach because they could go days without another kill.

4. THE DOMESTICATED HUNT

Well-fed domesticated cats will take their time while eating, often playing with their prey, carrying it back to their owners, or even abandoning it altogether. Having captured a mouse, for example, the cat will eat its head and work down the body, brushing aside fur and skin. (If consumed, the fur and skin are usually regurgitated later.) But hungry or not, the hunting instinct resides in cats, which will even kill unsavory vermin, including moles and shrews, animals that are not considered to be tasty to cats. The bird is considered the best hunt. Studies show that as many as 90 percent of chased birds escape, making a victory all the tastier. A cat will always devour a bird—a feline's delicacy.

5. THE HOUSEBOUND HUNTER

The hunt is what all cats crave, and for this reason, it is important that your cat have something to hunt. Whether it is a creative pull toy, a stuffed animal on string, or a ball, cats need the physical and emotional outlet of the chase and capture. (Be sure to be present when your cat plays with string or yarn as it may become entangled and panic or even be strangled.)

6. **THE INDOOR CHATTERBOX**

An indoor cat that spots a bird through the window may start chattering in frustration. Having seen a bird close at hand—or paw—the cat becomes transfixed, watching its prey's every movement. Slowly, the cat, imagining the kill of such tasty prey, begins to emit a strange chattering-clicking-moaning sound. Called the vacuum activity, this sound is the cat's emulation of the practice of delivering a killing bite, or a bite meant to give a fatal blow to the back of the prey's neck.

7. **THE METHOD: STALKING**

Eyes wide, ears forward, body hovered just above the ground, and legs primed ready to spring, the cat fixates on its victim and begins the stalking motion. The cat moves slowly and cautiously toward its intended victim, carefully gauging its own distance from the target and the movement of the prey. In what is known as the "slink run," the cat narrows the gap between itself and the prey, pausing periodically to assess its victim further. Ideally, the cat searches for a place of cover as it closes in so it can better surprise the victim at the last moment.

8. **THE AMBUSH AND THE KILL**

Tail twitching in anticipation, the cat crouches very low, waiting for just the right moment to pounce. When the timing is right, the cat leaps, claws and paws extended, onto its prey. No sooner does the cat make contact with the prey than it uses the claws of its powerful forepaws to bring the animal down, forcing it into a position for biting. The ideal kill is a bite at the base of the neck, severing the spine. But the plan does not always go smoothly, and for this reason, the cat will often strike the victim to daze it, thus allowing the cat to move in for the kill. To the untrained eye, this can be perceived as a "cat and mouse" game of torture. In truth, the cat is cautiously hitting the victim to be sure it does not bite back.

9. CAT'S GOT YOUR TONGUE

Leonardo de Vinci once said the cat was a masterpiece. Indeed. From its tail to its eyes, it appears to be the perfect machine of efficiency. In regard to hunting, even the cat's tongue is well designed. Covered in sharp hairlike points called papillae, the tongue enables the cat to effectively scrape blood and flesh from bones, cleaning off every last possible morsel for consumption.

10. THE PATROL

As you have read, the cat is such a mighty hunter because of its great physical abilities and instincts. But it is the cat's sense of territorialism that allows it to find food in the first place. Constant patrols are what hone the hunting skills of lions on the savanna and outdoor kitties alike. As the cat leaves its home base and picks up new scents—birds or mice nests—it learns and registers every nook and cranny of its territory. Whether a garden, the house, or a vast terrain, cats record anything new or different, and wait. Perhaps this is how the reputation of the lazy cat began, as it often appears that cats have nothing else to do but sit, looking sleepy-eyed and disconnected. That is, until something stirs.

II
Curiosity and
the Cat

Stories of Survival and Rescue

It has been argued that cats are among the strongest animals alive, pound for pound. Their abilities to climb, hunt, scale, and leap are surpassed only by their survival instincts. While stories of survival are in the thousands for domesticated felines, only a sampling can be offered here as testament to the amazing cat. These are my personal top ten.

1. **SEPTEMBER 11**

On that fateful day in American history, more than 150 pets were rescued from apartment buildings near the World Trade Center. Many required medical attention, and many others were killed and/or lost. In the days after September 11, it was often the little things that gave people hope and joy. In this particular story, that little thing was a cat named Precious. Left alone for eighteen days following the terrorist attack, Precious suffered from dehydration, burns, eye injuries from flying glass, and inhalation of dust and smoke, but somehow she managed to find her way to the roof and cried for help. She was discovered there by a search and rescue dog—oh, the horror! Precious's rescue story made national news—as one of the first good stories the nation had heard in a long time. Precious was later honored 2001's "Cat of the Year" at the Westminster Cat Show.

2. SEPTEMBER'S OTHER CAT

When the Twin Towers collapsed, too many lives went with them. Stories of survival—any survival—became a kind of lifeline for the men and women who risked life and limb to sift through the rubble. So when a mother cat was found amidst the destruction in what was once a restaurant, the wondrous news spread quickly. The mother cat, christened "Hope" by her rescuers, was emaciated, dehydrated, and suffering from the flu. Her babies—Freedom, Amber, and Flag—also survived and flourished, bringing much happiness in a time of great sorrow.

3. A LITTLE FAITH

In September 1940, during the World War II air raids on London, a small tabby named Faith appeared on the steps of St. Augustine's Church on Watling Street, looking for food and shelter. The rector adopted her, taking her to live in the rectory house adjoining the church. There, Faith had a small kitten named Panda, and they lived very happily until Faith decided it was time to move and carried the kitten down three stories to the other side of the house. When the rector discovered that Faith had moved with her kitten, he located Panda and carried her back up to his room. Faith retrieved the kitten and went back downstairs to her new nest. She and the rector swapped Panda three times. A few days later, when a bomb slammed into the side of the rectory house, no one believed the occupants could have survived. While the rector had luckily been out of the house when the bomb was dropped, he was sure Faith was gone. Still, he called for her until he heard faint mews from the corner of the house that was still intact, the place Faith had chosen for her new nest. Buried in rubble with Panda between her paws was Faith, unharmed. She was decorated for her courage during the war.

4. FIRE CAT

In the late 1990s Scarlett became a famous cat. A neglected and abused stray—like thousands of other abandoned cats—

she had a litter of kittens in an old building in Brooklyn, New York. Shortly after her kittens' births, Scarlett's life took a terrifying turn—the old building where she and her litter sheltered caught fire. Firefighters quickly appeared on the scene, but they were unable to control the raging flames. Suddenly, out of the smoke and fire came a small cat carrying a kitten. Both mother and baby showed the signs of having been nearly trapped by the overwhelming heat and fire. Firefighter David Gianelli saw Scarlett and went to help, but the cat dropped her kitten and raced back into the burning building. Again and again, she appeared with another kitten, each time taking longer to return and each time showing more signs of suffering from burns and smoke inhalation.

Finally, with the last kitten out, Scarlett collapsed by Fireman Gianelli, who found treatment for Scarlett and care for the kittens. Because of him, all of the cats survived and were adopted by loving families.

A story of sacrifice, pain, and recovery, Scarlett's tale illustrates the will and devotion of mother cats everywhere. To immortalize her selfless behavior, Jane Martin and Jean-Claude Suares have dedicated their book, *Scarlett Saves Her Family: The Heartwarming True Story of a Homeless Mother Cat Who Rescued Her Kittens from a Raging Fire* (Simon & Schuster, 1997), to her heroism. In fact, the book is also a tribute to Scarlett's people—the fantastic firefighter, the doctors, the caring rescuers, the adoptive families for Scarlett and her kittens, and to cat lovers everywhere.

5.   SOOTY THE NAVIGATOR

When Sooty's owner moved from Swansea, Wales, to Bath, England—a distance of about ninety miles—the black cat was content to stay around the new home as long as the owner's daughter remained with them. But when the daughter moved back to Swansea, Sooty took matters into his own paws: he set out to find her, making an arduous six-month-long journey to Wales. Animal psychologists believe this journey was possible because cats have strong navigational senses and can trace old hunting grounds. What is not clear is how Sooty found his young mistress in an apartment he had never seen, in a neighborhood where he had never been. Some powers, animal experts agree, just cannot be explained, and as we all know, much of what cats do remains a mystery to us humans.

6. SOONER OR LATER

Under the Texas sun in the summer of 2003, a small, frightened tabby sat in the engine compartment of an SUV for more than forty-eight hours, dehydrated and burned from his journey. His unexpected trip began in Oklahoma, where the kitten climbed up under the hood of the vehicle to escape the heat of the day. As a feral cat, he was used to wandering the vast farmland he called home. But when the car engine started, the kitten was too frightened to move. Car owner Audra Dahl had no idea she had the company of the feline, but when she kept hearing mewing from her car, she began to suspect something was wrong. Two more days passed before she located the cat, and it took another full day for the kitten to be coaxed out. Since the cat came from Oklahoma, it was aptly named Sooner. Today, Sooner works full-time as a mouser in a horse barn and is loved to ridiculous proportions.

7. BLIND FAITH

In a suburb of London a group of neighbors had watched with concern as a wild and malnourished tabby kitten took up residence with a family of foxes. Soon enough, as the fox pups grew, they appeared to be more and more aggressive toward the kitten, and neighbors knew it was only a matter of time before the cat would be their next meal. One of the neighbors, Barbara Jarman, decided she needed to rescue the cat, and borrowing a cat trap, she was able to catch the frightened kitten. Upon capture it was discovered that the kitten was completely blind—not because of natural causes but because of deliberate cruelty. On the day of Princess Diana's funeral, Jarman's vet was to put the kitten out of his misery, but instead—perhaps because of the outpouring of grief over Diana's sudden death—the vet offered to remove the cat's eyes for free, as long as Jarman promised to care for the cat.

Maybe because her own father had been blind or because the cat had been through so much Jarman agreed. Within a year, Arnie (named after Arnold Schwarzenegger) had learned to trust his new family and mind map every room in his new house and backyard, using his ears or whiskers to rub against walls, railings, and furniture. As a reward for this remarkable journey, Arnie was the winner of the Best Turn-Around Award at the Cats Protection Rescue Cat of the Year Award ceremony in 2003.

8. YELLOW CAT

In April 2004 Florida businessman Norman Goldberg got the surprise of his life, opening a shipment of four hundred birdcages that had recently arrived from China. When he opened the shipment, a severely malnourished cat jumped out from among the cages. Weighing only three pounds, this remarkable cat is believed to have survived the monthlong trip by chewing on cardboard boxes. Named China by Hillsborough County Animal Services in Tampa, Florida, the yellow-colored cat was given intravenous fluids and soon was feeding on her own. Few details of China's trip are known. She began her journey the first week of March at the factory where workers had loaded the cages into a forty-foot metal container. From China, the container arrived by ship in Los Angeles on April 1, 2004, and then traveled by train for the next two weeks to Tampa.

When Goldberg e-mailed the factory in China to tell them about the unexpected traveler, he received an immediate response. "We are very happy to know our cat is still alive. Would you please tell us more information about our cat? Is it a yellow or gray one? Because we have two cats, but they disappeared one month ago. . . . Please raise it, or you can give it to the animal asylum."

Sadly, there is no news of the gray cat, but China was quickly adopted. Flooded with phone calls from cat lovers around the world, Hillsborough County Animal Services was able to choose a loving home most suitable for China.

9. LILO AND CRATE

Named after Lilo of Disney's *Lilo and Stitch*, an eight-month-old kitten survived a month-long journey from Hawaii to Junction City, Kansas, in December 2002. On December 2, 2002, the kitten climbed into a set of box springs unnoticed and simply disappeared. Fearing he had trapped himself inside a crate, Lilo's family and their packers began pounding on their moving crates, hoping to hear the cat mew, but Lilo—frightened and alone—remained silent. It was not until January 8, 2003, that he decided to speak out. As the crates passed through Denver, a North American Van Lines worker reported hearing the sounds of faint mewing. Still, the crate passed on to Kansas. When Lilo was retrieved, he was immediately treated for starvation and dehydration. Incredibly, Lilo regained all his strength.

10. HELP! MAD CAT!

Sometimes, it is necessary to be rescued from a cat. A new mother cat turned aggressive when the owner of her home left, leaving an unsuspecting Elisabeta Costici of London to fend for herself. With the cat hissing and snarling wildly, Costici was held hostage for almost three hours until the local fire department could come to the woman's rescue, backing the mad mother cat away from the new homeowner.

The Cats of War

You'll never hear stories about bomb-sniffing cats or military-trained attack cats, but cats have been part of war history along with the canine. While their experiences were fewer in numbers, they sacrificed no less than their archrival—the dog. Cats have a long history of fighting alongside humans in battle. These are my top ten examples of cats showing great strength and resilience under fire.

1. **CAT CALLS**

Legend has it that cats were once set upon the Egyptians in time of war, rendering them helpless for battle. So great was the Egyptians' love for felines, they refused to fight in fear of killing the animals and lost the battle. This legendary battle aside, cats have been used in great war strategies throughout the martial history of humans. Everyone from the Egyptians to the Romans to Napoleon used cats to carry messages to and fro. More fortunate cats simply wore small canisters around their necks while others, it has been said, were fed top secret messages—which could not be discovered—only to be slaughtered at the receiving end.

2. **BIOLOGICAL CAT-FARE**

During the sixteenth century, when the Hapsburgs of the powerful Austrian/Hungarian Empire ruled much of Europe, cats were a favorite tool of warfare. Well before the Haps-burgs entered enemy camps, cats were sent in with poison strapped to their backs to infest enemy territories (and peo-ples) with disease and death. An early form of biological war-fare, leaking bottles or sacks allowed the poisons to seep out slowly, quickly spreading toxins through marketplaces, watering holes, and homes.

3. VALOR IN COMBAT

Simon, the only cat to have ever received the dubious honor of the People's Dispensary for Sick Animals (PDSA) Dikin Award for Valor in Combat, showed his mettle in 1948 when he came aboard the HMS *Amethyst*. Dubbed Able Sea Cat Simon by crew members, he was picked up along Hong Kong's Stonecutters Island. With full run of the ship, Simon shared quarters with Lt. Cmdr. Bernard Skinner for one year until the HMS *Amethyst* was caught between warring Chi-nese Nationalists and Communists. The ship was shelled heavily, killing Skinner and most of the crew. Simon, though slightly burned, survived and made daily visits to the wounded sailors. Upon return to England, Simon was quar-antined, where he died. Able Sea Cat Simon was buried with full naval honors.

4. THE BLACK CAT

In 1941 a small black cat was forced into the sea, paddling for hours, when the German *Bismark* was sunk by the HMS *Cossack*. British soldiers fished the cat with seven lives out of the ocean, promptly named him Oscar, and brought him back to live on the HMS *Cossack*, where he resided happily until it was struck and sunk five months later by the Ger-mans. Surviving the hit and the oceans once again, the cat was down to five lives when he was picked up by sailors from the HMS *Ark Royal*. Three weeks later a German U-boat struck the HMS *Ark Royal*, leaving Oscar down another two lives and paddling in the open seas. It is uncertain how many more hours Oscar had to swim before he was rescued again by another British ship. Nursed back to health, it was decided Oscar had seen enough action and didn't need to board any more of the Royal Navy's ships. According to naval records, Oscar resided at the Home for Sailors in Belfast until 1955 when he died—of natural causes.

5.   CAT BEARING NEWS

During World War II, a French soldier named Guillaume discovered that a German soldier on enemy lines not too far from where his unit was posted had just become a father. As it turns out, Guillaume was married to the German soldier's cousin, who sent word that the young German had become a father while he was away at war. The resourceful Guillaume tied a note to a cooperative cat and sent it across "no-man's-land," through barbed wire and enemy trenches, and the grateful German received the news.

6.   RUN, KITTY, RUN

During the siege of Stalingrad in 1942, a brave little kitty named Mourko the Cat was used to carry messages back and forth between two buildings occupied by the Allied forces while German troops were on the ground. It was common during this time for dogs to be used to carry messages back and forth; there are countless stories of incredibly brave canines, dodging bullets when it was discovered they were messengers. Though the Germans shot dogs so messages could not be delivered, no one thought anything about a cat. They probably didn't even see Mourko at all as he slipped easily between, under, and over debris from one side of the road to the other.

7.   BAY OF THE CATS

Recently declassified information from the National Security Archives revealed a little known cat caper that involved a kitten dubbed "Acoustic Kitty." An effort to listen in on top-secret conversations between communists involved a trained cat that would wander into a room and settle down for a cat nap, allowing the Western world to learn what the Cubans and Soviets were up to. Unfortunately, Acoustic Kitty had a penchant for wandering off during missions, and one day, though he had been well trained—and fitted with internal electronic listening devices—the expensive cat wandered into the street and was killed by a taxi. The plan was abandoned in 1967.

8. PRISONER OF DEVOTION

In times of strife, cats have always given comfort. During the reign of Elizabeth I, the third Earl of Southampton was imprisoned for treason. The Earl's cat, Trixie, was determined to do time with her master, who was taken to the Tower of London. Trixie traveled across London and maneuvered through the tower until she was able to climb down a chimney that led to his cell. Once with him, Trixie remained with her master until his release some two years later. So moved was he by Trixie's love and devotion, the Earl had a portrait made of Trixie and himself living in the cell.

9. WINDY, SUPER ACE FLYER

Forget everything you thought you knew about cats. Windy, a sidekick to Wing Cmdr. Guy Gibson V.C., the famous dam buster and ace fighter pilot of World War II, loved to swim, fly, and live life as a fighting cat. Windy and Gibson flew many dangerous wartime missions, putting in countless hours in the air and shooting down enemy planes. Windy reportedly loved the action and was inclined to take a swim whenever the chance arose. She is the only known ace flyer sidekick World War II vet cat.

10. CATS OF TEL AVIV

Today the term "war cats" has a new meaning. In Tel Aviv, while daily battles rage between the Israelis and Palestinians, hundreds of cats are abandoned as families are forced to evacuate and are unable to take along family pets. In many sad cases, the animals are made instantly homeless by a single, deadly blast. Feral colonies are left behind to fend for themselves. That is, they were before the creation of The Cat Welfare Society of Israel (CWSI), an organization that fights to feed and shelter lost cats of the war. For more information about this great cause, log on to *www.cats.org.il*.

Disaster Preparation for Your Cat

Over the years the lives of many pets have been lost to natural disasters such as tornadoes, hurricanes, and floods. In recent times, entire towns have been off-limits to homeowners due to the danger of overturned freight trains or trucks hauling hazardous materials. Since September 11, deadly acts of terrorism on U.S. soil seem to be a greater threat, and the devastating tsunami in Asia in December 2004 brought horrible images of human and animal suffering. To assure a fast and safe exit for your family—including your four-legged loved ones—rescue agencies and veterinarians believe a to-do list in the event of a disaster is essential.

1. HAVE A PLAN

Have a plan that everyone understands so that you, your family, and your pets can be ready to move in a matter of moments. The plan should include a fire route in your home. If you live in a flood plane or earthquake zone, you must know where to go in an emergency, what shelters take pets, where your family meeting point will be, and what kind of transportation you and your pets will be taking to safety. By having a list of instructions, should you be injured or taken ill, rescue workers and caregivers will know what to do with your cat.

2. **TALK TO YOUR VETERINARIAN**

It is vital that your vet is on board with your disaster plan. Find out about what services your vet plans to offer the community in the event of a disaster. Will he or she be on hand? What about the office staff? What will the office hours be? Should something happen to the established office, where should you seek care?

3. **IDENTIFY YOUR CAT PROPERLY**

Every year powerful storms sweep through small towns and cities, putting hundreds of animals on the run for their lives. In some cases, newswires report stories of animals traveling hundreds of miles from home. Identifying these confused and/or hurt animals is difficult, so it is important that your cat has some form of identification that will help locate either you or your veterinarian when your cat is found. Because cats must have a breakaway collar, in case it catches on tree limbs or brushes, you will need to talk to your vet about how your cat can be properly identified.

4. **UPDATE YOUR CAT'S MEDICAL RECORDS**

Keeping medical records up-to-date assures that you and your vet are clear about your kitty's health and welfare. Your cat's record should include all possible emergency contact numbers for you—even if this means giving the telephone number of your mom who lives on the other side of the country.

5. **RESTRAIN YOUR CAT**

Cat owners are often ill-prepared to properly restrain a frightened or injured animal. Because cats are so small and easy to carry, many owners opt not to use a carrier. Remember that there will likely be many agitated children, dogs, and other animals around should you need to move to a shelter, and in the excitement of an emergency, your cat will feel the need to take flight. Often owners try to carry their cats to the

vet in a pillowcase rather than deal with the trauma of putting
them in a carrier, but the real trauma begins when a frantic
cat is dropped, lost, or charged by another animal. Cats will
find more comfort in a darkened carrier lined with one of
your old T-shirts.

6. STORE EXTRA FOOD

Many people keep an emergency kit for the family, but they
forget to pack food for their feline. Keep at least four days
supply of food and water on hand for your pets. Extra food
may be stored in zip-lock bags and should be recycled every
two to three months to keep it fresh. If your cat takes a pre-
scription medication, be sure to have an extra supply in case
of an emergency. It is always a good idea to have a spare
kitty litter box and spare kitty litter on hand. If you must be
taken to a shelter, you should be able to keep your cat contained without hassle or mess.

7. MAKE A FIRST-AID KIT

With the fresh food supply and spare kitty litter, you should
also have an emergency kit that includes bandages and
medications for animals, as well as a guide for administering
pet care. Ask your vet for a list of supplies needed to build
your first-aid kit. Also, talk to your vet about how to apply
medication or first aid to a cat that may be agitated.

8. HAVE AN ALTERNATIVE PLAN

Do not rely on having just one vet in the event of an emergency. Compile a list of vets, including names, addresses,
and phone numbers in your city and neighboring cities in
case you need to move quickly. You will also need to have a
list of animal caregivers who might be able to come into your
home should you/your family be unable to care for the cat.

9. GET HEALTH INSURANCE FOR YOUR CAT

Talk to your vet and get on the Internet to check out animal
health insurance. A 2002 survey among pet owners with in-

surance conducted by the American Veterinary Association found that unexpected accidents or disasters were most often what sent cats to the vet. Those who responded to the survey said having health insurance relieved much of the financial burden.

10. **TAKE TURNS**

Be prepared to help neighbors, friends, coworkers, and family when they are sick, traveling, or in need of assistance. Exchange pet information, including names, medical needs, feeding times, favorite toys, and if applicable, walking/outdoor schedules. Research shows that people in hospitals heal much more quickly when they know their pets have proper care.

Ten Cats Who Risked Nine Lives

Gone are the days when only dogs are considered brave and loyal. Today, cats are used for a variety of functions, including police work. Russia's only "sniffer cat," Rusik, was used to sniff out smugglers of sturgeon, whose eggs are eaten as caviar. Quickly leading police to Stavropol, a known mafia region, Rusik was seen by criminals as a major threat to the $2 billion black market caviar industry. In 2003, just one week after his story was made public, Rusik was hit by a mafia-owned car.

Everyday cats are performing equally amazing acts of bravery and loyalty to their owners.

1. TEABAG TO THE RESCUE

Late in the night in 2001 someone broke into David Simpson's home in the quiet English suburb of Bradford and had no intention of letting him out alive. After the house was robbed of personal items, including a TV, a fire was deliberately set. While Simpson and his neighbors slept, his cat Teabag became aware of the fire. Simpson claims to have awakened to the usually docile Teabag jumping up and down on his bed, screeching at him. Darting back and forth, constantly yowling and screaming, Teabag drove Simpson out of bed. Only then did Simpson understand what was happening; he scooped up his cat and was able to make it out before the house was fully engulfed in flames.

2. **CAT VS. MACHINE**

Harry Dostie, who suffers from a disorder known as sleep apnea, used a breathing machine to keep his airway open as he slept. Working the night shift, he usually went to bed as his wife left for work and almost always fell instantly to sleep. With the snorkel-like device from the CPAP (continuous positive airway pressure) affixed to his face, Dostie was gone to the world. So, it was with great vexation that he was awakened by his cat, Shadow, sitting on his head and batting at Dostie's face with his paws. Fully awake, Dostie smelled plastic burning and found the CPAP machine was smoking with noxious fumes moving up through his breathing tube. At the tender age of six months, Shadow, wise beyond his years, saved Dostie's life.

3. **OH, JOY!**

Bob Gilliland likes to say his cat, Joy, paid him back for adopting her from a cat rescue group. One day, a year after Joy's adoption, the retired fire chief from Mission, Kansas, became incoherent and unable to call for help when his normally low blood pressure plummeted. While Gilliland was rendered helpless, Joy sprang into action, howling and pacing back and forth between the living room and the bedroom, where Gilliland's wife lay sleeping. Eventually, Joy woke her mistress and brought her into the living room to find Gilliland. Gilliland saved Joy, and now, Joy has saved Gilliland.

4. **ÉTOILE DE NUIT, A TRUE STAR OF NIGHT**

Guylaine Labonté loved her three-year-old kitty, but never imagined that Étoile might save her life. Then, one predawn morning in Quebec, Étoile's fanatic and persistent cries awakened Labonté to find a fire raging through her home. Labonté, a muscular dystrophy sufferer, hurried to wake her neighbors, losing track of Étoile in her efforts to save her human friends. Forced from the building by the smoke and fire, she begged the firefighters to help her find her cat. Despondent with her lost hope, Labonté looked up to see a police officer coming toward her with her frightened and ash-covered Étoile. The officer proclaimed Étoile a heroine, and the Purina Hall of Fame agreed. In 2000 Étoile joined 103 other animals—eighty-five dogs, seventeen cats, and one horse—honored over thirty-two years as very special pets that acted with bravery to rescue their owners from danger.

5.   FOR BEAU, NO BARRIER IS TOO GREAT

At four in the morning in May 2002, Mona Melanson slept in her Chateauguay, Quebec, apartment while trouble brewed. Four-year-old Beau, a beautiful black cat, literally threw caution to the winds, repeatedly hurling himself against a bedroom door to waken his owner. The home's fire alarm was sounding, but Melanson could not hear it behind the closed door. Beau's unflagging efforts finally got his owner's attention and both escaped the fire unhurt. Want to guess where Beau sleeps now?

6.   CALI, NATURE'S SECURITY SYSTEM

Six-year-old Cali (an appropriately named calico) is her owner's private security guard. While Lauren MacLaren slept in her Toronto, Ontario, apartment, Cali noticed a stranger outside the apartment window and took action when the would-be intruder tried to break in. Unable to rouse her owner by meowing, she jumped up and down on her until MacLaren awoke. Fortunately, a quick call to the police, who immediately responded, resulted in the arrest of the thwarted criminal.

7.   HOBBES, THE HERO

Sheri Coull and her family were astonished to be awakened in the middle of the night by the yowling of their five-year-old orange tabby, Hobbes. The battery-operated smoke detector in the Ontario apartment had failed to go off, so

Hobbes took over and raised the alarm. The family quickly fled their apartment and warned their neighbors of the fire. Within minutes of getting everyone out, the apartment building was engulfed in thick smoke and poisonous carbon monoxide fumes.

8. JACK, THE BRAVE BABY

Jack was only *two months old* when he saved his family's life in Montreal, Quebec. Jack's owner, Corrie Owens, says that Jack gave her and her son Brandon the best gift ever, when he woke her up with his loud, nonstop meowing on Christmas morning in 1991. Owens saw flames everywhere, grabbed Brandon and Jack, and ran. The fire destroyed everything and left fourteen tenants homeless—but alive.

9. OLLIE, THE SNIFFER CAT

Ollie is a red tabby with a great nose. He sniffed out a fire that had started in a crack in his house's fireplace in Waterloo, Ontario. With great insistence, Ollie got owner Brian Rozee out of bed and led him to the living room, which was beginning to fill with smoke. Thanks to Ollie, the fire was contained, damage was minimal, and the family was safe.

10. NAPOLEON, THE CONQUEROR

In Ennismore, Ontario, Marjorie St. Amour was awakened early one morning by her Siamese cat, Napoleon, but not in the usual way or because there was a fire. Napoleon discovered St. Amour's electric blanket and mattress smoldering and beginning to flame, so he attacked the problem. He found the fire with his paws, scratched at the blanket and his owner, and finally, in desperation, began biting the flames and St. Amour to get her awake. Like his namesake, Napoleon demonstrated a fearless determination to defeat the enemy.

The Mother in All Cats

It has often been said that felines are the most maternal of all animals, taking great care of their litters, risking their lives to protect their kittens, and often taking responsibility for caring for other animals and even people. These top-ten cat moms demonstrate the wonderful nurturing nature of felines.

1. WHILE THE MICE ARE AWAY

When mice were discovered in the Wellers home in Cranbrook, Canada, the family knew they had to dispose of the pests and pitched the mice nest outside. The Wellers had enough babies as it was; Patches, the family cat, was nursing her seven-week-old kittens. But the morning after they dispelled the mice nest, the Wellers woke up to a big surprise: Patches had managed to rescue two of the baby mice and was caring for them in addition to her own young.

2. A SQUIRRELLY KIND OF LOVE

When Fluffy appeared on CNN, the story of a young mother taking care of her brood wasn't so unusual. But when word got out that she took on five babies in addition to her own seven, people were impressed. In October 1997 Fluffy, an ordinary housecat from Argos Corner, Delaware, amazed everyone by stepping in to care for five baby squirrels after their mother died. Fluffy took care of the squirrels alongside her own kittens until they were strong enough to live on their own.

3.   ARE YOU MY MOTHER?

In 1997 five newborn puppies from Portsmouth, Virginia, were abandoned by their mother. Local animal shelter workers quickly put out word that they were looking for a possible adoptive mother to nurse the newborns. While no dogs stepped forward, a pregnant tabby cat came to the rescue of two of the Labrador-rottweiler mixes, while the three remaining newborns found their new mother in another cat who accepted the puppies into her litter of kittens.

4.   PLAYING CAT AND MOUSE

For years Huan was reputed to be a great mouser, so when Huan's owner, Charanai Nanoontum of Thailand, found a baby mouse in her closet, with Huan by her side, she had no doubt what would happen next. What she wasn't expecting from her cat was . . . love at first sight. Huan instantly adopted the mouse, raising it as her own and protecting it from the other cats and dogs (who were reportedly confused and disturbed by Huan's behavior). Huan and her new mouse friend, Jerry, played and slept together, and were often seen lapping milk from the same bowl. Love, it seems, has no bounds.

5.   KIT KAT AND COMPANY

Kit Kat, a mother cat from Paarl, South Africa, raised her litter of kittens quite happily until a powerful storm blew through her farm near Cape Town. It was then that a squirrels' nest was blown from a tree, leaving the baby squirrels abandoned and helpless. A neighbor, not knowing what else to do, gathered up the babies and carried them to Kit Kat. Although Kit Kat had a penchant for hunting squirrels, she was also known to be a good mother. And she didn't disappoint, readily taking on the baby squirrels to raise.

6. SANTA CLAUS CALLING MOUSE

Mouse is an especially caring mother cat who agreed to add a newborn, orphaned Chihuahua puppy to her litter of four three-week-old kittens. One evening Mouse, who did not have a litter box, asked to go outside. When she didn't return to the house or answer when she was called, her owners thought she just wanted a night off from caring for her now six-week-old kittens and three-week-old puppy. They went to bed unconcerned. The next morning they found Mouse in her bed, snuggled up with her babies and purring loudly. Shocked as to how she got back into the house, the owners began to look around for clues and soon realized she had come in through the chimney. Determined to be with her babies, Mouse had climbed up on the roof of the house; slid down the chimney, landing in the ashes in the fireplace; pushed away the glass fireplace screen; and leaving black paw prints through the den, living room, and kitchen, made her way to her litter. When Mouse is through being a mom, perhaps she would like to work with Santa.

7. A MOTHER'S WORK IS NEVER DONE

Philosopher and author St. George Mivart told of watching a cat leap into a rushing stream to rescue her drowning kittens in the countryside of England. The mother cat fought raging waters, swimming to her babies and bringing them, one by one, to the shore. When all were safely on land, she began to care for them—to dry them with her tongue and paws, to soothe them with her mothering sounds, and to feed and warm them. Asking for no help, responding instantly and so courageously to what seemed an impossible task, the remarkable mother acted as if she had simply done what was expected in a normal day.

8. SOMETIMES "MOTHER" IS A MALE

An Arizona doctor tells the story of Footsie, a male kitten who ran away from a neglectful farmer and was rescued by her parents, who were living in Bavaria. Footsie and his adoptive family were very happy together. About five years after Footsie came to live with the doctor's parents, he appeared one day in the kitchen with a kitten in his mouth. It seems that Footsie had returned to the farm from which he had escaped and rescued another kitten. Footsie's adoptive family suspected that the kitten was Footsie's daughter, and they were able to convince the farmer to let them keep the kitten. Named Minko, the young cat adores "Mother" Footsie and has become the constant companion of the doctor's father (a former cat-hater changed by the special love of feline family members).

9. ANOTHER "MOTHER"

When a feral cat suddenly appeared in Angela Baines's barn in rural England, Baines guessed him to be about six months old. When it became clear that the cat, who she named

Author's collection

Sooner the tabby spends his nights snuggled on top of Cookiedough the goat.

Harry, intended to stay in her barn, Baines "rugby-tackled [him] with a towel" to take him to be neutered. Harry didn't fully trust Baines for nearly a year after the towel incident. So, why did he stay? Baines's favorite horse, a Welsh named Sultan, was diagnosed with incurable Cushing's disease. While Harry, obviously aware of the horse's illness, would have nothing to do with anyone or anything else, he would shadow Sultan, always looking after him. Shortly after Sultan died, the still-devastated Baines learned that her other beloved horse, a thoroughbred named Alex, had skin cancer. Even before Baines had gotten the diagnoses, she had noticed that Harry had taken an interest in Alex. In fact, although there were many other animals in and around the barn, Harry kept company exclusively with Alex. In 2003 Harry was honored Rescue Cat of the Year in the Best Personality category, a fitting award for such a sympathetic friend.

10. A Nanny Kind of Love

Sometimes a cat needs a mother. Sooner, a two-month-old orange tabby, was separated from his family in Oklahoma after a dangerous and frightening ride in the engine compartment of a car. While he survived the 250-mile trip, he was suddenly orphaned in Midlothian, Texas. Adopted by this author's family, Sooner now shares a barn with three horses, three goats, and another young cat, but he found most comfort in a nanny goat named Cookiedough. During the day, after his morning butterfly-chasing and grasshopper-killing adventures, Sooner can be found in the field, no farther than two or three feet from Cookiedough while she grazes. Come nightfall, Sooner curls up on top of Cookiedough's back as she settles in for the night. While Cookiedough has two kids of her own, Sooner gets preferential treatment.

Cats in Court

Heroic deeds and motherly love aside, our cats are not without controversy. Whether they are acting as plaintiff or defendant, cats are no strangers to the courtroom.

1. HIS AND HER CATS: DIVORCE COURT

In Europe during the tenth century, so important was the cat, it weighed heavily in cases of divorce. When a husband and wife separated, their goods and chattels were evenly divided—except for the family cat. If the couple had only one cat, it went to the husband.

2. RATS SUE AND WIN

In the sixteenth century a Frenchman named Bartholomew Chassenee represented rats in a lawsuit against cats. Chassenee complained before the court that his clients, the rats, were unable to appear in court at Autun because of the heavily cat-populated countryside. If his clients were required to appear in court, he said, it would surely cost them their lives. While the details of the lawsuit are unclear, records indicate that he successfully defended his rats.

3. MARINE LAW

Marine insurance does not cover damage done to cargo by rodents. However, if the owner of the damaged cargo can prove that there was no cat aboard the vessel to combat the vermin, the owner can collect damages from the shipmaster. According to English law, a ship found at sea without a living being aboard is considered a derelict and is forfeited to the admiralty, the finders, or the king. Once again, cats come to the rescue. Faced with a choice between the waves and staying aboard a damaged or deserted vessel, sea cats often opt to stay on board. In doing so, cats ensure that the ship will not be condemned.

4. CATS-R-US

Yes, there really is a Cats-R-Us. But the London-based charity for cats almost went belly-up when toy conglomerate Toys "R" Us found out about it. In 1998 the million-dollar company sued the charity, stating that "R Us" is a trademark and that consumers may be confused by the similarities. Although the charity proprietor, Marion Maychell, had registered the name in 1996 without incident, she was suddenly facing the possibility of losing everything, including her cats. Because Maychell and Cats-R-Us have been praised for saving and placing thousands of cats in homes and for working to control the cat population in England, there was a huge outpouring of support and protest against Toys "R" Us. Several months later the toy distributor backed down, giving a sizeable contribution to the cat cause.

5. CAT KILLER

In August 2002 Eric Grossnickle entered the Myersville, Maryland, home of his tenant, April Ritch, after he had warned her that he would kill her roaming cats if they were not restrained. Grossnickle then shot Babe and Angel with a 12-gauge shotgun and tossed their bloodied carcasses in a nearby creek. He was tried in the Frederick County Circuit Court on felony animal cruelty charges but was acquitted of these charges by Judge Mary Ann Stepler, who based her decision on the loose wording of Maryland's animal cruelty law. Stepler instead found Grossnickle guilty on two counts of malicious destruction of property, a misdemeanor that carries a $1,000 penalty and up to ninety days in jail.

6. CALL OF THE WILD

Sentiment about animal protection is much different in the United Kingdom. In the late 1970s, when a cat killed a number of pigeons belonging to a neighboring breeder in Perth, Scotland, the judge ruled that while it was unfortunate the birds had been killed, this act was the will of mother nature. Cat owners have no obligation to restrain their animals to the house. "The plaintiff's plea is that the natural instinct of the feline race is to prey on birds as well as mice." So it was argued that the owner of the cat should prevent the possibility of its coming into contact with its favorite sport. But it is "equally true that the owner of a bird should exercise similar precaution to prevent its coming within the range of a hostile race."

7. CAT FOOD

In 1971 the U.S. Congress mandated a program that would save wild horses. The U.S. Bureau of Land Management's Wild Horse Burro Program was designed to prevent cowboys from rounding up wild horses and burros to sell to slaughterhouses. It put a federal adoption program in place that allowed ordinary citizens or animal groups to care for wild horses and, in some cases, to break and train the animals for personal use. When the program began it involved just over ten thousand horses, most living in Nevada. By 1998 the horse population had grown to more than forty thousand, and with the increased number of horses and burros came new problems. With so many horses grazing on limited federal land, more open adoptions were conducted, until it came to light that some groups were buying the horses for cat food. Today, the Wild Horse and Burro Program sends horses to prisons to be saddle broken in an effort to teach the inmates life skills. With the horses come barns, hay, and you guessed it—cats. Cats are very popular with the inmates fortunate enough to work with the animals.

8. THE MURDER SPREE

In August 2003 Denver, Colorado, had a possible serial killer on its hands with no suspects. More than thirty-five Denver-area cats had been killed—split open with their organs removed and tossed to the side. While the police department maintains that this was the possible work of dogs or coyotes, canine experts disagree. Coyotes, for example, don't kill for the fun of it. They drag their kill, organs and all, off to be eaten; they do not leave good food out in the open. Indeed, a different kind of predator was at work, and with no clues, Denver cat owners were urged to keep their cats indoors and to be on the lookout for a feline murderer.

9. THE TALKING CAT

On November 15, 1982, the U.S. District Court in Augusta, Georgia, ruled in the favor of the City Council of Augusta, saying that Blackie, the talking cat, needed to have a business license if he was going to continue to take money for his talent. Blackie could intelligibly say, "I love you" and "I want my Mama" (yes, that's right), and his owners, Carl and Elaine Miles, enjoyed the good life as their cat made national headlines and television appearances, including a cameo on *That's Incredible!* By June 1981 the City Council required the Miles couple to file for a business license for soliciting contributions from pedestrians in the downtown Augusta area who wanted to hear Blackie talk. Evidence indicates that Miles also asked an off-duty police officer for money in exchange for some Blackie "I love yous." After several complaints from Augusta residents who did not like the prospect of hearing cat talk, Blackie became police business.

10. OH, THERE'S MORE . . .

The Miles family filed with the U.S. Court of Appeals, stating that Blackie's rights of speech had been violated. The court reviewed the history of the Mileses' relationship with their talking cat. The Mileses found Blackie while they were living in a rooming house in South Carolina. Mr. Miles discovered Blackie could talk and began to cultivate his cat's talent. Over time Blackie the Talking Cat lost his appeal with South Carolina audiences—go figure—so the Miles moved to Georgia, looking for better fortune. It was there, the lawsuit contends, that Blackie's freedom of speech was violated. On August 4, 1983, the court ruled that although Blackie had a real talent, he could not be considered a person and, therefore, was not protected by the Bill of Rights.

Cats on the Books: The Most Unusual Laws

From the moment cats reached divine status among the Egyptians, we have had laws about the keeping of, caring for, and purchasing of cats. A record from 59 B.C. shows that a Roman official sent to Egypt accidentally killed a cat and was promptly hanged. In modern times laws have changed with regard to dealing with cats. Old laws pertaining to owner responsibility in the event of a ruined garden or murdered pet pigeon are easy enough to interpret and understand. Some of the laws, however, are not so easy to understand.

1. GIVE US YOUR SHEEP, YOUR GOATS

Old laws read that in countries where rats were plague-carriers and cats were rare, any man or woman who killed a cat would be forced to pay the price in livestock—giving up at least one sheep and one goat.

2. THE FLINGING OF FELINES

In 1818 a decree was issued at Ypres in Flanders forbidding all from flinging felines from high towers in commemoration of a Christmas spectacle, as was once customary.

3. NO DUCK CHASING ALLOWED

In more modern times the unusual continues: In Morristown, Louisiana, cats are prohibited from chasing ducks through the city.

4. TAIL LIGHT, PLEASE

In Berea, Ohio, a law decreed that all cats on public streets after dark must display a red tail light.

5. BIRDS OF A FEATHER

Reed City, Michigan, had once made it illegal to have a bird and a cat living under the same roof.

6. TINKER BELLS

In Lemonine, Montana, domesticated cats must wear three bells as a warning to birds.

7. LET'S SEE YOUR I.D.

Drinking beer can only bring out the bad side of cats. In Natchez, Mississippi, drinking beer is an illegal activity for cats.

8. HEADLIGHTS REQUIRED

In Dallas, Texas, cats should not let the sun go down without wearing proper headlights. The law requires that cats running in the streets after dark must wear headlights.

9. THE CAT WHO SWALLOWED THE CANARY

In Canada the court overturned a case in which a man sued his neighbor after the neighbor's cats ate his pet canary. The court ruled that cats "may be regarded as still undomesticated and their predatory habits are but a remnant of their wild nature." While it is legal to kill a dog that destroys one's property, including livestock, cats have found the "predatory habits" loophole helpful.

10. **LEASHES REQUIRED**

In Westerville, Ohio, where there is a strict leash law for dogs, cats are allowed to roam free, causing many citizens with prize gardens to complain. It is their contention that free-roaming cats defecate on and dig up gardens. One home-owners association in the Columbus suburb lobbied hard enough to have a rule established that all cats must be leash-walked while a leash-free zone has been established for dogs.

Legal Heirs:
Everlasting Love

For many, man's best friend has always been the cat. The Egyptians wanted to take cats, their constant companions in life, with them into the afterlife, taking special care to even mummify mice so that their dear feline friends would have something in the afterworld to nibble on. But those who couldn't take their cats with them often took special precautions to make sure their cats were cared for well after the owners were gone.

1. CARDINAL GIFTS

By the seventeeth century, cats had returned to public favor, and once again, owners were lavishing great gifts upon their feline friends. Cardinal Richelieu was known to keep dozens of cats at court with him and, in preparation of his own death, set up endowments for the cats so that they would be well taken care of.

2. TWO CATS

In 1963 two cats named Brownie and Hellcat became the sole beneficiaries of $415,000—a sum left to them in the will of Dr. William Grier of San Diego. Two years later, when the cats died, the remaining money went to George Washington University in Washington, D.C.

3. **THE CAT'S ORCHARD**

Approximately A.D. 1280, the Egyptian Sultan El Daher Beybars decided that all cats in his region should be cared for, for all time. He ordered that after his death a garden known as Gheyt-el-Qouttah (the Cat's Orchard), situated near his mosque outside of Cairo, should be used to support cats in need. Although the garden has been bought and sold many times over, the last words of the Sultan are still honored by the owner today. At the same afternoon hour every day, meat is brought into the center of the garden, and cats from all over the city hurry to get their share. It is a sight to behold, with hundreds of cats jumping from house to house, sliding down the walls, and appearing from under bushes to fight for their share of the booty.

4. **CAVENDISH CATS**

The daughter of a former beauty queen and a wealthy businessman, Patricia Cavendish O'Neil inherited a sprawling estate in South Africa called the Broadlands. An animal lover, O'Neil owned chimpanzees, dogs, cats, horses, birds, reptiles, and exotic animals of Africa. But her most treasured pet was said to be her lion, with whom she spent eleven years. Twice divorced, O'Neil never claimed to be good at marriage—she was only good with animals. Still, she shocked the British and South African communities, not to mention her husband, when she created a new will leaving her entire estate to her animals, including her fourteen house cats.

5. **THE FAT CAT**

A forty-eight-pound, striped tomcat named Joseph became a millionaire in 1969 when his owner, Ms. Agatha Isabel Frazer Higgins, died and left her feline friend her entire fortune. Joseph lived happily in his mansion with a full staff and family members until his death, at which time the fortune was dispersed among family.

6. **THE LADY AND THE TRAMP**

Years before she died, Mrs. Margaret Layne adopted a black stray cat in London, where Layne had been living alone. Tinker kept Mrs. Layne company, going for short walks with her and spending time in the small backyard, until Layne went to a nursing home. Tinker meant the world to the elderly woman, and eighteen months after Layne died, friends and family found out exactly how much Tinker's companionship was worth. In her will, Layne placed her house and £100,000 in a trust fund so that Tinker could remain in her home. A magistrate ruled that until Tinker died or decided to take to the road again, Layne's friends and neighbors named in the trust would care for the cat and house. Only when Tinker was gone would the house be sold.

7. **CONTESTING THE WILL**

John, second Duke of Montagu, loved his cats so much that he decided he would leave his part of his estate to his animals. When he died in 1749, his cats continued to live in luxury since he had no remaining relatives left to dispute the will.

But seventeenth century French harpist Mademoiselle Dupuy's cat was not so lucky. Mademoiselle Dupuy believed she owed her skill as a musician to her cat, who sat beside her while she performed, expressing—she believed—pleasure or annoyance, depending on how she played. Consequently, she left him both a town house and a country house with sufficient income to keep them up properly. Her relatives, however, succeeded in wrestling this bequest away from the unfortunate feline, who probably was not even allowed to be present in court.

8. **KITTY TRUST FUND**

If Floridian Irene Wright were to die tomorrow, her ten cats and four dogs would still live out their lives comfortably in her home. That is because, through an attorney, Wright has set up a trust fund that will provide for the animals and allow a pet caretaker to live in her home rent- and utility-free. She also has appointed a board of friends, relatives, and a veterinarian to choose the caretaker after her death and periodically check up on that person. She has appointed a different board to dissolve the fund and sell the property when the pets die or the situation becomes economically unfeasible.

"This is their home, and I want them to be able to stay here if something happens to me," Ms. Wright explains. "It gives me great peace of mind."

9. INSEPARABLE

While no written agreement was made between assisted-living patient Francis Powe and the staff of Rosemont in Houston, Texas, his cat was taken care of all the same. Time and again, Powe had expressed his love and concern for the welfare of his Siamese, Missy. Regular visits and errands were made specifically for Missy by the staff but, when Powe was sent to the hospital—never to return to his home or his cat—Missy continued to live in the apartment alone. With her own television and regular constitutionals around the halls of Rosemont, Missy continued to stay on the patient list and was fed along with all the other (human) residents. But after sixteen years of constant companionship, the friendly Rosemont staff was not enough to take Missy's mind away from her missing owner, and she stopped eating. The two friends died within four months of each other.

10. VICTIM OF CIRCUMSTANCE

Jean Mason of Kent, England, does not have great peace of mind right now. Mason lived with her sister and brother-in-law, Sheila and Peter Holmes, from 1970 until 1985, before moving into an apartment of her own nearby. Even after her move, she took care of her sister, who had fallen ill with cancer, everyday until Mrs. Holmes died in 2001. (Mr. Holmes had died in 1986.) In 2002 Ms. Mason moved back into her sister's home, saying that her sister—in her final days—had wanted Mason to have the house but did not have a chance to change her will before she died. In her will as it stands, Mrs. Holmes left her sister £25,000, and left her house—worth £385,000—to animal charities, including the Cats Protection League. Ms. Mason has spent most of the £25,000 contesting the will, to no avail. She was evicted from the house in March 2004 and forced to return to her apartment.

The victims of deceased pet owners' unclear intentions, whether human or feline, are many and have been for centuries. The good news is that pet wills and trusts may now be set up to care for your four-legged children after you are gone. Many decisions must be made and written down while setting up these trusts (such as who will care for the animals) because humans left behind don't always honor the dying wishes of their loved ones. To protect your wishes and your pets, see these websites for instructions on setting up unchallengeable wills and trusts: *http://www.abcny.org/pubprovforpet.html; http://www.greatlakesbcrescue.org/Simmy Project/PetWill.htm;* and *www.cvm.tamu.edu/petcare/.*

The Nature of the Beast: Laws of Cat

W hatever laws humans may have had or may still create in regard to the health, welfare, or ownership of cats, cats have always had their own sense of law and order in the feline world. And, in keeping with the nature of the beast, they don't really care how these laws affect us.*

1. THE LAW OF THE SLEEPING CAT

All cats must sleep with people whenever and wherever possible, and must do so in the manner most uncomfortable for the people involved.

2. THE LAW OF COUNTER-SNIFFING CATS

A curious cat must be able to stretch just long enough to reach any countertop that may be of interest to the said cat.

3. THE LAW OF COUNTER-JUMPING CATS

Legally, there is no such thing as off-limits counter space. Therefore, it is perfectly reasonable that all cats have complete and total access to countertops when deemed necessary.

*These ten laws of cat can be found at www.jfort.co.uk/jonathan/feline.html.

4. THE LAW OF NECESSITY FOR CATS

If a cat wants something, it is deemed necessary. If a cat is curious about something, it is deemed necessary to investigate. If a cat is hungry, it is deemed quite necessary to eat. If a cat is tired, it is deemed necessary to sleep upon what item or person the cat chooses. If there is something that is of no interest to the cat, it is unnecessary and, therefore, may be destroyed at any given moment.

5. THE LAW OF CAT DISINTEREST

A cat's level of disinterest is in direct correlation to the amount of effort a human puts forth trying to interest said cat.

6. THE LAW OF RUG CONFIGURATION

No rug shall be left in a naturally flat-lying state as long as a cat is nearby to mess it up.

7. CAT PHYSICS

A cat shall move in a straight, forward moving gait unless there is a really good reason to move laterally or backward.

8. THE LAW OF THE CAT HAIR

All cats shall be drawn to navy blue or black sweaters, and shall feel extremely affectionate when humans are wearing said garments.

9. THE LAW OF THE NAP AND STRETCH

A cat must stretch in direct proportion to the length of time said cat napped.

10. THE LAW OF CAT OBSERVATION

If a cat watches a refrigerator long enough, someone will assuredly come along and take something out that is good to eat.

Ailurophiles: Famous Cat Lovers

Anyone who truly loves cats appreciates the mysterious ways of cats—their amazing agility and grace, their sense of humor and honor—and empathizes with the feline's refusal to be made fun of. Cats, to so many, are honorable and dignified creatures that have served as excellent companions for centuries. While the list of those who adore cats is too long to recount, there are at least ten who have recorded their love of cats on paper. In the words of Thomas Jefferson, owner of many cats: "The written word endures," as does the love affair between humans and their cats.

1. RAYMOND CHANDLER (1888–1959)

This famous author once owned a black Persian named Taki. Chandler used to call his cat his personal secretary because Taki would sit on his manuscripts as Chandler revised them. The two spent many long hours together.

2. WINSTON CHURCHILL (1874–1965)

This famous prime minister saw it as a sign of good luck when a cat suddenly appeared on his doorstep just after he had delivered a very successful speech at Margate in 1953. So, in honor of the town, Churchill adopted the kitten and named her Margate. Within two weeks Margate won over Churchill completely—he even shared his bed with her. After

Margate died Jock came into the prime minister's life. Churchill was so taken with his new cat that he refused to eat dinner at the table until his cat was beside him. His staff were often sent out to find Jock before Churchill would take his seat at the head of the table.

3. ALBERT SCHWEITZER (1875–1965)

This Nobel Prize–winning French missionary/doctor lived with his favorite cat, Sizi, in his famous African clinic. The left-handed Schweitzer often wrote his prescriptions right-handed so as not to disturb Sizi, who habitually fell asleep on the doctor's left arm. Visitors noted that Schweitzer doted on the wants and needs of his cat more than on his guests.

4. ERNEST HEMINGWAY (1899–1961)

The often-eccentric writer, who described great adventures on the open plains of Africa, had a great affection for domestic cats. Hemingway shared his Key West home with more than fifty felines. Today, his home stands as a museum, where visitors will find not only artifacts from the author's life but also descendants of his many cats, approximately half of which are polydactyl (having extra toes).

Cats also influenced Hemingway's son, Patrick, who lived in East Africa for twenty-five years. For many of those years Patrick was the epitome of the Great White Hunter, but in his later years the beauty of the land and the magnificence of the animals, especially the cats, inspired Patrick to become a conservationist.

5. CHARLES DICKENS (1812–1870)

An avid cat lover, Dickens always had cats about. But when one of his favorite cats, Williamina, had a large litter of kittens and insisted on moving into his study, Dickens decided enough was enough; he would get rid of all the kittens. One of Williamina's babies, however, had other ideas and fought for the author's constant attention. She became known as the Master's Cat and lived quite happily among Dickens's

Jack Church

Einstein seems deep in thought.

works. It is rumored that she would get his attention by snuffing out his reading candle.

6. MARK TWAIN (1835–1910)

On Twain's Connecticut farm there were many animals, but none so favored as his cats. Eleven cats were under the care of Mark Twain and his daughter, Susy, who was heard to have declared, "The difference between Papa and Mamma is that Mamma loves morals and Papa loves cats."

7. HARRIET BEECHER STOWE (1811–1896)

The seventh child of a well-known Protestant preacher, the mother of seven children, and the author of *Uncle Tom's Cabin*, Stowe found a fast and true friend in a feline named Calvin. The Maltese cat appeared at Stowe's home one day, taking over the house and Stowe's daily routines. Calvin, she wrote, was assertive, domineering, and prone to sit on her shoulders while she wrote her manuscripts, overseeing her every word.

8. EDGAR ALLAN POE (1809–1849)

Poe loved watching his cats; he was infatuated with their movements and their manner of hunting. Many of the more gruesome descriptions in Poe's stories were drawn from his observations of the cats' stalking and hunting techniques. It was his favorite tortoiseshell cat, named Catarina, who was the inspiration for "The Black Cat," a story of destitution, death, murder, and insanity. In this story a husband, driven by a distrust (and perhaps fear) of his wife's favorite cat, becomes angry when he thinks the cat is ignoring him. (Cat owners everywhere are saying, "So?") He punishes the cat and actually tries to kill him, but the cat survives. Feeling stalked by the cat, the husband plans to hang the cat, to make sure he dies, only to have another cat come into his life. The husband's attempt to drive away the second cat, who bears an uncanny resemblance to the first, results in an accident that kills his wife. Driven insane by the cats, the husband hides his wife's body in the walls of their house, but is found out when police and neighbors hear a cry from inside the walls. The husband had inadvertently sealed the cat in with his wife's body. Ah, the irony. It was the man's suspicions about a cat that drove him to violence and a cat that revealed him as a murderer.

9. COLETTE (1873–1954)

The untamed French writer Colette likened herself to her cats. She lived life on her own terms, often shocking and always entertaining the world around her. While some argue her own antics were much more pleasurable to read about than her creations, two of her more popular works were based on her cats. *Sept dialogues de betes*, or The Seven Dialogues of Beasts (1927), is a fictionalized debate between cats and dogs featuring a gray male Angora resembling her own cat and, *La Chatte*, or The Cat, is a story based on her own Russian blue. It is believed that author Jean Cocteau, who wrote beautifully of cats, learned to truly love cats through his association with Colette.

10. BRONTË SISTERS

The three Brontë sisters (Charlotte [1816–1855], who wrote *Jane Eyre*; Anne [1820–1849], who wrote *Agnes Grey*; and Emily [1818–1848], who wrote *Wuthering Heights*), are well-known cat lovers. Their poetry and novels reflect their lifelong relationships with their feline friends. Charlotte and Anne often referred to their precious cats in their diaries.

BONUS CAT LOVER:

Sir Isaac Newton (1642–1727) must be distinguished from even the best of cat lovers as his love for cats was so grand he could not bear to see his cats shut up or kept from doing anything they wanted to do. He invented the cat flap (also known as the cat door) so that his cats could come and go as they pleased throughout the day. Among cat lovers, it is agreed the famous mathematician and physicist may be the greatest cat lover of all!

Ailurophobes:
Famous Cat Haters

A h, yes. There are always those who do not understand the finer things in life, and so cat haters have always been among us. Politicians, workingmen and women, clergymen, knights, kings and queens, conquerors, writers, and artists have despised cats out of fear, superstition, and ignorance. It is interesting to note that many who tried to conquer the world could not stand an animal that could not be conquered.

1. JOHANNES BRAHMS (1833–1897)

Famous for his piano concertos, Johannes Brahms was also well known for his dislike of cats. Apparently, one of his favorite pastimes was to sit at his window and shoot at his neighbor's cats with a bow and arrow. Could there be a connection between his hatred of cats and his unlucky love life—three loves, all unrequited?

2. NAPOLÉON BONAPARTE (1769–1821)

This infamous general and emperor of France (1804–1815) was terrified of cats. Once his aids discovered him wildly stabbing into the tapestry in his room with his sword, sweating profusely, lunging in and out, and cursing loudly. Upon investigation, his men found a kitten in the corner of the room. Napoléon's superstitions about cats were so potent that the hopeful conqueror could not abide the presence of a cat in the room with him.

3. HENRY III (1551–1589)

Napoléon was not alone. While Henry III of France was a ferocious, unforgiving king in his efforts to destroy the Protestant church, he was rendered helpless against the mew of the cat. In Henry's time, cat superstitions were extreme. To kill a cat could bring death, to injure a cat could bring demons and destruction, but to live among certain cats could bring great misfortune. At the mere sight of a cat, Henry III was known to faint.

4. GEORGES LOUIS LECLERC, COMPTE DE BUFFON (1707–1788)

French naturalist de Buffon felt so strongly against cats that he preached that these animals were indeed evil, as evidenced by their sneaky manner of hunting and their vile slaughter of birds.

5. NOAH WEBSTER (1758–1843)

In his early dictionaries, Webster refers to "the stealthy-stepping cat." He goes on to say, "the domestic cat is a deceitful animal and, when enraged, extremely spiteful."

6. ALEXANDER THE GREAT (356 B.C.–323 B.C.)

It is somewhat puzzling that Alexander, as a world conqueror, had no use for cats. He kept his interest in animals to large dogs and horses. Alexander was responsible for crossbreeding one of the most powerful war dogs of all time, and was known to set his dogs upon any cat so that he could watch while the feline was ripped to pieces.

7. JULIUS CAESAR (100? B.C.–44 B.C.)

Caesar is widely reputed to have been so fearful of cats that he would become faint upon seeing one. Like Alexander the

Great, Caesar bred large, fighting dogs and would use cats as bait for his canines.

8. WILLIAM SHAKESPEARE (1564–1616)

This world-famous playwright made no secret of his dislike for cats. His frequent references to the annoying feline make clear his feelings. In *Cymbeline* (act 5, scene 5), Cornelius talks of "killing creatures vile, as cats and dogs, Of not esteem." In *Coriolanus* (act 4, scene 2), Volumia refers to a gathering mob as cats: "Twas you incensed the rabble: Cats, that can judge as fitly of his worth As I can of those mysteries which heaven Will not have earth to know." In *Othello*, Shakespeare wrote of drowning cats and similarly useless beings, including people who are a burden on society. Although he was a great writer, Shakespeare's empathy did not seem to extend to all of earth's creatures.

9. ROCKWELL SAYRE (1848–1930)

A successful Chicago banker in the 1920s, Sayre started a campaign to rid the world of cats by 1925. He offered financial rewards to anyone who would kill the "filthy and useless" animals. He claimed to have inspired the killing of 7 million cats and in 1925 extended his campaign for another ten years. Fortunately, the new timeline did not take effect; Sayre died only five years after making his announcement, and no one else came forward to finish his campaign.

10. ELIZABETH I (1533–1603)

A true cat hater, Elizabeth let her subjects know how she felt about felines. In 1558 her coronation parade included a dummy of the pope (who was hated by the Protestant Elizabeth) that was made of wicker and filled with live cats. After the parade, the wicker dummy was thrown in a huge bonfire. Elizabeth's Protestant supporters said the cats' shrieks were "the language of the devils within the body of the Holy Father."

Quotable Cats: Best-Known Lines about the Feline

Cats have been feared, worshipped, persecuted, and adored throughout history. Always entertaining, always engaging, always mysterious, the cat has given us much to write about.

1. "Cats are mysterious kind of folk. There is more passing in their minds than we are aware of."

—Sir Walter Scott

2. "No matter how much cats fight, there always seem to be plenty of kittens."

—Abraham Lincoln

3. "When my cats aren't happy, I'm not happy. Not because I care about their mood but because I know they're just sitting there thinking up ways to get even."

—Penny Ward Moser

4. "Cats refuse to take blame for anything—including their own sins."

—Elizabeth Peters

5.   "She could never be made to comprehend the great difference between fur and feathers, nor see why her mistress should gravely reprove her when she brought in a bird, and warmly commend when she brought in a mouse."

—Harriet Beecher Stowe

6.   "There are two means of refuge from the misery of life: music and cats.

—Albert Schweitzer

7.   "The cat is a guest and not a plaything."

—Colette

8.   "So it is, and such is life. The cat's away, and the mice they play."

—Charles Dickens

9.   "Cats are absolute individuals, with their own ideas about everything, including the people they own."

—John Dingman

10.   "Thou are the Great Cat, the avenger of the Gods, and the judge of words, and the president of the sovereign chiefs and the governor of the holy Circle; thou are indeed . . . the Great Cat

—Inscription of the Royal Tombs of Thebes

Bonus:

"Cats are smarter than dogs. You can't get eight cats to pull a sled through snow."

—Jeff Valdez

Cat Lines: Cat Expressions

Cats have entranced and inspired humans throughout their thousands-years-long relationship. It is not surprising that many popular sayings reflect our feline friends' behaviors.

1. CAT GOT YOUR TONGUE?

This expression first appeared during medieval times, when it was commonly believed that cats and witches worked together—and were often considered one and the same—against good people, preventing them from crying out for help. Many people thought that a cat, an agent of the devil, could take over a person's will and soul, rendering the person helpless and speechless, and many of these possessed souls were executed for associating with evil.

Another source of the saying was the "pussy will and the cattail," named for the plants' resemblance to cats' swinging tails. The plants and cat tails were compared to the "cat-o'-nine-tails," a whip used to flog people during medieval times. The nine "tails," or knotted cords, fastened to the whip were likened to the nine lives of cats. Just the notion of a beating with the cruel whip (usually called "the cat") could cause victims to lose their speech. Indeed, the cat got their tongues.

2. **IT'S RAINING CATS AND DOGS!**

In the sixteenth and seventeenth centuries, when streets were narrow and poorly designed for proper drainage, heavy rains and flooding often swept strays away and drowned them.

3. **HE LET THE CAT OUT OF THE BAG.**

This expression dates back to the eighteenth century, when con artists tried to pass bags of cats for bags of piglets, hoping to convince would-be buyers that they could not open the bags for fear of releasing the wild piglets. Sometimes, however, a cat would struggle free of the bag, exposing the con.

4. **SHE THINKS SHE'S THE CAT'S MEOW.**

This expression comes from 1920s slang and describes a person who thinks very highly of herself.

5. **TO GET ONE'S BACK UP**

When cats sense danger or fear an attack, they instinctively arch their back. The bigger they appear, the better their chance of scaring off their attacker. This response is the basis for the phrase "to get one's back up," which describes humans when aroused to anger.

6. **THERE'S MORE THAN ONE WAY TO SKIN A CAT.**

This saying comes from the British, who used the expression, "there are more ways of killing a cat than choking it with cream." This idiom implied that there was often a better way to reach an end—particularly since cats like cream and were unlikely to choke on it. The Americanized version of this saying—"there's more than one way to skin a cat"— means there are often several ways to accomplish a goal.

7. **IT'S THE CAT'S PAJAMAS *and* IT'S THE CAT'S WHISKERS.**

Coming from the Roaring Twenties, these expressions reflected cats' ability to look very pleased with themselves.

They described something—an action, a hairstyle, clothing—that was very fashionable or extremely desirable.

8. CATHOUSE

Since the fifteenth century, prostitutes have been referred to as cats because a female cat can attract tomcats from miles away when she is in heat and can mate with them one after the other. In the 1400s it was common to warn men away from "chasing cat tails" or "chasing tail."

9. LOOK WHAT THE CAT DRAGGED IN.

Americans borrowed this popular expression, which references the disheveled condition of a person's appearance, from the British as well. For centuries cats have brought home dead or half-dead vermin and insects that have been played with until they are sufficiently messy. Americans use this saying not only to describe tousled visitors but also in a teasing way to welcome unexpected guests.

10. TO GRIN LIKE A CHESHIRE CAT

Charles Lutwidge Dodgson, better known as Lewis Carroll, made the Cheshire cat popular in *Alice's Adventures in Wonderland* (1865). In Carroll's story the Cheshire cat leaves a scene, gradually fading from view with his smile the last to disappear. In fact, this saying may have originated before Alice's adventures, coming from Cheshire cheeses that were once molded into the forms of smiling cats.

III
Breeds

Best Breeds for Kids

Over the years cats have been notoriously (and unfairly) pegged as unfriendly toward children. While certain breeds are less comfortable with active children (as there are within the dog world), a large number of breeds are very kid-friendly. Countless stories of cats befriending lonely children, saving their lives, and serving as therapy for children with terminal illnesses or physical challenges dispel the notion that dogs are our only best friends.

The top ten cat breeds listed as kid-friendly have been compiled through the cooperation of many veterinarians and animal behaviorists.

1. Abyssinian

2. American and Exotic Shorthair

3. Birman

4. Burmese

5. Maine Coon

6. Manx

7. Persian

8. Ragdoll

9. Somali

10. Tiffany (also known as Tiffanie or Chantilly)

Non-Kid-Friendly Kitties

Just as you may find exceptions among breeds that do typically like children, you may find exceptions among typically non-friendly breeds. There are many endearing stories about Siamese, for example, who have shared a strong bond with children. However, the list below identifies breeds that either do not care for the loud and unpredictable movements of children or are prone to be one-person cats, jealous of children or other animals in the house.

1. American Wirehair
2. Bengal
3. Bombay
4. Cymric
5. Egyptian Mau
6. Korat
7. Siamese
8. Scottish Fold
9. Sphynx
10. Singapura

Like many of the breeds listed above, the Singapura is affectionate but quiet. These cats tend to be creatures of habit and do not like change. They treat strangers with caution. The origins of this cat's are up for debate. Some claim that the Singapura's suspicious nature stems from its treatment by Singaporeans, who dislike cats intensely. Also known as the "drain cat," this breed is said to roam the streets for scraps and has endured great abuse.

Most Popular Breeds

The most popular breed of cat is the mixed breed. Everyday mixed breeds have consistently proven to be stable, loving, loyal pets that blend easily with children, other animals, and hectic lifestyles. Still, cat fanciers identify pure breeds as personal favorites. In order of popularity the following is a list of the most beloved pure breeds.

1. Persian

2. Maine Coon

3. Bengal

4. Siamese

5. Abyssinian

6. Oriental Shorthair

7. American Shorthair

8. Birman

9. Burmese

10. Tonkinese

Most Unusual Breeds

Unlike the Nebelung or Tiffany (also known as Tiffanie or Chantilly)—which are truly rare breeds fighting for recognition and to keep the breed pure—the breeds in the following list are not difficult to find. Instead the breeds below exhibit some of the more rare and unusual traits in the cat world.

1. BENGAL

Not only do Bengals not fear water, they actually like it. Leaving the shower door open is a Bengal's invitation to jump in and play. Bengals are also unusual in their doglike characteristics. Called man's best friend in the cat world, these felines have a powerful build and love to roughhouse, fetch, and play games with their owners.

2. BOMBAY

In literature the Bombay has been compared to the exquisite black panther and, like the panther, has keen hearing and is ever alert and suspicious of strangers. Unlike the panther, this cat is extremely affectionate and enjoys quality time alone with its owner. After a long, hard day of listening to every sound in a one-mile radius, the Bombay enjoys nothing more than a nice, long walk with its owner.

3. JAPANESE BOBTAIL

One of the easiest breeds to teach, the Japanese bobtail loves to learn new tricks—and try them out again and

Tuesday Marie Essa

The appeal of the beautiful Bengal.

again—almost as much as they love their owners. Even without being taught to "shake" or "how do you do," these cats like to paw at their owners, raising a paw when people walk into the room to get attention. And, like the Bengal, these cats enjoy playing in water. Unlike the Bengal, however, the Japanese bobtail isn't afraid to jump in the water and paddle around.

4. **MAINE COON**

Known for their unusual style of sleeping—flat on their backs and spread-eagle or sprawled out as though they were a stuffed animal carelessly tossed to the side by a child—the Maine coon also has a great sense of humor. As much as they enjoy hunting outdoors and protecting their territory, they love to socialize in the house. Perhaps the most amusing thing about the coon is how they like to splash and play in water. Unusually adept with their paws, coons are also known to scoop up food in a paw to eat.

5. **MANX**

One of many legends about the Manx is set in 1588, when the Spanish Armada wrecked off the Isle of Man, located in the Irish Sea between England and Ireland. The Spanish cats, known for their ability to persevere under difficult circumstances, swam ashore and soon created their own flourishing colony on the isle. The Manx has been associated with the Celts, the Vikings, and pirates—all fitting companions for the strong hunter. In addition, this breed is recognized for its bravery when protecting an owner.

6. **NORWEGIAN FOREST CAT**

A frequent character in Norwegian and Swedish folktales, the "huldrekat" or "fairy cat," remains an extremely popular cat in the Scandinavian countries. They are the only cats that can climb down the full length of a tree headfirst. These clever cats can also open doors, often helping themselves to whatever they desire. Extremely affectionate cats, they will sit for hours with their owner.

7. **RAGDOLL**

The ragdoll has an unusually high threshold for pain, often making it difficult for owners to know if their kitty is injured or not. They are infinitely patient with children, love other animals, are fearless, healthy, and love being held—often melting into a person's arms like, well, a rag doll.

8. SCOTTISH FOLD

A cat with folded ears is unusual of and by itself, and this breed has not been without controversy in the cat world. It is, however, the personality of this breed that puts it in the unusual category. The origins of the Scottish Fold can be traced back to 1960s Scotland, where these cats became known as strong, ferocious mousers. This breed is healthy, resistant to disease and, by all appearances, very serious—until you see them sleeping: laid out, flat on their backs, with not a worry in the world, Scottish Folds morph into balls of fluff. This cat is also known to sit up like an otter, to the amusement of his owners.

9. SIAMESE

Can anything the Siamese do be construed as unusual? Yes, this fiercely independent cat enjoys a good walk with his owner wearing a leash and collar. For every time a veterinarian or animal behaviorist warns a prospective cat owner against getting a Siamese because of its loner ways, somewhere a Siamese cuddles up to his owner with leash in mouth, begging to go for a walk. This is the way of the Siamese.

10. SOMALI

The Somali is a long-haired Abyssinian with a gorgeous coat and, yet, this cat cannot stand the cold. Somalis should live indoors, especially during the colder months. Unlike the Maine coon, who loves the cold and will use its tail as a shield against the cold and winds, the thick tail of the Somali is for decoration only.

BONUS UNUSUAL BREED:

Look up the Turkish Van in any cat book and you will likely find a picture of a white cat swimming in pools, lakes, streams, or even bathtubs. And just like humans, this cat tends to have a unusually large appetite after a good swim.

Most Doglike Cats

Most doglike cats. In some circles, this could be considered a great insult. But those who own such cats know this comparison is made with great love, affection, and admiration. The cat is notoriously independent and self-centered—qualities that turn many people off of cats—but a large number of breeds are quite the opposite. In fact, some cats do not do well when left alone, crave companionship, love walks on a leash, perform tricks, and follow their owners around—like a puppy. These cats are happy, loyal, affectionate pets that defy the stereotypical (often negative) image of the cat.

1. ABYSSINIAN

Much like the Labrador retriever, this cat will find some way of entertaining himself—which could involve your drapes, a houseplant, or your stack of CDs, if it's left alone for too long a period of time. When given a choice, the Abyssinian will choose the company of an owner over another cat. The Aby likes to perform tricks, fetches, and enjoys long leash-walks.

2. BOMBAY

These extremely loving cats like to cuddle in bed together and enjoy being under the covers. Because they tend to be possessive of owners, these felines are not considered to be good with kids or other animals. They enjoy a one-on-one relationship and like nothing better than a good game of fetch.

3. **CHARTREUX**

This muscular, deep-chested cat enjoys fetching and some tug-of-war with its owner. It is said that the Chartreux, particularly the male, is easily trained and enjoys working. If well exercised, they are calm and gentle. The Charteux responds to his name and, in short spurts, will romp around with human pals in the backyard or around house in an enthusiastic game of chase.

4. **EGYPTIAN MAU**

Potential dog owners should analyze their lifestyle before investing in a canine. An active bird-hunting dog, for example, is not a good match for sedentary, apartment-dwelling people. Similarly, the Egyptian Mau is not a good match for sedentary, apartment-dwelling people who keep long hours away from home. Just like many smart hunting dogs, the Egyptian Mau—a cat that loves to learn tricks and play with its owner—will also teach itself how to escape from an apartment or house. The Egyptian Mau is quite adept at opening door and window latches.

5. **MAINE COON**

Like many hearty dogs, the Maine coon enjoys napping by a warm fireside as much as it loves hunting during the day, romping through the snow, playing with water, and defending its turf. This cat is the "King of the Jungle" in the domesticated cat world.

6. **OCICAT**

A large cat, this breed is often likened to a puppy. Exuberantly happy and eager to play, the ocicat is a fast learner, enjoys long leash-walks, and likes to play fetch.

7. **THE REXES**

Within the rex family are the Cornish rex and Devon rex along with new breeds named Dutch rex, Selkirk, and (unofficially) Si-rex. While there are variations to rex breeds and temperaments, they are all doglike in manner. Highly social, the rexes wag their tales with pleasure and trot along, beside, or behind their owners, always wanting to be part of the pack.

8. **RUSSIAN BLUE**

Also known to be excellent parents, Russian blues spend as much time with their owners as possible. The Russian blue is loving, loyal, and highly intelligent, but can also be destructive if neglected or ignored. This breed has been called the Doberman pinscher of cats.

9. **SIBERIAN**

Also known as the Siberian forest cat, the Siberian cat is a muscular, powerful feline that loves the outdoors. Like the Maine coon, this breed is very friendly. A Siberian will happily move from room to room with an active owner just to be nearby, and when given the chance, is a big face kisser, showering a willing owner with lots of love.

10. **TONKINESE**

The Tonkinese loves a good trick. Even better, this breed loves the time spent learning a new trick with an owner. An ideal breed for learning to come when called and shaking paws, Tonkinese have a wonderful sense of humor—often trying to trick their owners. Owners of this breed often wake up fifteen minutes early every morning to allow themselves time to deal with their loving Tonks. Just as dogs require attention in the morning, Tonkinese need some human time before their owners leave for the day.

Cats Who Rule the House

While all cat owners would say their cats are one-of-a-kind and certainly all kinds of breeds have intelligent, loving personalities, the following group of cats will especially disrupt the average household with its acrobatics, often in the middle of the night. With a passion for climbing drapes, skidding down hallways, leaping over furniture, and getting into everything they can possibly get into—and unconcerned with what you think about that—these cats are not for the fainthearted. You must be prepared to give lots of attention, affection, and exercise, and to have patience with these fun-loving felines—and batten down the hatches!

1. American Wirehair

2. Balinese

3. Egyptian Mau

4. Havana Brown

5. Norwegian Forest Cat

6. Ocicat

7. Oriental Shorthair

8.   Siamese

9.   Singapura

10.   Tonkinese

Facts about Siamese
. . . If You Please

M ost Americans were introduced to Siamese cats by way of song. In the 1955 animated Disney movie *Lady and the Tramp*, two mischievous Siamese, Si and Am, sang, "We are Siamese if you please. We are Siamese if you don't please." It had been fifty-six years since the first Siamese came to America, but the movie generated real interest in this fascinating cat among breeders and pet owners alike. The first several litters of Siamese kittens born in the United States were very weak, and many died of feline enteritis. However, the breed is tough and soon began producing healthy kittens. The Siamese have always been something of a breed apart; between legends about their Eastern heritage and stories of unusually strong personalities, they remain shrouded in a bit of mystery.

1. **SIAMESE ART**

At times there seems to be too little information about cats and early humans. Because cats were not seen as a threat nor a hunting partner, no cave drawings of early cats have been discovered. Although the Egyptians celebrated the cat, there is not one cat artifact from the early Romans, not even a cat bone from the ruins of Pompeii. So, it was all the more exciting that illustrated manuscripts from the ancient capital Ayutthaya in Siam (now Thailand) were found depicting a variety of cats from the years 1351–1767. What was even more compelling was the description of the cats—pale seal point Siamese, similar to today's breeds, showing how little the breed has actually changed.

2. THE FIRST SIAMESE IN THE WEST

The West didn't know the Siamese until the late nineteenth century when two cats, Pho and Mia, were sent to the British consul general by the king of Siam. In 1885 the breed first appeared in London, where Pho and Mia's offspring took ribbons at the Crystal Palace Cat Show. Pho and Mia were seal points with characteristic cream-colored coats and brown markings on their faces, paws, and tails.

3. CATS OF THE TEMPLE

The temple cats of Siam were regarded as sacred protectors of the souls of the dead. Only priests and royalty had the honor of keeping these cats, and anyone who attempted to steal the treasured felines was put to death. From the beginning, Siamese were held in the highest regard, rumored to be of great healing and magical powers, and kept secret from the rest of the world until the 1880s. The Temple Siamese were squinty-eyed with kinks in their tails—characteristics that were bred out over time.

4. THE STUFF LEGENDS ARE MADE OF

The Siamese were used as guards of Buddhist temples, protecting treasures from pirates. They were fierce warriors that would chase away, even attack, would-be robbers. So, it is said, the eyes of the Siamese were made squinty because of the long hours the cat spent gazing at the temple's treasures, never taking its eyes from its keep. And the cat's tail was kinked because it would curl around the treasure chest, always on the lookout for nighttime thieves. It was also believed that princesses, when bathing, would give their faithful Siamese their rings to hold. The clever cats would kink their tails to hold the jewelry and keep it from being lost or stolen.

5.   THE FAMILY TREE

The eight breeds of Siamese all have their trademark blue eyes in common. The family includes: Balinese, Birman, Burmese, Colorpoint longhair, Oriental shorthair, Siamese, Snowshoe, and Tonkinese.

6.   THE MAJESTIC BIRMAN

The long-haired Birman was also regarded as a temple cat. These cats, used to protect the temples and priests, were reputed to have descended from one pure white cat known as Sinh the Oracle, who resided in the Temple of Lao-Tsun. According to legend, when vigilantes attacked the temple one day, Sinh leapt to the rescue of his master, high priest Mun Ha. Although Sinh fought with all his strength, his master was struck down. As his master lay dying, Sinh's paws turned the purest of white where he touched the priest's body, while the rest of his fur took on a golden tinge and his eyes turned sapphire blue. Since, that time, all Birmans have had white paws, a gift from Sinh's tremendous act of bravery.

7.   APPLE HEAD

The 1960s were a time of change—a generation of people tried to "find themselves," while one of the Siamese lost a couple defining traits. Once a larger, heavyset cat with what was described as an apple head, today's Siamese is more slender and slight with a wedge-shaped head. Only the characteristic Siamese markings and the breed's penchant for talking remain the same. For Siamese fancier Diana Fineran, this change was unacceptable. Fineran, determined to bring back the apple head, contacted breeders with the more traditional looking Siamese in 1987 and established the Traditional Cat Association (www.traditionalcats.com) to preserve breeds as they once were.

8.   HAVANA BROWN

Evidence suggests that the Havana brown first appeared as early as 1888 in Britain and again in 1894, listed as a Swiss mountain cat or a brown cat. In the 1930s the brown cat appeared again, believed to be the result of a cross between a Siamese and a shorthair carrying the chocolate brown gene. It then disappeared, and was not to be seen again until the 1950s, when two British breeders mated a Siamese and a black shorthair with seal point ancestry, producing a beautiful litter of kittens, dubbed Havana browns, that were shown in 1953. Since then the American and British breeders of the Havana brown have used different methods: the British have continued to backcross the breed to the Siamese, making sure they captured the proper features, while the Americans have prohibited Siamese crossings (which limited the gene pool). And like the breeding methods, even the origin of the name is disputed: some claim Havana brown came from the brown rabbit breed, while others contend it came from the color of Havana tobacco.

9. OLD FAITHFUL

The primary characteristic of the Siamese is its great passion. Cat owners are warned not to adopt Siamese unless they are willing to invest time and energy to satisfy their cats' demands. Siamese are known to bond with just one owner and can be highly jealous if the object of their affections is looking elsewhere. Still, they are extremely loving and loyal cats, as noted in Siam legends. There is no greater example of the Siamese's devotion than that of Poo Jones, the cat of actress Vivien Leigh. Leigh and Poo Jones were inseparable, and the two sailed on the *Queen Elizabeth* in 1960, taking daily strolls together on deck. Poo Jones remained by his mistress for the rest of her life, lying at Leigh's bedside when she died in 1967.

10. SIAMESE TALK

Considered one of the Oriental breeds, the Siamese is the fourth most popular cat in the United States, and the most talkative of all the felines. Owners say that the Siamese have their own language, with more than a dozen yowling sounds that each have different meanings.

Most Popular Names for Female Cats

1. Sassy
2. Misty
3. Princess
4. Missy
5. Molly
6. Sophie
7. Maggie
8. Cleo
9. Chloe
10. Sadie

Most Popular Names
for Male Cats

1. Max

2. Sam

3. Simba

4. Charlie

5. Oscar

6. Buddy

7. Toby

8. Buster

9. Bailey

10. Simon

The Mysterious Sphynx

Many cat fanciers believe the sphynx comes from Egypt, but the breed is not nearly so ancient. Although one legend has it that the sphynx lived among the Aztecs, scientist refute this as nothing more than legend. So, what is the true origin of this hairless, unusual looking feline? Following are ten interesting facts about this rare breed.

1. PLACE OF BIRTH

Although the sphynx looks like the cats from ancient Egyptian drawings, it originated in Toronto, Canada, in 1966. When a hairless kitten was born to a black and white domestic cat named Elizabeth, a natural genetic mutation was recorded and cat breeders took notice. To get the sphynx line started, breeders bred the hairless cat to a cat with hair, and then bred it back to a hairless. By 1973 the sphynx became more common, and Cat Fanciers' Association (CFA) judge David Mare named the breed. Reminded of a famous Egyptian cat statue in the Louvre, he settled on the name sphynx.

2. APPEARANCE

Barrel-chested with long, slim legs, sphynx appear to be hairless but are covered with peach-fuzz-like fur. They have unusually large, wide-based ears, lemon-shaped eyes, and they are covered with wrinkles. Their feet have extra thick

Joe Patalano of Mythmakers Sphynx

A grand champion sphynx.

pads, making them look as though they are walking on air cushions. They are particularly nimble, using their unusually long toes as fingers. While they are medium-size cats, their weight is often more than one would think. They are particularly dense and muscular, coming in a variety of colors and markings.

3. NATURE OF THE BEAST

Sweet-tempered and loving, this cat has been compared to many dogs. They are known to run to the door to greet guests and climb up on visitors' laps. The sphynx enjoys playing one-on-one with its owner but will also play with another cat. They tend to be possessive of their owners, and were once believed to be best suited for single-cat families. In truth, sphynx are highly social creatures who love company. "They love to be taken for walks on leash as well as go for rides in the car," says breeder Diana Scott.

4. TO THE TOUCH

Sphynx breeders say that people who have never touched a sphynx are often surprised by its feel. Because a fine layer of peach-fuzz covers the cat's body, it is soft to the touch. Some sphynx have a suede-like feel while others feel more rubbery. Because it is hairless, this breed sweats (mildly). The sphynx is also surprisingly warm. One myth regarding this breed is that its body temperature is one to two degrees higher than that of the average cat. In truth, its body temperature is the same as other breeds but because it has no fur to insulate its body heat, it feels much warmer to the human touch.

5. IN THE EYE OF THE BEHOLDER

In the early 1990s the International Cat Association (TICA) in North America granted championship status to the sphynx. By 2002 the Cat Fanciers Association (CFA) of the United States had also granted them championship status, but the United Kingdom has been less forthcoming. While the Governing Council of the Cat Fancy (GCCF) recognizes the breed, they do not allow the cats to be shown. Despite the on-going debate regarding the breed's show status, the sphynx is TICA's eighth most-registered cat breed.

6. BY ANY OTHER NAME

The sphynx continues to be one of the most debated breeds in the cat world, and its name is no less controversial. These cats are often referred to as Mexican hairless, which is incorrect. Correct alternate names for the breed include Canadian hairless, temple cat, Chat sans Poils, and moon cat.

7. THE ALLERGY-FREE CAT

Not quite. One misconception about sphynx is that they are hypoallergenic. Many believe that because they are relatively hairless, these cats are good pets for people with allergies. But it is cat dander and saliva that causes the allergic reactions of cat owners and fanciers. The best benefit of the hairless sphynx is they won't get cat hair all over your furniture.

8. AN EASY-CARE CAT

Contrary to popular belief, this cat requires more grooming than most. The high-maintenance sphynx must be bathed every seven to ten days because oily secretions otherwise absorbed by a fur coat stay on their skin and collect dirt, dust, and debris. Heavy oil secreted from the cuticle area also collects dirt, so the cats' claws must be cleaned frequently. And because sphynx do not have eyelashes or fur protecting the ears, their eyes and ears collect goop that must be cleaned out regularly. Without a regimented cleaning routine, the sphynx can fall prey to serious infection.

9. FOR THE INDOORS ONLY

Though they need constant cleaning, sphynx are very sturdy cats. They are primarily indoor cats, due to their lack of protection against the elements. But a good rule of thumb is, if you are comfortable, your sphynx is comfortable. While sphynx, like humans, may not enjoy the outdoors on a chilly fall morning as much as Persian cats, they are strong, healthy felines. However, don't forget to cover your sphinx with sunscreen; also like humans, this breed is prone to sunburn.

10. STRIKE A POSE

Sphynx have a characteristic pose that is unique to their breed. Although no one is quite sure why, this cat often stands with a foreleg raised, much like a pointing bird dog.

For more information about the sphynx, contact Diana Scott at www.kkfa.com/sundancenbare or www.sundancen bare.com.

The Maine Coon

The Maine coon is often referred to as the all-American cat. The breed has a number of legends about its origins and, if possible, an even greater number of supporters. Not long after the breed was recognized its popularity soared, in part because of the cat's pleasant temperament and also because, like every great story, the Maine coon was not without controversy.

1. A STAR IS BORN

At the beginning of the French Revolution in 1789, says one of several stories, Marie Antoinette planned to flee France for America, and in preparations she sent her beloved cats ahead of her. Her feline entourage included Persian and Angora cats. Although great care was taken in transporting the cats, they escaped once they landed on American soil and, so says the legend, interbred with American feral cats. Thus, the Maine coon was born.

2. NORWEGIAN FOREST CAT

Rumors persist about the origin of the Maine coon. Many say the first coon was the result of a cross between a domestic cat and a raccoon or a cross between a housecat and a spotted bobcat. Since both of those options are genetically impossible, the breed is more likely a direct descendant of the

Norwegian forest cat, which may have been introduced to America by Leif Eriksson or those who followed him on his travels in the eleventh century.

3. CAPTAIN COON

Then, again, there was a sea captain by the name of Coon who traveled up and down the New England coast in the early 1800s with his many Persian and Angora pet cats. Whenever the captain went ashore, so did his cats. When longhaired kittens began showing up in coast towns, local inhabitants called them "Coon's cats."

4. AMERICA'S SETTLERS AND THEIR CATS

It seems most likely that the Maine coon is a successor of the cats that came to America with the early colonists. Later trading ships probably brought additional cats, including longhaired cats that bred with the local shorthairs. Cats that survived the first cruel New England winters were probably the Maine coon's first ancestors.

5. SNOW CATS

Because Jeff Valdez said cats could never be made to pull a sled through snow, we can assume he never met a Maine coon. Unlike other cats, the Maine coon enjoys a good romp in the snow. This breed was designed to survive the harsh winters of the area bordering Canada, where the average annual snowfall is over seventy inches and the frost remains for over six months of the year. The Maine coon has developed a rugged coat, which acts as a blanket against the wet snow and as insulation for their bodies. Its large feet have great tufts of hair between the pads, allowing them to cross over snow and ice—perhaps another indication that the Maine coon is related to the bobcat.

6. BEST OF SHOW

Thanks to Mrs. E. R. Pierce, who documented the early breeding and showing history of domestic cats in the United

States, we know that twelve Maine coons appeared in America's first cat show in Boston, January 1878. In 1895 a Maine coon won Best Cat at the first national cat show, held at Madison Square Garden in New York City. Cat shows were popular as early as the 1870s, especially at county fairs, where they offered excitement for breeders and cat lovers alike.

7. "SOME PRETTY GOOD CAT"

The intelligent and industrious Maine coon was a favorite of the early settlers, both as a family pet and as a mouser. A story in coon history reports that in the 1860s a Maine farmer, besieged by mice, brought home a coon in hopes of restoring order to his farm. Reportedly, his wife was not pleased about the new addition to the family until she saw how quickly the mighty hunter ridded her henhouse of mice. "That is some pretty good cat!" she exclaimed. Noted less for their beauty and more for their robust stature, Maine coons have long been renowned as great barn cats and continue to enjoy the reputation of "pretty good cat" today. They are the second most popular cat in America and the number one choice among farmers and ranchers.

8. BUILT FOR SURVIVAL

The Maine coon is an excellent example of adaptation to the environment. Having to survive in the harsh New England winters has given the cat a heavy, water-resistant coat that is unlike the fur of any other cat. Longer under the neck, on the stomach, and on the hindquarters, it protects the cat from snow and wet weather; short on the back and top of the neck, it doesn't get caught in bushes and other entanglements. While it might not sound so, the Maine coon's fur is smooth and—here's the best part—requires very little care. Brushing once a week will make your Maine coon look splendid. Coons also have a long, bushy tail that they wrap around themselves for warmth. Extra fur in and around their ears and huge, tufted feet (snowshoes) also protect them from the cold. Big eyes and ears enhance the cats' chances of survival, giving them greater sight and hearing capacities. If your Maine coon is an indoor cat, you may notice another trait linked to its development: coons are not as vertically oriented as many other breeds. They are not inclined to jump up for things, but prefer to chase objects on the ground and grab them with their big paws—appropriate behavior for mousers.

9. ONCE A KITTEN, ALWAYS A KITTEN

Maine coon cats develop slowly. They are not fully grown until they are between three and five years old, and their behavior is kitten-like throughout their lives. They have been described as "big, gentle, good-natured goofs." They are affectionate, enjoy the company of children, dogs, and other cats, and seem to like being around lots of people and activity. While a Maine coon will not constantly demand affection, it does like to "hang with the guys." Your coon will almost always be close at hand, just being there and being nice. Even the Maine coon's voice—a soft sound that some describe as similar to the chirping or trilling sound made by raccoons—is pleasant and so quiet that it doesn't seem to fit the cat's size. On average females weigh nine to twelve pounds and males weigh thirteen to eighteen pounds, and with the winter coat added, the coon is a big cat—which makes his kittenish behavior even more endearing.

10. SO YOU THINK YOU WANT A MAINE COON

Then you need to do your homework: read more about the breed, find local breeders, and learn about breeding ethics. One of the things you need to know is what special medical problems might exist in the breed. All breeds have genetic strengths and weaknesses—the Maine coon's sometime health problems are hip dysphasia and cardiomyopathy—but knowing your breed and working with reputable breeders will significantly lessen the chance of a serious problem arising in your cat. Cat associations recommend visiting local cat shows to meet breeders and see their cats firsthand. Cat magazines list breeders, and breeders lists are also available online. The Fanciers Breeder Referral List (FBRL) includes Maine coon breeders. Have fun looking, and enjoy your Maine coon!

Munchkin Facts

W hat is the munchkin? No, not a little person from the *Wizard of Oz* (although a cat named Eureka did appear with Dorothy in the *Wizard of Oz*). The munchkin is a breed of domestic cat with unusually short legs. While some cat lovers contend these are perfectly natural cats, others protest the continuation of breeding a genetic defect. As animal rights activists and enthusiasts battle back and forth, here are ten facts to consider about the controversial breed.

1. THE ORIGIN OF THE MUNCHKIN

Most people did not know about this breed until it was formally introduced to the public at Madison Square Garden in March 1991, but it had been previously identified in England during the 1930s. Four generations of munchkins were described in the *Veterinary Record* in 1944, but the breed disappeared during World War II. Munchkins resurfaced in Stalingrad in 1953, only to disappear again until the 1970s, when they reappeared in New England.

2. FIRST KNOWN MUNCHKIN BREEDERS

In 1983 a woman named Sandra Hochenedel found a pregnant black cat with very short legs living under a pickup truck. Christened Blackberry, the cat soon had a litter of kittens, half of whom had the same short legs their mother had.

Blackberry reportedly continued to have litters of kittens, throwing the munchkin gene to at least half of each of her litters. One of her male kittens, named Toulouse, was given to a woman named Kay LaFrance, who established a colony of munchkins.

3. THE DWARFISM GENE

Munchkins are the product of dwarfism. The gene for dwarfism is autosomal dominant, which means that it can be passed from either parent (autosomal) and that it only takes one parent to pass the gene to offspring (dominant). Kittens of a parent with the dwarfism gene have a 50 percent chance of inheriting it. If both parents have the dwarfism gene, the chances of its inheritance are greatly increased. A kitten embryo that receives a copy of the dwarf gene from both parents is a homozygous lethal and is unable to survive the womb. For this reason, munchkin breeders mate a "nonstandard," or long-legged, cat of either sex to a "standard," or short-legged, cat of the other sex.

4. THE CAT

Munchkins have large, wide-set, walnut-shaped eyes, which give them an open, alert expression. Their typical body size is about that of nonstandard cats (perhaps a little smaller), but they have significant shortening and mild bowing of the nonstandard cats' long bones; specifically, munchkins have short legs. They are amusing to watch because of their running gait, which has been likened to that of a ferret, although they can achieve great speed and can, according to one munchkin expert, "outrun an alligator" and "scramble up trees." However, their shorter legs make them unable to achieve the kind of leverage a typical cat achieves and most often cannot jump onto countertops or high ledges (a characteristic some breeders/owners find preferable).

5. THE TYPE

At the present time the munchkin appears to come in every sort of body type, head type, coat length, and color. The only thing these cats have in common is their extremely short legs. Since their gene pool is unlimited, no clear guidelines can predict the cat a munchkin will ultimately resemble; some munchkin breeders mate to Persians, others to Siamese, and still others to Abyssinians. So all that sets them apart at this point in time are their distinctively short legs.

6.   THE PERSONALITY

Munchkins maintain kitten-like personalities for their entire lives, making them perfect for people who desire a kitten that never grows up. They are affectionate, social, and outgoing cats, who love to be around people of all ages, other cats, and dogs. They readily accept a harness and leash and seem to enjoy taking their owners for walks. Munchkins are very playful and love to run, chase, climb, and play with toys. Their short legs give them an advantage over long-legged cats when it comes to chasing because they can scramble faster and corner more sharply. Finally, munchkins are often called the magpie cat because they love to collect little jewels and knickknacks, just like the magpie, and hide them under furniture.

7.   THE ARGUMENT AGAINST

While breeders of this cat contend that the munchkin survived in feral communities in Europe, present day veterinarians argue that history is not a license to continue to breed a mutated gene, which poses physical threats to the animal. Munchkins can suffer from a condition called thoracic lordosis, which causes back pain and pressure. Because the body of the munchkin cat is still long, excessive pressure is placed on the cat's spine. Evidence also suggests that this breed is susceptible to compressions in the chest, which can put extra pressure on the heart and lungs. When munchkins are bred with heavy-boned cats, their kittens' often have leg bones and elbows that protrude, causing more pain or other ailments.

8. THE ARGUMENT FOR

Professional munchkin breeders say they are aware of these potential health problems and are therefore very selective in their breeding. Breeders point out that dwarfism occurs in other animals as well. In the canine world the basset hound, dachshund, and corgi are products of the dwarf gene—having been bred specifically as working/hunting/herding dogs. (Dachshunds, for example, are bred to hunt badgers and must have short legs so that they can follow the badgers into their holes.) Munchkin breeders argue that these dogs are also full-bodied, short-legged animals who are active and successful hunters and live full lives (although all three breeds are also subject to back problems because of their long spines).

9. THE BREEDING DEBATE

Many cat enthusiasts were alarmed by the official introduction of the munchkin, fearing that the munchkin gene would begin to find its way into other breeds of cats. However, serious breeders, munchkin breeders say, would never mix breeds. Still, veterinarian groups worry that the munchkin is bred strictly for a specific look or body type. This is not only a worry in the cat community but in all animal breeding circles. Animal breeding for looks only always raises red flags because such careless breeding so often leads to all kinds of medical problems and complications. On the one hand, munchkin breeders note that corgi and dachshund breeders have been dealing with this for decades; on the other hand, vets point out that corgis (herding dogs) and dachshunds (hunting dogs) have a purpose for their size and are also bred for temperament and agility. Another example of breeding for purposeful appearance in the canine world is the Great Pyrenees, a large white herding dog, which was specifically bred with a white coat so herders could distinguish between the dog and a wolf in the dark.

10. **WHAT'S NORMAL?**

It is important to understand what is deemed acceptable in one organization may be unacceptable in another. There are often vast differences between the American and the European definitions of "abnormality," "defect," and "deformity." What American breeders see as short legs may be considered a deformity in Europe, and vice versa. According to the American Veterinary Association, good health and strong bodies are the most important qualities to look for in your cat. Whether or not all munchkin breeders are breeding a specific look, there is no doubt that at least one of them is doing just that—to the detriment of the animals she is breeding.

In 1944 documentation appeared regarding a breed of cats in Japan that appeared to have a genetic mutation of the feet. These cat had a condition called radial hypoplasia, or in the more extreme form, radial aplasia, in which the long bone of the leg was absent and the wrists/paws were attached close to the shoulder. The cats' feet were either deformed (twisted) or absent, leading to severe medical problems. These cats had to use their back legs to hobble along, earning them the name the kangaroo cat. In recent years a woman in Texas, Vickie Ives Speir of Karma Farms, declared these cats "cute" and began breeding what she calls twisty cats (or Karma Kats). Almost no one in the cat and medical communities disputes that these cats live in great discomfort for the duration of their lives. Unfortunately, no laws in Texas prevent the breeder from continuing this practice. For more information about twisty cats and other breed mutations, visit these websites: www.simplypets.com, www.cfainc.org.

Feral Cats: Facts vs. Myths

Feral cats are domestic cats living as wild animals, a result of either being abandoned by humans or having been born into the wild. However they became feral, these cats are the topic of a growing debate around the world. Large communities of feral cats are blamed for property destruction and disease, and they are real sore spots for bird lovers. Animal activists also cite problems for the cats themselves—starvation, predators, disease, and abuse. Too many people believe that cats can be dumped in the countryside or left to fend for themselves in the city because they are the ultimate survivors. "They'll be just fine," they often reason. If you have uttered these words, this chapter is for you. Here are the facts and myths about the feral cat.

1. FERAL CATS ARE MAN-MADE.

Fact. These cats are the offspring of cats that have been abandoned, dumped, and neglected. Researchers know that a colony can grow rapidly, with one unspayed queen responsible for up to seventy kittens and one tom able to father an infinite number of cats. Because these animals are survivors, they can create colonies almost anywhere, hunting prey or raiding dumpsters to exist.

2. FEEDING A FERAL IS A GOOD THING.

Myth. We've all done it. We've fed a helpless stray and sent it on its way with a full belly. The American Veterinary Medical Association has estimated that millions of people feed feral cats. So how can feeding a stray be a bad thing? This practice, though well intentioned, actually increases the chances that a colony will increase by sustaining the feral breeding machine. Animal activists encourage kindhearted stray feeders to trap feral cats and have them spayed instead. Often local humane societies will spay strays free of charge (check feral information with your local society).

3. FERAL CATS CANNOT BE SAVED.

Myth. Feral communities subsist on remote islands, where, speculation has it, they are the survivors and descendants of shipwrecks. These cats rely on their ancestral hunting instincts to feed and survive. These remote colonies have perpetuated the myth that feral cats cannot live among and interact with humans. In fact, kittens that have been trapped and cared for can learn to tolerate (and trust) humans.

4. FERAL CATS DESTROY THE BIRD COMMUNITY.

Myth. In truth, cats have been hunting birds for centuries—and then some. Amazingly, both species have coexisted well enough. While fewer cats are always better for bird populations, humans have had the most devastating effect on our feathered friends. Every day humans destroy the birds' natural habitats, forcing them into suburbs and parks where they are prime pickin's for hungry felines. A feral community that is controlled in numbers has far less impact on the bird community than human habitat destruction.

5. FERAL CATS ARE WILD, AND THEREFORE, COMMUNITIES CANNOT BE MANAGED.

Myth. When citizens work with city or county officials in an effective trapping and neutering program, the population of feral communities can be controlled. When trapped, the animals are vaccinated and, at times, tagged for research. The Ocean Reef Club in Key Largo, for example, adopted a trapping and neutering program in 1995 with the help of three veterinarian technicians. The numbers of the cat population in their community fell from more than two thousand to only five hundred in eight years (and are reportedly still dropping). The biggest threat to this program is humans who use the feral communities as a dumping ground for the felines they no longer want. Still, evidence shows that a well-managed community allows for ferals to dwell successfully and healthfully among human populations.

6. FERAL CATS CARRY DISEASE.

Fact. Unmanaged feral communities can carry (and transmit) rabies, feline leukemia, and toxoplasmosis—to name only a few diseases—to other animals and humans. This is a compelling reason for trapping and neutering programs, which greatly reduce cat suffering with no risks to the human community, to be implemented in all communities.

7. FERAL CATS ARE DANGEROUS FOR THE COMMUNITY.

Myth. "Feral cats attack humans!" This headline has run several times in small beach communities battling with feral communities, which have become drop off points for unwanted cats. With an estimated 2 million feral cats in Britain and possibly more than 6 million in the United States, there is no question that a management program has to be adopted to care for these creatures. In fact, more people are scratched, bitten, or attacked by domesticated felines than ferals. In June 2003 in New Milton, England, the Royal Mail was temporarily shut down after postal workers protested against an eleven-year-old domestic cat named Purrdey that attacked, bit, pounced on, spit at, and scratched seven carriers. In 2002 a housecat named Boo Boo temporarily shut down the mail. More often than not, ferals are timid around humans and will flee rather than have any contact.

8. THE FLORIDA CONTROVERSY

Florida, just one of several states tackling the problem of feral cats, made national headlines when a seven-member commission appointed by Governor Jeb Bush decided to capture and euthanize its feral population. The commission's biologist described feral cats as predatory machines, killing rare beach mice, ground-nesting birds, endangered rabbits, the rare Key Largo woodrats, and other animals. Further, the commission argued that large feral communities took food away from the state's other natural predators, including the hawk, fox, owl, and bobcat. In defense of the feral, cat advocates cite human construction and destruction as the greatest contributor to animal extinction, but developers, including those in Florida, the third most populous state in the nation, have more powerful backers than cats do.

9. THE LIFE OF THE FERAL

Just twenty years ago the life expectancy of the domestic cat was four to five years. Today, the life expectancy is fifteen years or more. The feral, in contrast, is not so fortunate with a life expectancy of only five to six years. Because the feral cat spends much of its day hunting or finding a place to stay warm and secure, it is more lean and smaller-boned than the house cat. In an unmanaged community, the greatest health threat to the stray is respiratory viral infections, which can run rampant through a feral community. Traffic, abuse, inhumane traps, and accidental poisoning are other hazards ferals must face. Worse, because the feral is so vehemently despised by many humans, they are often shot. In England one gamekeeper claimed to have killed over three hundred ferals, while another brought home pelts to his wife so that she could design rugs from cat skins as a source of secondary income.

10. FERALS AND ABORIGINIES

Like all other cat species, the feral seem to have its own folklore. For years anthropologists have wondered how feral cats came to Australia. Although no cats species are indigenous to Australia, several kinds of cats can be found there. How? According to aboriginal folklore, the Great Hunting Cat was and is part of their ancestry. When the aborigines, who traveled across the continents settled more than 50,000 years ago, they brought hunting cats with them from the islands. Although they arrived before the early colonists, the cats of Australia are the truest form of feral.

The Big Cats

Just how different is your homebound kitty from the big cats? The term "big cat" in fact, denotes only five of the large, muscular cats of the wild. Known as *Panthera*, these five have distinct physical and behavioral characteristics that differ from those of other large cats such as the lynx, puma, cheetah, and bobcat. The great roaring cats, as they are also known, are the most sought after prey for trophy hunters—and three of them are listed as endangered species.

1. KING OF THE JUNGLE

Only folktales and legends have made the lion the king of the jungle. The male's regal mane makes him a majestic character for story time. In truth, this big cat lives in open plains with antelopes, zebras, and giraffes. The "king" prefers to live in a pride—a large group of lions that share hunting responsibilities. In the pride, the pressure is on the male to establish dominance and effectively fight off hyena or leopards that attack the young. The female lion is the mighty hunter that stalks and kills to feed the young.

2. LAST OF ITS KIND

The lion that once roamed all over Europe, Africa, and South Asia is now confined to Africa, south of the Sahara. As late as the 1850s lions were seen in India, but their numbers decreased sharply because of big game hunting. Today, a very small number, fewer than 250, dwell in northwestern India where a lion sanctuary was created in 1966. North Africa was once home to a large species of lion whose males had manes that covered their entire bodies, but this species had been killed off by the early 1920s. One remaining colony of lions on the Atlantic coastal strip of Namibia were destroyed by 1991. Although the lion has always been referred to as fierce and rugged, humans threaten the long-term existence of these quiet, graceful animals.

3. JAGUAR

Native to the Americas, this big cat inhabits tropical forests and open plains from southern Mexico to Argentina. As late as the 1940s the jaguar also lived in Texas. Preferring to reside by the water, the powerful cat became a symbol of grace, strength, stealth, and agility to the Aztecs of Mexico and South American Indian tribes. These tribes hunted the cat, using its glorious coat for headdresses and ceremonial covers. Weighing from ninety to three hundred pounds, larger jaguars are capable of bringing down a horse, cow, water hog, or any other large animal that happens to its waterhole for a cool drink.

4. LEOPARD

The most widespread of the big cats is the *Panthera pardus*—the leopard. Found throughout most of Saharan Africa, Asia Minor, and southern Asia, this cat has adapted from the jungles and scrublands to the deserts and swamplands. Archeologists have found prehistoric remains of the leopard that indicate it once lived throughout Europe. Today, the leopard continues to be the most agile of all the big cats, scaling trees or running down large prey. Unlike other cats, these big cats do not bury their prey. The leopard avoids dinnertime confrontations with other big cats by dragging its prey up into a tree where he can eat in peace.

5. SNOW LEOPARD

The endangered snow leopard lives in the rocky terrain of the Himalayas and Central Asia, above the snowfields and glaciers during the summer months and just below the snow-lines in the winter. As food is often scarce in this harsh environment, snow leopards will raid livestock herds, making themselves targets for farmers and herders. Because the coat of the snow leopard is thick and plush, it has long been an ideal pelt for hunters. With fewer than five thousand in existence, the snow leopard continues to be in great danger as long as its coat is bought and sold on the Asian market.

6. CLOUDED LEOPARD

Very little is known about this cat, and what is known comes from observations of captive cats. The clouded leopard is approximately half the size of the snow leopard with short, powerfully built legs. This cat was discovered in the nineteenth century, although it may have been around in ancient times. Unlike the other large cats, the clouded leopard has unusually long upper canines, similar to the prehistoric saber-toothed tiger. Living in the forests and swamplands of southern and southeast Asia, this is the only big cat besides the cheetah that is unable to roar.

7. *PANTHERA TIGRIS*

The tiger is the largest of all the big cats, often tipping the scales between 250 and 500 pounds and sometimes as large as 700 pounds. A native of the southern and southeastern Asian jungles, northeastern China, and Siberia, it is also the only striped big cat. Eating up to sixty pounds in one sitting, these big cats feed on young elephants, buffaloes, wild pigs, and even other cats, including the lynx. Much of their day is spent in the shade of trees. They actively dislike the heat and enjoy a good swim. The tiger is always on the move, covering as much as six hundred miles within a month. Some of its characteristics, however, are not so different from those of the demure housecat. Like so many in the cat family, the tiger is reputed to be an excellent mother, moving her cubs often for safety. Unlike the feral cat, which often dies young, the wild tiger lives to be twenty to twenty-five years old.

8. DRIVEN TO EXTINCTION

In 1900 there were more than 100,000 tigers worldwide. Just ninety years later fewer than five thousand remained. In Indonesia, on Sumatra, there are thought to be fewer than five hundred tigers, and in the whole of southern China there are no more than fifty. Siberia's numbers are down to five hundred and the Caspian tiger, a native of central Asia, has not been seen since 1970. Human population increase, natural habitat loss, and the use of tigers for ancient herbal medicines in Asian and Indian communities have had a devastating impact on tiger populations. Fortunately, the government of India implemented Project Tiger in 1973 to preserve the country's tiger population; the program saved the Royal Bengal just in time. In 1970s these tigers numbered fewer than two thousand. Today they have flourished; there are now more than forty thousand. (See projecttiger.nic.in for more information.)

9. A CLASS BY ITSELF

The cheetah is unlike any other big cat. The sole member of the *Acinonyx jubatus*, it is the only large cat unable to retract its claws. And unlike all the other cats that stalk and pounce, the cheetah chases down its prey, reaching speeds up to seventy miles per hour. With its claws constantly exposed, the cheetah brings down its victim with a final spring. As a young hunter, the cheetah is quite effective, but because of its impatience (the cheetah will not wait or stalk like the other cats), it suffers as it become less agile in old age. The life span of the cheetah is only five to seven years, and because they leave their dens more often to hunt, their cubs often have to face hyenas and lions alone, making the fatality rate very high for cheetah young. Fewer than ten thousand chee-

Marc Powe

Cheetahs are shut out of their territories by
East African landowners.

tahs live in the wild in Africa; in Asia and the Middle East the
numbers are far fewer. Iran, which once had 230,000 cheetahs in the early 1900s, now has fewer than sixty.

10. THE DOMESTICATED CHEETAH

The ancient Egyptians captured and domesticated the cheetah for their own hunting purposes. After dogs had flushed
out the prey, the Egyptians released a hidden cheetah to
bring the victim down. They used this hidden cat as much
for its agility as for sideshow entertainment. The ancient Persians adopted this sport from the Egyptians, carrying it over
to India where royalty hunted with the big cats. As late as the
twentieth century, cheetahs were regarded as royal pets.

Interestingly, a new mutation called the king cheetah has
been included in the cheetah family. The king cheetah can
interbreed with normal cheetahs and create a healthy, fertile
cheetah of both variations. Bigger in body with more spots,
the king is a perfect name for this cat.

Wild Facts about European Cats

The small cats of Europe, not to be confused with domesticated house cats or small feral cats, still run wild throughout the world. These cats, members of the *Felis* genus, are unable to roar—unlike the members of the *Panthera* genus whose voice box and skull are connected by tough elastic cartilage. The *Felis* genus is without this cartilage, and their deep roars are only mews. Despite their softer voices, however, these cats are equally powerful hunters.

1. THE SABRE-TOOTHED COUSIN

Some 35 million years ago, saber-toothed wildcats roamed present-day Europe. From this prehistoric cat came the lions, leopards, and other jungle cats that gradually migrated in response to external pressures of human settlements and climate changes. Many of the cats moved to warmer climates, but not all. Today, three small cats remain in Europe: the Spanish lynx, Northern lynx, and the European wildcat.

2. THE RAREST LYNX

Of the lynx species, the Spanish lynx is the most rare. Revered for its luxurious coat, the Spanish lynx has been so heavily hunted that, as of 1990, it was feared there were fewer than two hundred left. The third largest of the small cats (weighing up to thirty pounds), the Spanish lynx now lives in the remote mountainous regions of Spain and Portugal. This beautiful cat is listed on the United Nations' endangered species list.

3. **THE EURASIAN CAT**

Also known as the Eurasian cat, this wildcat has been hunted almost to extinction. Weighing between forty-five and eighty-five pounds, the thick-coated lynx moves and hunts easily in the snowy regions of northern and central Europe. Once a great hunter that stalked through prehistoric Britain, the Eurasian cat was known to be a ferocious killer of small prey, including mountain sheep and deer. By the end of the twentieth century, Europeans finally began to see the worth of this cat and protected it from hunters. From Norway and Sweden to the Balkans, Russia, Switzerland, Finland, and the Czech Republic, the Eurasian cat is protected by hunting regulations or is offered complete protection.

4. **THE MYSTERIOUS EARS**

The beautiful lynx has thick tufts of hair that extend from the ends of their ears, which zoologists believe act as antennas to help catch sounds.

5. **THE COMEBACK CAT**

Today the *Felis silvestris* is the most widespread wildcat to dwell in Europe, with habitats ranging from France to Poland. But the European wildcat was once on the verge of extinction. Until the fifteenth century the wildcat was quite common; however, as church and state turned against the cat, hatred for the European wildcat grew to great proportions. Farmers hated the wildcats because they threatened livestock and poultry. In the nineteenth and twentieth centuries, when farms began to decline and hunting estates became less numerous, the European wildcat population began to grow, and by the 1940s the species could be seen throughout Europe. Its revival, however, was short-lived. The European wildcat . . .

6. ... IS SLIPPING AGAIN.

Although hunting is not as prevalent as it was in prior centuries, it is still a factor in reducing the numbers of wildcats. More significantly, human population growth and the outward spread of cities and suburbs throughout Europe have had a major impact on the cats' habitats. Today the wildcat exists only in scattered populations in parts of France, Germany, Belgium, Spain, Portugal, Italy, England, Greece, Eastern Europe, and around the Black Sea.

7. TRUE TREE-HUGGERS

The European wildcat primarily lives in the forest. There seems to be a difference of opinion among the cats about the kind of forest they prefer—some favor conifers, while others choose deciduous wooded areas. Naturally, the wildcats' homes determine their diets. They primarily eat wood mice, pine voles, water voles, and shrews, with birds, small reptiles, and insects as supplements. Interestingly, wildcats do not usually eat fish, unlike their domestic cousins that seem to love fish. Perhaps it is the act of fishing that puts off the wildcats.

8. THE SCOTTISH WILDCAT

In Africa there are numerous subspecies of wildcat, usually divided by regions. In Europe, however, there are only three subspecies: *silvestris*, which makes up most of the European population; *caucasica*, which lives only in Turkey and the Caucasus Mountains; and *grampia*, found only in Scotland. The Scottish wildcat does not live in the forests; rather, it prefers the low shrubs of the heathland and the rocky, swampy moorland. The cats subsist mostly on rabbit and hare, which are plentiful in the open Scottish countryside.

9. THE WILD SIDE

Unlike the feral cat, the European wildcat has yet to be tamed when caught. They remain wild and fierce in captivity.

And when domesticated cats have mated with the wildcats, the hybrid kittens are usually untamable.

10.   **THE GREATEST THREAT**

Greater than the danger posed by hunters and more worrisome than human encroachment on the shrinking wildcat habitats is the threat to the species raised by inadvertent crossbreeding. While many wildcats live in remote areas, many also live close to farms, villages, and even cities. The wildcats introduction to domestic and feral cats both exposes the wildcat population to domestic cat diseases and to the possibility of interbreeding. As wildcats become more and more genetically mixed, we risk losing not only the species but the environs that the cats help to maintain.

Small Cats of the Americas

Relatives of the modern-day cat have existed in the Americas for more than 10 million years. Both lions and jaguars crossed the land bridge to the Americas from Asia, with lions occupying the Americas as far south as Peru until climatic change killed them off. But other smaller cats, with varying shapes, sizes, and behavioral characteristics, roamed the Americas as well.

1. KODKOD

This unusual cat remains a mystery to present-day zoologists. In fact, most of what we know about the kodkod comes from information recorded by a Jesuit priest more than two hundred years ago. Juan Ignacio Molina observed the small (four to nine pounds), nocturnal wildcat in the Amazonian rainforest. Today the kodkod, the *Felis guigna*, lives in the Andes foothills of Chile and Argentina.

2. PAMPAS CAT

The *Felis colocolo*, once a natural forest dweller, survives in the scrubland, forced out of the woods by excessive logging by humans. Ranging in size between eight to fourteen pounds, the pampas cat is reputed to be very aggressive and fearless. Fortunately, this rare cat is protected in Argentina. It also lives in Ecuador, Peru, and Brazil.

3. GEOFFROY'S CAT

Named after the nineteenth century French zoologist Etienne Geoffroy Saint-Hilaire, one of the pioneers of zoology species classification, this cat is quite similar to the pampas cat in size and coloring, but unlike the pampas cat, Geoffroy's cat prefers the lowlands of Bolivia, Argentina, Chile, Uruguay, and Brazil. Geoffroy's cat (*Felis geoffroyi*) is another wildcat involved in a breeding program with the domesticated cat. As one breeder reported, in every attempt to breed the two species, the male Geoffroy's cat killed the domesticated females.

4. TIGER CAT

The tiger cat (*Felis tigrina*) looks more like a rat than a cat, but it is indeed part of the American cat family. Also known as the little spotted cat, the tiger has small white spots over its coarse light brown coat and a hint of stripes. Very little is known about this rare breed, which is believed to be threatened by the deforestation of the Amazon basin.

5. CANADIAN LYNX

The fur trade took its toll on the Canadian lynx (*Lynx canadensis*). Today the numbers hunted are being counted. The biggest threat against this lynx is the diminishing snowshoe hare population, which it relies on heavily for its diet. When outside elements (human hunters, loss of habitat) affect the snowshoe hare population, they in turn affect this lynx. Tipping the scales at twenty-plus pounds, the Canadian lynx lives throughout Canada and Alaska and occasionally moves down to the northern regions of the United States.

6. OCELOT

Author Michael Pollard put it best when he wrote that the downfall of the ocelot has been its beauty. While this cat is said to be an extremely ferocious hunter, it has not fared well against hunters from the pelt industry. Its coat, similar in markings to the jaguar's, has made it a popular target in its southern United States and Argentinean homelands. Ranging in weight between twenty-five and thirty-five pounds, the *Felis pardalis* prefers the rainforest and bush country to the open range and is most active at dusk or night.

7. BOBCAT

Most Americans are familiar with the bobcat (*Lynx rufus*), who has survived all kinds of climates from the northern United States to southern Mexico. Slightly smaller than the Canadian lynx, the bobcat is powerfully built and is most known for its stumpy tail. The bobcat preys on rabbits, young deer, and occasionally young livestock such as goats. In harder times the bobcat is not opposed to killing and eating frogs and lizards. Because the bobcat does not have great speed, it must rely on other methods and diet options when hunting.

8. JAGUARUNDI

Otherwise known as *Felis yagouarondi*, the jaguarundi lives throughout Central America from Brazil to Paraguay, as well as in the southern regions of Texas. Described to have an almost weasel or otter-like face, this cat has short legs with an elongated body, making it a good stalker in brush. Its name is derived from the Tupi Indian language, and like the ancient cats did with the Egyptians, it appears to have developed a relationship with villagers in South America. There is documentation of jaguarundis being domesticated, working in farming communities to control rodents and reptiles. Most of these cats that live in the wild, however, are not territorial and are given to wandering great lengths.

9. MARGAY

The margay is known by several names: *Felis wiedii*, tree ocelot, and long-tailed spotted cat. It lives in the tropical forests and scrublands of Central and South America. A small cat, ranging in weight between six and eleven pounds, the margay lives happily in the trees. Because of its small stature and beautifully spotted coat (it's often likened to a miniature leopard), there have been many unsuccessful attempts to capture and domesticate this wildcat.

10. ANDEAN MOUNTAIN CAT

Called the Andean highland cat or mountain cat, the *Felis jacobita* is a medium-size cat (between eight and fifteen pounds) that lives on the slopes of the Andes from southern Peru to northwest Argentina. Very little is known about this species of cat except that it prefers to live along the snowline on the treeless, rocky terrain. Like the lynx, the Andean mountain cat has long tufts of hair extending from the tips of its ears, which may act as a hunting aid in such a remote region of the world. Its thick, luxurious coat is desired among fur traders.

The Great American Cat

The puma has become a mascot for shoe and sports apparel, dozens of colleges and high schools, and little league teams around the United States because of its power, grace, and athleticism. This all-American cat is the lion of the Americas: mysterious, ferocious, and endangered. There are many myths, legends, and unknown facts about this cat, which still faces the unrelenting threat of extinction by humans. Part of the mystery of the puma can be attributed to the fact that there are more than forty names for this elusive cat; many (or most) of them come from Native American folklore. The most common and most recognizable names for the puma are cougar, mountain lion, panther, Mexican lion, mountain devil, catamount, and painter.

1. THE BIG "SMALL" CAT

The puma (*Felis concolor*) ranges from 100 to 130 pounds, although there is documentation of males as big as 250 pounds in Mexico. This large cat, able to leap as high as forty feet in a single bound, is known for its climbing abilities and tremendous power, yet it is considered part of the small cat family.

2. MYTHOLOGY OF THE PUMA

The puma is deeply entrenched in Native American mythology. The Cheyenne, Cherokee, and Hopi, for example, tell stories in which the puma is part of the creation of the world. In one such legend the Great Spirit created the world long before humans were created and instructed all living creatures to stay awake for seven days and seven nights—but most plants and animals could not stay awake. Those plants that fell asleep were punished by having their leaves fall at the coming of each winter season. Only the pine and cedar, who remained awake, kept their clothes. Of the animals, only the puma and owl stayed awake and therefore were rewarded with night vision. The Pawnee tribe believed the puma to be invincible and named it as one of the four beasts that guarded the Evening Star. This big "small" cat, once abundant, was and is a part of almost every Native American tribe folklore. It is said to have the power to heal and offer hope.

3. LEGENDS FROM AROUND THE WORLD

Mountain lions or pumas that inhabited Mexico and South America had a heavy impact on the cultures in those regions. Mixtec society believed the puma was present at the moment of creation of the world. Ancient Peruvians gave the name puma to some of their most famous families because the animal was worshipped as a sign of greatness. Puma skins were used for dress representing bravery. And in the Inca civilization, villages, wards, cities, and mountains were named after the puma. The South American tribes, like northern Native American tribes, also believed the puma was part of the initial creation of the world and therefore had strong medicinal powers. When Mother Earth was first created, the mountain lion learned it would be used for ceremonies—and so its skin was used for saddle blankets and wardrobe; its gall bladder fought evil; and its claws and teeth decorated headdresses and necklaces and offered healing powers. Medicine men dangled dried paws and claws of the mountain lions over sick tribe members to ward off evil spirits, illness, or death. Killing pumas for sport was appalling to tribal communities. These cats were killed only for ceremonial purposes; otherwise, they were left alone and admired from afar.

4. EARLY COLONISTS VS. THE CAT

While Native Americans lived harmoniously with the puma, America's first settlers were not so pleased to cohabitate with these seemingly threatening cats. Journals of early settlers in Virginia report seeing "lions" and being quite frightened of the animals; consequently, settlers chose to kill these animals whenever the opportunity arose. In turn, the puma was delighted to see livestock brought by the Europeans. While deer was the cat's favorite meal, the sudden availability of goats, sheep, cattle, and poultry were a welcome addition to their menu, and the puma dined on these luxuries whenever it could. The cat's feasting became a major threat to the settlers' existence, and so their intense hatred of the mountain lion began. Into the 1800s, when settlers moved west, rewards were offered for puma pelts as a way to control the population of this carnivore. As a result, by the twentieth century, the puma population had been almost wiped out.

5. ALIASES

Puma? Mountain lions? Why so many names? When Europeans arrived in America, mountain lions roamed freely. In fact, the only large mammals more widely distributed throughout the Western Hemisphere than the puma were humans. Pumas could be found from as far north as Canada to the most southern regions of South America, from the Atlantic to the Pacific coasts, to the peaks of the Appalachian, Rocky, and Andes mountains. This large "small" cat was seemingly everywhere, and thus, with so many homes in so many different regions and cultures, this widely traveled cat naturally acquired many names. Early Spanish explorers to North and South America called it *leon* (lion) and *gato monte* (cat of the mountain). Puma is the name given by the Incas; cougar comes from the South American word *cugaucuarana*; panther was a common term used for solid-colored coats. Whatever the region, the cat was as quickly named as it was feared. As one Lakota Indian once said, "They are very bashful, yet dangerous, for no animal can tell what they are up to. If one sees you first, he will not give you a chance to see so much as the tip of his tail. He never makes any noise, for he had the right sort of moccasins." The *leon* or *gato monte* or *cuguacuarana* was the ultimate hunter.

6. **THE HUNTER**

While the puma cannot roar, this cat is known through legend and firsthand accounts for its hair-raising, skin-tingling scream. The scream of the mountain lion was believed to be a death warning by the Apaches and Walapais of Arizona.

An excellent climber, a puma can go almost anywhere. Mountains, rocky terrain, trees, or open plains are all perfect hunting grounds for the wildcat. Although deer are the pumas' main source of food, a vast array of other animals make up their diet. An analysis of the stomach contents of puma carcasses has revealed cows, buffalo, horses, elk, moose, sheep, beavers, antelope, coyotes, wild turkey, mountain goats, fish, and household pets. Pumas rarely confront their prey, instead striking from behind. Although they are large animals, they are particularly adept at blending into bushes and against rock. The mountain lion kills by leaping on its victim and breaking the neck, usually with a blow from a forepaw.

7. **THE HUNTED**

Navajo mythology claims that humans and animals were once the same—that people became animals and animals turned into people over time. For this reason, the Navajos (like most North and South American Indian tribes) had tremendous respect for animals, but not all humans shared in their reverence. Between 1916 and 1971 more than twelve thousand mountain lions were killed for bounties and for sport in the state of California alone. While tall tales were told of the hunt and stuffed snarling mountain lions (the handiwork of a taxidermist) were displayed, few hunters bragged about the steel-jawed leg hold traps, hunting dogs, snares, and poison they often used to fell this beautiful and noble animal. In the end, the trophy justified the means for far too many hunters.

In 1971 then-governor Ronald Reagan signed a moratorium against trophy hunting of mountain lions in California. Fifteen years later the National Rifle Association (NRA) and the Safari Club pushed Proposition 197—a claim that trophy hunting was needed for public safety—through legislature without a single voter signature. Fortunately, the proposition was defeated, but hunters continue to ignore humane behavior for the sake of having stuffed mountain lion heads to display on their walls. The hunting, trapping, and killing of these cats by people who want to sell fur and by farmers and ranchers who want to protect their livestock continue. While some progress has been made over the years in increasing the puma population, mankind clearly remains the puma's greatest enemy in what may be a losing battle for existence.

8. THE TERRITORY

Each year thousands of acres of land that were once hunting grounds for the puma are converted into housing developments. Less habitable land and more hunters are virtually wiping out the puma. Today there are only a few pumas on the East Coast; most are in Florida, which began legally protecting the cats in the 1950s. An estimated thirty to fifty adult pumas live in fragmented pockets of land in the state. Perhaps the largest puma population—some five thousand cats—is believed to live in the mountains, forests, and southern deserts, ranging from the southwest of Canada down the western states of northern America and throughout most western parts of South America. Conservationists and animal protection workers can only guess at the numbers of pumas because it is so difficult to track them. They are solitary animals who roam over vast territories.

9. LIVING IN HARMONY WITH HUMANS

Scientists believe the number of puma attacks against humans has increased in recent years because we are encroaching on their territory by hiking, camping, and jogging, not to mention building. In the foothills in California, a woman cyclist was mauled by a puma in January 2004. While she and a friend biked through a wilderness park, the cat hit her from behind and began dragging her off of her bike and away from the trail. Her friend grabbed her leg and a tug-of-war ensued until several other bikers appeared and began throwing rocks at the puma. Vastly outnumbered and frightened by far more noise than any puma likes, the cat let go of his prey and fled. Later the body of a man was found on the very same trail, leaving experts to believe he was attacked by the same rogue puma. There have been only fourteen attacks against humans in California since 1890. Experts agree that this number is extraordinarily low because pumas are generally not interested in attacking humans.

When allowed to thrive, the puma provides a great service to humans as an important predator in the food chain, controlling deer and rabbit populations. But, interestingly, since pumas have been hunted and displaced to near extinction, deer populations in America have exploded, and states have had to begin hiring professional bow hunters to kill the growing and troublesome population of deer.

10. JUST TO BE SAFE . . .

If hiking, jogging, or biking in puma territory, always bring a buddy. While cyclists can use their bike to protect themselves, hikers and joggers are advised to carry walking sticks. What should you do if you cross paths with a mountain lion? Shout, wave your arms, and hold your jacket open to look as big as possible—just as you would if attacked by a grizzly bear. Maintain eye contact with the animal and remain as calm as you can. Do not run; running is what the cat wants you do to. Do not crouch, and if you are with small children, pick them up to make sure they do not panic and try to run. If the lion strikes, fight back! And never jog with a goat in puma territory.

Small Cats of Asia

S imply stated, the small cats do not have nearly the mass appeal that the big cats have. Depending upon whom you talk to, this could be good or bad. Because so many of the small cats remain relatively unknown, they do not face the hunters or trappers that many of the better known big cats face. But this lack of information about the small cats' habitat and role as predators in the food chain means most conservationists are not as interested in the lesser known cats. In the instance of the Chinese desert cat, only sketchings and drawings provide information about the species, which does not appear to be alive today. Just as the Asian continent is vast and diverse, so too are the small cats that live there.

1. LEOPARD CAT

Sadly, this beautiful cat is one of the better known cats in Asia because of its coat. In just three years during the 1980s more than 2 million leopard cats (*Felis bengalensis*) were slaughtered for their pelts. Similar in appearance to the great leopard, this cat weighs in at just six to nine pounds, living in trees throughout southeastern Asia, from India to China, Japan, and the Philippines.

2. JUNGLE CAT

Also known as the swamp cat or reed cat, the *Felis chaus* prefers to live outside human settlements, feeding on livestock. Biologists believe the jungle cat originated in the swamps or marshes in the Middle East where it used riverbeds and streams for its hunting ground. Most interestingly, mummified remains of this medium-size cat (weighing fifteen to thirty-five pounds) have been discovered in the ancient ruins of Egypt. Today the hardy jungle cat lives in southern Asia, reaching the Caucasus, the eastern Mediterranean coast, Turkistan, and Uzbekistan.

3. FISHING CAT

As the name suggests, this cat does most of its hunting along rivers or streams, diving in after fish. Like the domesticated Turkish Van and the tiger, this cat has no qualms about swimming, much less getting wet. At twenty pounds, this cat is agile with long legs and a long body. Its paws have webbing to help with swimming and claws described to be as sharp as fish hooks. Today the *Felis viverrina* continues to be hunted in India and Pakistan for its skin.

4. PALLAS'S CAT

With unusually large eyes, a flat head, and low-riding ears, the *Felis manul* has often been described as the owl cat. Now living in Central Asia between the Caspian Sea and Mongolia, this cat was named after German doctor Peter Simon Pallas, who traveled throughout southern and eastern Asia on the instruction of Russian Empress Catherine the Great.

5. RUSTY-SPOTTED CAT

Living in or near human settlements in southern India and Sri Lanka, this is the smallest of the small cats, weighing only two to four and a half pounds. Feeding on small rodents, the rusty-spotted cat (*Felis rubiginosa*) is easily domesticated and makes a good pet.

6. MARBLED CAT

The *Felis marmorata* spends most of its life—whether hunting or sleeping—in trees, feeding on birds, reptiles, and squirrels. Resembling a leopard, this typically twelve-pound cat lives throughout Malaysia, Burma, Thailand, and Indonesia.

7. BAY CAT

Also known as the red cat or the Bornean red cat, the *Felis badia* is found only in the scrubland of Borneo. Weighing only four to seven pounds, this extremely shy cat is not very well known, but it is believed to prefer living in the thick forest and marshes, where cover is heavy.

8. IRIOMOTE CAT

Naturalists believe that the South American kodkod could be related to the iriomote cat; however, the real connection between the species may simply be that they live in very similar environments. Unlike the other small cats of Asia, the iriomote cat survives on a remote island off the east coast of Taiwan, near the Ryukyu Islands. While the *Felis iriomotensis* was not identified until 1967, fossils resembling the iriomote cat on a neighboring island are believed to be more than 2 million years old, which suggests that the cat existed as a separate species.

9. TEMMINCK'S GOLDEN CAT

First identified by Dutch naturalist Conrad Temminck (1778–1858), Temminck's golden cat, or the Asian or Asiatic golden cat, was once thought to have ancestral roots to the Siamese. The *Felis temmincki* survives today in the forest and mountains of the Himalayas and throughout southern China, as well as on the Indonesian island of Sumatra, where it's known as the rock cat, fire cat, and yellow leopard. This fierce hunter is very similar in appearance to the puma, weighing only thirty-five pounds.

10.   **FLAT-HEADED CAT**

Found only in Borneo, Malaysia, Thailand, and Sumatra, the *Felis planiceps* weighs only twelve to eighteen pounds. While it does not swim, the flat-headed cat dwells near water, so that it can fish for a large portion of its diet. It also hunts waterfowl and frogs.

BONUS CAT:

As mentioned previously, the Chinese desert cat remains a bit of a mystery to cat lovers. In 1889 Henri, Prince of Orleans and one of a family of pretenders to the French throne, was denied access to Siam and was forced to reroute his travels through Sichuan, a Chinese province in the Yangtze basin. There the prince was shown the skins of two cats called Chinese desert cats. Most of what is known today about the *Felis bieti* is based on the prince's descriptions of the pelts themselves and of accounts from those hunters who killed the cats for him. Recent sightings of the Chinese desert cat have been reported by adventurers who have traveled along the small mountainous region in western China at an altitude of over ten thousand feet.

Small Cats of Africa

While the small cats of the Americas and Europe survive along riverbeds, in dense forests, and in the trees, it can be argued that the small cats of Africa are the greatest survivors of all. Undersized predators, they compete against the most aggressive, powerful big cats in the world in some of the most dangerous and difficult terrain in the world. Biologists argue that *because* of the big cats, the small cats of Africa have been unable to flourish. Still, these remarkable cats survive.

1. SAND CAT

Also known as the sand-dune cat, this very small cat (approximately four pounds) has unusually large ears, with internal ear mechanisms. It is believed these oversized organs enable the cat to detect the slightest sounds of small desert creatures. The sand cat needs every advantage to survive. It is a very fluffy orange tabby by appearance, but make no mistake, everything has a purpose. Its hair color blends perfectly with the color of the sand and its coat acts as a shield against the scorching heat. It is named *Felis margarita* after the French general Jean Auguste Margarita, who is responsible for claiming the western Sahara for the French Empire in the 1860s.

2. **CARACAL**

Unlike most wildcats, the caracal hunts for the thrill of killing. This cat, while under scientific observation, has killed far more prey than it needs for feeding. A fierce hunter, the caracal is a nomad, spending a solitary life (except when mating) in the semidesert and mountainous regions of South Africa and Uganda. Weighing up to forty-five pounds, this cat has been observed attacking birds as large as eagles. The caracal (*Felis caracal*) will take on anything for the challenge.

3. **AFRICAN WILDCAT**

The *Felis silvestris libyca* is often compared to the European wildcat. While the two are similar in build and coloring, the African wildcat has a less thick, less dense coat than that of its European cousin. And, unlike the European wildcat, the African cat actively seeks out humans, establishing itself near or just outside human settlements so that it can use them as a food source. This cat is found throughout Africa, except in West Africa, and across India and southern Asia.

4. **SERVAL**

Most commonly found in Central Africa, the *Felis serval* is considered to be endangered. Weighing between thirty and forty pounds, it has a spotted coat similar to the leopard's and large, wide ears. An accomplished hunter, its favorite technique appears to be finding, then digging out moles. Ears down toward the ground, used like funnels, the serval has excellent hearing, even underground. One current myth suggests that this cat is vicious, but animal activists believe this falsehood has been spread to justify the practice of hunting these wildcats for their beautiful pelts.

5. **AFRICAN GOLDEN CAT**

This cat is also surrounded by myths and folklore—all favorable. Prominent in western and central Africa, the *Felis aurata* is majestic, brave, and powerful. Good luck is promised to anyone who lays eyes on this usually human-shy cat. Unfortunately, however, native chieftains also believe the tail of the African golden cat brings good luck, and its coat is sought for royal robes. Similar in appearance to both the Asian golden cat and the puma, this cat (weighing fifteen to twenty-five pounds) is part of local African folklore from coast to coast, and is thought to be a mystical creature brought forth during the creation of earth.

6. **BLACK-FOOTED CAT**

While its name was derived from the blurred black marking on its feet, the black-footed cat (*Felis nigripes*) looks like a miniature leopard, weighing only about four pounds. Although it is small in size, the legends that surround this cat are large. Found only in the semidesert and grasslands of southwest Africa, this cat leaps on to the back of its prey—no matter the size—and hangs on until at last the jugular has been pierced. Legend holds that the tiny black-footed cat can even kill a giraffe.

7. **JUNGLE CAT**

While the jungle cat (*Felis chaus*) lives in Asia, this cat also dwells in northeastern Africa. Weighing in at fifteen to thirty-five pounds, the jungle cat feeds on hares, mice, birds, snakes, and domestic poultry. Known to be active at night, they can be seen near human settlements, often denning in old buildings. These cats share the distinction with the African wildcat of having been mummified in ancient Egyptian tombs.

8. **FERAL CAT**

It is believed that Arab sailors introduced the feral cat (*Felis catus*) to the coastal ports of eastern Africa as a way to control the rat population. Certainly, cats were kept on board ships that traded in that region of the world and could have escaped from the ships, making the islands of Mauritius and Madagascar home. While many new species have been introduced to the African continent, one of most damaging is the feral cat, which has been blamed, in part, for the extinction of land tortoises and lizards in Mauritius. Today the feral cat is actively trapped and killed.

9. CAT IN NAME ONLY: THE MIERKAT

The mierkat is actually a mongoose with many catlike characteristics that lives on the African grasslands. For example, mierkats hunt with amazing grace and agility. They are one of the few predators that attack with no warning, in a manner mierkat admirers have called the ultimate in sneak attack. Mierkats are very social (unlike other species of mongoose), living in large family groups and taking care of each other. These fascinating creatures love to eat poisonous scorpions; they quickly bite off the stingers and then gobble down the rest. And they really admire a good sunrise, rushing out of their burrows and stretching up tall, obviously enjoying the warmth of the early morning sun. Mierkats are cute, friendly, and smart. In fact, they are a lot like Timon, the adorable, funny mierkat in the Disney movie, *The Lion King.*

10. CAT IN APPEARANCE ONLY: THE GENET

Although catlike in appearance and habit, the genet is not a cat. Rather it is a member of the Viverridae family, which also includes civets and mongooses. The ancient Egyptians, who kept genets as pets, believed this creature to be a member of the cat family. From the Greek empire to the Middle Ages, the genet was admired for its rat- and mouse-catching abilities and trainability. Like the cat, it has retractable claws, excellent for climbing trees and catching rodents and reptiles. At just four to five pounds, this spotted brownish-gray animal also purrs, spits, hisses, and arches it back like a cat. It is believed the ancient Egyptians eventually replaced the genet for domesticated cats because of its smell. The genet secretes a powerful, foul-smelling scent from its anal glands when frightened and a heavy, musky odor to convey messages of sexual or territorial behavior.

IV
Celebrity Cats

Cats on Camera

In June 2003 the cable channel Oxygen launched the premiere television show, *Meow TV*, with video segments made specifically for a feline viewing audience. With segments such as "Squirrel Alert," a fifteen-second spot of intense squirrel watching, or "Cat Yoga," *Meow TV* has made a bold statement about the way we see and feel about our cats. For decades cats have been some of the biggest stars of the silver screen, on our television sets, and in print.

1. MORRIS THE CAT

While Morris wasn't known for his work in the film industry, he is arguably the most famous feline celebrity. Animal trainer Bob Martwick discovered this stray in 1968 at the Humane Society in Hinsdale, Illinois, and became intrigued by the orange tabby. When the not-yet-named Morris passed several tests of concentration, Martwick paid five dollars for the cat and took him away. Just one year later Morris won the role of spokescat for 9Lives cat food. His star power was so great, the ad scripts were quickly rewritten to feature him as the star. Morris was made honorary director of StarKist Foods, Inc, the then-parent company of 9Lives, and was given power to veto any cat food brand he didn't like.

In 1973 Morris was awarded the Patsy Award (the animal equivalent of the Oscar) for Outstanding Performance and starred in *Shamus* with Burt Reynolds and Dyan Cannon. He had his own staff and personal chauffeur, visited the White House (where he signed a bill by making an ink impression with his paw), and often feasted in fancy restaurants with kitties of the opposite sex.

2. **DOUBLETAKE—MORRIS II**

When Morris died in 1978, a nationwide search began for the new Morris. Frantic to find another spokesanimal, the 9Lives corporation participated in the search. Hundreds of photographs were reviewed and analyzed until a young orange tabby from the East Coast made the cut. The new cat looked like Morris's twin and had an unbelievable ability to stay where he had been put, enduring dozens and dozens of flashing lights from photographers and constant applause. Like the first Morris, this young cat lived and trained with Bob Martwick, making regular public appearances. Morris II has his own book and has appeared in dozens of national magazines and commercials. He continues to be one of the most recognizable animals of all time.

3. **ORANGEY**

Another orange cat became very popular in the 1960s when he appeared in a dozen of movies, including *Gigot* and *Breakfast at Tiffany's*. But what the adoring public didn't know was that behind this cat's cute and cuddly facade lay the heart of a tiger—a mean tiger. Once called "the world's meanest cat" by a movie executive, Orangey was often violent with his costars, scratching and spitting after a scene was complete. During a scene, he showed the same star quality the Morris cats did several years later, able to stay for indefinite hours. But once the scene was a wrap, he would often flee, shutting down production until he could be found again. Trainer Frank Inn was known to place guard dogs at the studio's entrance doors to prevent Orangey from running away.

4. ANOTHER ORANGE CAT

Otherwise known as the *Mary Tyler Moore* cat, this little mascot was used to play off the old Metro-Goldwyn-Mayer film studio's roaring lion. Looking for a mascot of their own, the MGM folks used a litter of newborn kittens belonging to the son of one of the company's film editors. Setting up a camera crew in hopes of catching a toothy snarl as the kittens played, not one kitten made a peep, roar, or snarl. It was only when a kitten yawned that the camera crew got a shot of fangs.

5. NEW CAT IN TOWN

At a time when the cat most favored by showbiz was clearly the orange tabby, a Siamese named Syn Cat stepped into the limelight. In 1964 a simple movie called *That Darn Cat*, the story of a cat who became entangled in a botched bank robbery, an FBI investigation, and an international mystery, launched Syn Cat as a superstar. Unlike other star cats, Syn Cat was reportedly down-to-earth, easy to deal with, and able to perform all his own stunts.

6. PEPPER

In the 1930s when the Keystone Kops were at the height of their popularity, it seemed everyone was trying to get into the action. A star waiting to be discovered, a slender black cat crawled through the floorboards and sauntered onto the set. So captivating was the cat, director Mack Sennett worked the cat into the next scene and declared, "From henceforth you shall be known as Pepper, and I predict a long and brilliant career for another member of the Sennett realm." And so it was. Pepper went on to star with Charlie Chaplin, Fatty Arbuckle, and the Keystone Kops. Pepper also worked with a Great Dane named Teddy, with whom she formed a strong bond. When Teddy died, Pepper went into mourning, refusing to work. Several other dogs were introduced to her but she refused them, and one day she simply disappeared, never to be seen again.

7. STARS OF THE UNITED KINGDOM

In 1963 Britain had a Morris-like star of its own. Superstar Arthur was the spokescat for a large cat food manufacturer until the cat food company decided to have Arthur's teeth removed. It appeared Arthur liked the cat food a little too much and tried eating during the scenes, ruining the shots. Unbelievably, the executives honestly believed removing Arthur's teeth would solve their problem. The cat's owner/trainer refused to have the procedure done, and the case went to court, where a judge determined that Arthur was the property of the cat food company. In an act of desperation, his owner deposited Arthur in the Russian embassy where he could not be touched.

Today the Animal Consultants and Trainers Association (ACTA) is always on hand to be sure that animal stars in Europe are treated kindly. While Arthur is long gone, Glitter, a silver tabby British shorthair, works as a spokescat for Whiskas. Fat and happy, Glitter even takes twenty-minute naps between her sets.

8. SALEM—HALF CAT, HALF ROBOT

As the story goes, the witches counsel sentenced this warlock to live as a cat for a hundred years when his plan to dominate the world was revealed. Starring as Sabrina's sidekick in the popular show, *Sabrina the Teenage Witch*, the character of Salem, a sleek, black shorthair, was awarded the Nickelodean Kid's Choice Award in 2002. While more than half of his scenes actually feature a mechanical cat, Salem is a primetime feline star. Working alongside Melissa Joan Hart and Soleil Moon Frye (who incidentally began her acting career as a sidekick to a golden retriever puppy in 1984's *Punky Brewster*), Salem depicts the typical cat—self-centered, entertaining, loving, and loyal.

9. SASSY

The Himalayan Sassy of the 1993 production *Homeward Bound* fared far better than her counterpart in the 1963 production *The Incredible Journey*. Sassy I was chased by dogs and tossed into swift-moving streams. No doubt, she used up most of her lives during filming. But with the American Humane Society on set in 1993, every stunt and every move of Sassy II was closely monitored. While the audience sees poor Sassy thrown into water, tossed down a waterfall, chased by wild animals, and forced to cross narrow passages, the real Sassy had two stunt doubles: a robot and a stuffed toy. In the scenes that called for Sassy to run, a buzzer was used as a trigger for her to go. After each buzzer stunt, she was rewarded with treats. An interesting piece of trivia: Sassy became tolerant of the water during the takes and retakes of *Homeward Bound*'s famous water scene, and she became a proficient swimmer.

10. SNOWBELL

Four Persians played the part of one Snowbell. Shhh. We'll never tell. Doubles Ruffy and Tuffy were called in for the stunts, while Rocky was used for running sequences, and Lucky Prince was used for the close-ups. (Monty the Alley Cat was actually two tabby cats.) For the more complicated scenes involving Snowbell being launched through the air, a toy cat was used. But how did they make him talk? Food was, and continues to be, the training tool of the trade.

How to Break Your Cat into Showbiz

It's been estimated that 80 percent of the top canine stars in Hollywood are former strays, saved from animal shelters around the nation. While those numbers aren't quite so high with feline stars, a good number of print and picture cat stars have been rescued from the shelter. Because animal trainers know what to look for in a cat, it is easier to rescue a cat than screen hundreds of hopefuls from owners convinced their cats are the greatest. Following are ten "musts" your cat has to have to become a star.

1. MUST GET ALONG WITH STRANGERS

Star cats must be able to withstand being around dozens of people, whether those people are physically touching the felines or bustling around on a busy soundstage. Camera and sound crew members, photographers, makeup artists, other actors/models, producers, and assistants surround the cat.

2. MUST GET ALONG WITH OTHER ANIMALS

This is not the time to be a prima donna. It is one thing for star cats to be the certain of attention with humans, it is quite another if they can't abide other animals or want to play with them. Animal actors must be able to resist the call to fight or play with other animals while they are working. British animal trainer Olive Tate was once asked to supply sixty cats for a French commercial in which they were all released on the word "Action!" to run through streets and across fields to

Olive—out of sight—who was calling to them. Remarkably, every cat came! And not one cat fight occurred.

3. MUST KEEP FOCUS

Ever been on a soundstage? It's not quiet. While animal actors are on set, a very distracting and stressful place for Hollywood hopefuls, they must be able to focus on the trainer, taking cues only from the trainer. With people yelling, cameras clicking, horns sounding off, lights flashing, and radios blaring, it can be virtually impossible to hear commands being given. This is all the more reason a cat must be willing and able to focus on the trainer and the trainer only, often times taking physical cues.

4. MUST WORK LIKE A DOG

Dare it be said: Working cats must be trained like dogs, learning basic commands so that they can have the confidence to work in a distracting, often confusing environment. Teaching basic obedience to your cat—yes, it really can be done—is essential in acting or modeling.

5. MUST START YOUNG

Teaching kittens a variety of tricks helps them learn to accept physical and verbal cues, thus opening the possibility of learning more cues for standard obedience. Read the chapter titled "Top Tricks for a Super Kitty."

6. MUST SIT AND STAY ON COMMAND

For some cats, sitting still for hours on end comes naturally. Morris the Cat became a megastar for this gift alone. But for other cats (e.g., Snowbell and Sassy), training techniques were used to teach the basic commands of sit and stay. But teaching your cat the command is just the beginning. A cat star must be able to sit and stay while a scene plays out, often with unbelievable distractions.

7. MUST DOWN AND STAY ON COMMAND

During the shooting of *Stuart Little*, Snowbell was often asked to work a scene as though Stuart Little, an animated/

mechanical mouse, was present. This required long stays for the Persian during which he was asked to move his head back and forth as though a conversation were taking place. Stuart Little was dubbed in later. Learning how to sit and lie down on command was essential for many of the shots.

8. MUST BE ABLE TO STRIKE A POSE

Just as with the sit/stay and down/stay commands, a cat should be able to hold a pose standing. In cat shows, cats are asked to remain still while judges look them over, but the standards for Hollywood can often be a little more demanding. While cameras are adjusted or lighting is set and reset, star cats must be able to hold their positions. The work can be tedious and exhausting, all the more reason animal trainers insist that acting or modeling is a career a cat must want to pursue. British actress cat Glitter reportedly enjoys all the fuss and attention and, in exchange, is willing to stand patiently for her next cue.

9. MUST HAVE A FLEXIBLE OWNER

If you're in it for the money, leave now. First, remember the competition is fierce as most directors and producers go to animal trainers with a proven record in the film industry. Second, the payoff is usually minimal in comparison to the time and effort you have to put in. Having a showbiz cat should be fun for both owner and feline, and not be driven by the idea of making money, which will only result in additional stress for you and the cat.

10. MUST HAVE AN AGENT

No matter how brilliant your feline, you won't get work if no one sees the cat. Talk to an animal casting agent to learn how much time, money, and energy are involved in making your fabulous feline a star. These professionals will be able to give sound advice and answer any questions you may have about your kitty.

Casting Agencies
for Animals

1. **HOLLYWOOD PAWS**

www.hollywoodpaws.com

2. **ANIMAL ACTORS INTERNATIONAL**

www.animal-actors.com
(800) 803–9606

3. **HOLLYWOOD ANIMALS' ANIMAL ACTORS AGENCY**

www.animalactorsagency.com
4103 Holly Knoll Drive
Los Angeles, CA 90027
(323) 665-9500
info@animalactorsagency.com

4. **EXTRAS FOR MOVIES**

www.extrasformovies.com/
animals_actors_talent_extras.asp
(760) 599-5400

5. **HOLLYWOOD ANIMALS: EXOTIC ANIMAL TRAINING SCHOOL**

www.hollywoodanimals.com
4103 Holly Knoll Drive
Los Angeles, CA 90027

(323) 665-9500
info@hollywoodanimals.com

6. CASTING 4 HOLLYWOOD

www.casting4hollywood.com

7. ANIMAL ACTORS

www.animalactors.com
animalactors@groups.msn.com

8. ANIMAL CONSULTANTS AND TRAINERS ASSOCIATION

www.acta4animals.com
Warwick House Business Centres Ltd., 2nd floor
181/183 Warwick Road
London, England W14 8PU
0207-244-6999
acta4animals@blueyonder.co.uk

9. CRITTERS OF THE CINEMA

www.crittersofthecinema.com
(661) 724-1929

10. TRAINING UNLIMITED

www.miriamfields.com
Stafford, Virginia
(540) 659-8858

Top Grossing Cat Movies of All Time

1. **Cat People** (Nastassja Kinski, 1982, Universal)

2. **Lion King** (animated, Matthew Broderick, James Earl Jones, 1994, Disney)

3. **That Darn Cat!** (Hayley Mills, 1965, Disney)

4. **That Darn Cat** (Christina Ricci, 1997, Disney)

5. **The Incredible Journey** (1963, Disney)

6. **Aristocats** (animated, 1970, Disney)

7. **Cats & Dogs** (Tobey Macquire, Alec Bladwin, 2001, Warner Bros.)

8. **Cats Don't Dance** (animated, Scott Bakula, Jasmine Guy, 1997, Turner)

9. **Milo and Otis** (1989, Columbia/TriStar)

10. **Homeward Bound** (Michael J. Fox, 1993, Disney)

First Felines

Since John Adams set foot in the White House, pets have been able to call the 1600 Pennsylvania Avenue residence home. Between Theodore Roosevelt and Calvin Coolidge, there were animals at and in the White House of such variety that the National Zoo must have felt rivaled. Lions, cubs, five bears, a flying squirrel, a coyote, a piebald rat, a donkey, raccoons, antelope, a wallaby, guinea pigs, and even a zebra have all been presidential pets. But it comes as no surprise that some of the most engaging, entertaining, and beloved presidential pets of all time were of the feline persuasion.

1. ABRAHAM LINCOLN AND TABBY (1861–1865)

Of Lincoln's four sons (three of whom died before they reached the age of eighteen), Thomas had a special affection for cats. Nicknamed Tad (short for tadpole) for his oversized head, he owned a small tabby cat named, cleverly enough, Tabby. The fruit didn't fall far from the tree as Lincoln was a huge animal lover himself. On a visit with General Grant during the Civil War, Lincoln discovered three small kittens in a tent who appeared to be lost. He gave special instructions for their care and continued to check up on their status long after his departure.

2. MRS. RUTHERFORD B. HAYES AND FIRST LADY OF SIAM (1877–1881)

David Sickels at the U.S. consulate in Siam sent Mrs. Hayes, as a gift, the first Siamese cat to live in the United States. Initially, the cat was named Miss Pussy, but she was quickly renamed the First Lady of Siam, called Siam for short.

3. WILLIAM MCKINLEY AND IDA'S CAT (1897–1901)

When the First Lady Ida McKinley's prized Angora cat gave birth to four kittens, the press made much ado about the precious kitties and the first lady promptly named each kitten after a prominent leader in the world, including the governor of Cuba and the ambassador of Spain. But when war broke out with Spain during the McKinley administration, the first lady attempted to make a political statement by ordering the cats to be drowned. Sadly, her order was carried out.

4. THEODORE ROOSEVELT AND SLIPPERS (1901–1909)

Slippers, a gray tabby, was distinguishable from other cats because he was polydactyl, that is, he had extra toes—a fact that greatly amused the president. Slippers was also a demanding cat who commanded a lot of attention. Roosevelt doted on him, feeding his ego. Slippers always seemed to know when and how to put in an appearance at White House dinners, strutting into the room and waiting to be admired. On one legendary evening, just as the procession of dignitaries began to make way to the dining hall, Slippers lay down in the middle of the floor. What did everyone do? Why, the guests gingerly stepped around the cat as he rolled on the carpet. Obviously, they understood cats.

THEODORE ROOSEVELT AND TOM QUARTZ (1901–1909)

Although an avid hunter, Roosevelt was a great fan of the feline. In a letter to his son, Kermit, on January 6, 1903, he expressed his affection for his cats in a long and loving description of this kitten's antics:

Tom Quartz is certainly the cunningest kitten I have ever seen. He is always playing pranks on Jack and I get very nervous lest Jack should grow too irritated. The other evening they were both in the library—Jack sleeping before the fire—Tom Quartz scampering about, an exceedingly playful little creature—which is about what he is. He would race across the floor, then jump upon the curtain or play with the tassel. Suddenly, he spied Jack and galloped to him. Jack, looking exceedingly sullen and shame-faced, jumped out of the way and got upon the sofa and around the table, and Tom Quartz instantly jumped upon him again. Jack suddenly shifted to the other sofa, where Tom Quartz again went after him. Then Jack started for the door, while Tom made a rapid turn under the sofa and around the table and just as Jack reached the door leaped on his hind-quarters. Jack bounded forward and away and the two went tandem out of the room—Jack not cooperating at all; and about five minutes afterwards Tom Quartz stalked solemnly back.

5.   CALVIN COOLIDGE AND TIGER (1923–1929)

Like Roosevelt, Coolidge was known and admired around the world for his love of pets. In fact, this often caused great consternation for the staff of the White House as animals of all shapes and sizes were sent to the White House from all over the world. Goats, raccoons, dogs, cats, and birds were common pets during Coolidge's administration. Coolidge had three cats—Bounder, Tiger, and Blacky. Of the three, Tiger was clearly his favorite, and when Tiger disappeared from the White House, a desperate Coolidge made a radio broadcast pleading for the return of his beloved pet. The broadcast worked and Tiger was found. Unfortunately, the cat had the soul of a wanderer and soon disappeared again, never to return.

6.   JOHN F. KENNEDY AND TOM KITTEN (1961–1963)

Tom Kitten, who belonged to JFK's daughter, Caroline, was the first kitten to grace the floors of the White House since

TR's Slippers. Upon Tom's death on August 21, 1962, an obituary in the *Alexandria Gazette* read: "Unlike many humans in the same position, he never wrote his memoirs of his days in the White House and never discussed them for quotation, though he was privy to many official secrets."

7. GERALD FORD AND SHAN (1974–1977)

Shan, a sassy Siamese, belonged to Gerald Ford's daughter, Susan. Shan did not like men, except for the president. He was the first cat in the White House to send out photos autographed with his own paw print.

8. JIMMY CARTER AND MISTY MALARKY (1977–1981)

His full name was Misty Malarky Ying Yang, and he was a social male Siamese who traveled with the Carter family for the duration of the presidential campaign and their four years in the White House.

9. BILL CLINTON AND SOCKS (1993–2001)

Until Socks, the White House had not seen a cat since Amy Carter's Siamese. The Clintons' cat, subject of countless websites, books, magazine articles, and political cartoons, made headlines when it was discovered he and newcomer Buddy, a chocolate Labrador, didn't get along. Socks, who was apparently very fond of the White House secretary, was sent to live with Betty Currie in 2001. He made such good tabloid news, the Bush administration couldn't resist the publicity and issued a press release offering to supply food, shelter, and employment to the displaced feline.

10. GEORGE W. BUSH, ERNIE AND INDIA (2001–   )

While on the campaign trail, Bush's cats were his constant companions and helped to keep him relaxed. He said he liked to start everyday by feeding them. Whether he made these statements for politics or out of true affection, political analysts agree it was smart for the president to talk about his love of felines. Less than a decade ago, the politician's best friend was always the dog, but as cats have become the number one pet in America, candidates probably do better with cats by their side. The Bush cats, orange and white tabbies discovered stuck in a tree, quickly became part of the family. Ernie, named after Ernest Hemingway, was noted to have extra toes. Too wild for the White House, he was eventually sent to California to live with a new family. The other cat, who stayed with the family in the White House, was named India.

Cats of Royalty

While the cat has not always fared well through the ages, there have always been cat lovers, and the feline has often lived in the lap of luxury. Behold the ten most majestic of cats.

1. ABYSSINIAN

While it has been difficult to identify an absolute origin for this beautiful cat, cat enthusiasts and animal experts have noticed similarities between today's Abyssinians and royal cat depictions in early Egyptian art. What may have been an early Abyssinian has been found in several renderings of ancient Egyptian life in the royal courts. So close were ancient royal cats to their owners, they were often mummified with their pharaohs so that they might guide and protect their masters in the afterlife. Mice were mummified and buried with the cats, it is thought, so the feline would have food and in turn would offer comfort and security to the pharaoh.

2. EGYPTIAN MAU

Wall paintings found in the temples of Thebes on the Nile, believed to have been built around 1400 B.C., show spotted cats very similar to the Egyptian Mau flushing out waterfowl from thick marshes, suggesting the important role this breed played in ancient Egyptian culture. Archeologists have found even earlier recordings of the cat, from between 1850 and 1650 B.C., in *The Egyptian Book of the Dead*, a book that taught early Egyptians how to ensure their safe passage into the afterlife. This book included several references to the spotted cat that killed serpents, safeguarding the pharaohs against evil.

The close relationship between the Mau and its humans did not stop with the pharaohs. As recently as 1953 Russian princess Natalie Troubetskoy, traveling through Egypt, was so taken with the breed she brought back two cats to her cattery in Rome and showed them in the International Cat Show in 1955. By 1956, with kittens in tow, the princess came to America, introducing the breed to the United States.

3. THE KING'S KHORAT

In Siam, the Khorat, believed to be good luck, was often presented to new brides to ensure a prosperous marriage. In *The Cat-Book Poems*, a nearly six-hundred-year-old manuscript now kept at the National Library in Bangkok, the Khorat is described with great affection—as a cat of the people and royal descent. It had "roots like clouds and tips like silver," and its eyes, "like dewdrops on a lotus leaf," were the eyes of a cat that offered good fortune. The khorats were invited into rice fields in the hopes of bringing a strong harvest and a good rain season. Known today to the people of Thailand as Si-siwat, the cat was named Khorat by King Chulalong-korn when he learned the cat originated in the Khorat region of eastern Siam.

4. SIAMESE

To this day the Siamese is one of the most beloved cats in royal courts around the world. With its regal origins, not to mention its stoic, regal characteristics, it is easy to understand how this cat has sat on thrones throughout Asia, the Middle East, and Europe.

5. BIG CATS IN THE ROYAL COURT

Smaller, domesticated cats were not the only favored felines among royalty. The cheetah was a popular cat in the royal court, not only as a status symbol but also as a hunting partner. From ancient pharaohs, Mongol warrior Genghis Khan, and King Charlemagne to the emperor of Abyssinia, Haile Selassie, cheetahs were kept as pets, complete with collar and chain. Ramses II, the pharaoh of Egypt, owned a lion named Anta-M-Nekht, and Nero, emperor of Rome, owned a tiger named Phoebe.

6. ROYAL DEPICTIONS

In Paris, France, on August 31, 1997, one of the most beloved figures of our time, Princess Diana, was killed in a tragic car accident as she and her companion, Dodi Fayed, fled from paparazzi. In the days, months, and years that followed Diana's sudden death, people around the world struggled to make sense of this loss.

Princess Di was a woman of grace, beauty, and charm. Dubbed Queen of the People's Heart, she worked endlessly to ease human suffering and bring about awareness of causes such as fighting AIDS and purging war-torn nations of destructive landmines. Caricatures of the princess as a cat began to appear in editorials, posters, and cartoons. What better animal than the feline to represent Diana? Today, one of the most popular caricatures is a stamp called Pretty Persian—a cat replica of Princess Diana with a crown of pearls from Great Britain.

7. STAMPED OUT

Since the Middle Ages cats have won the hearts of royals as well as commoners. In recognition of their loyal service and devotion, royal families have decreed that their beloved felines adorn the postal stamps of their countries—so that everyone can admire them. In Poland, Yemen, Luxembourg, Spain, the Netherlands, Romania, and Yugoslavia royal cats have been honored with stamps of their own.

8. A BUSHEL'S WORTH OF CATS

In the ninth century A.D., when the cat rebounded from the stigma of being a wanted member of the community, royals welcomed the cat with open arms. Cats returned once again to castles and vast lodges that also housed undesired vermin. King Henry I believed the cat to be so valuable as a pest-killer, he decreed that killing a cat would cost the offender sixty bushels of corn.

9. QUEEN VICTORIA'S CAT

An avid animal lover, Queen Victoria was known for her love of horses and small dogs, but her favorite pet was a large cat named White Heather. Whether or not White Heather was a good mouser, she was certainly well fed. Living with the queen in Buckingham Palace, White Heather spent many of her days with Victoria. Upon the death of the queen, it was requested that White Heather be kept as she had lived with Victoria—in the lap of luxury. King Edward II, Victoria's successor, honored this request and kept White Heather until her death.

10. THE RUSSIAN BLUE

With its origins unknown, the Russian blue cat is surrounded by legends and mystery, almost like Russia itself. The darlings of Russian royalty, blues were pampered and petted. Peter the Great's cat, Vaska, is even mentioned in Russian historical documents. Catherine the Great gave these cats as gifts to other rulers. One of the mystifying things about blues is that everywhere these cats went, they became natives: In Spain, they were known as blue Spanish cats; the French called them blue Chartres; on the island of Malta, the cats are Maltese. In 1893 an English industrialist brought two blues, Lingpop and Yula, from Arkhangelsk to Britain. These two cats are widely credited for being the Adam and Eve of Russian blues in Europe and North America—from Russian royalty to happy cat owners around the world. The bluish-gray haired cat remains highly valued and exceedingly popular, particularly in England and the United States. Blues are also gaining in popularity in Russia, Czechoslovakia, Sweden, Denmark, and Holland. They are still rare in France and Germany, and if you want to buy a blue in Italy, you may choose from only one blue breeder in the country.

Best Loved
Animated Cats

1. **FELIX THE CAT**

Felix the Cat was not the first big-name cat to hit the cartoon circuit. (Krazy Kat had reached a certain popularity as a minor character in 1910; he progressed to his own comic strip in 1918.) In 1917 cartoonist Pat Sullivan created Thomas Kat, perfecting the image until he drew the beloved Felix the Cat in 1919. Still one of the most popular cats of all time, the character of Felix has appeared in hundreds of films in the sixteen years between his debut and the death of his creator, American cartoonist Pat Sullivan, in 1933. Felix was the first animated star to peak, beating out Mickey Mouse who debuted a year later and, most critics agree, was based on the character of Felix. A regular cartoon strip featuring the antics of the comical cat appeared in 1923 and continued for decades. In 1928, when NBC made its first experimental television transmission, Felix was the star of one of the first television shows.

2. **GARFIELD**

The undisputed king of cats in more modern times, Garfield took the attitude of the typical housecat to a new level, and fans adored him for it. Created in 1978 by cartoonist Jim Davis, the cartoon continues to run in more than eight hundred newspapers around the nation and has been the feature of countless books and cartoons. The lasagna-loving, dog-hating feline friend of character Jon Arbuckle drives his owner crazy, endlessly tortures his fellow four-legged house-mate, Otis, and just like the real thing, manages to be love-able despite it all.

3. HEATHCLIFF

Although Heathcliff, the smart-aleck, fast-talking, streetwise alley cat was created five years before Garfield, he never reached the same level of success. Some argue that because Heathcliff had no owner to irritate and berate, he was harder for fans to identify with. Still, Heathcliff was featured on ABC Saturday morning cartoons, appeared in hundreds of news-papers around the world, and was the subject of the book *Heathcliff Banquet.*

4. KLIBAN'S CATS

You've seen them. You've probably drunk from a coffee mug featuring these cats, or purchased a card for a sick friend and didn't even know you were supporting the now more than $70 million dollar business. When Bernard Kliban created his cats in the best-selling book *Cat* in 1975, he truly had no idea what he was starting. Calendars, coffee mugs, posters, cards, stationary, wrapping paper, gift items, and more fea-ture the unusual looking, striped cats.

5. PERIWINKLE

In 1996 Angela Santamero created a children's show differ-ent from any other. Using the unconventional approach of speaking directly to the viewing audience, actor Steve Burns and his animated pet, Blue, stole the hearts of millions. The show was a huge success, winning multiple awards, includ-ing the Television Critics Award for Outstanding Children's Show, and it continues to have a strong following. What few people know is that Blue, the darling blue puppy of daytime TV was intended to be a kitten. Santamero wanted to use a kitten to teach preschoolers, but when it was discovered another kitten cartoon was already in the works, she used a puppy instead. After several seasons, Santamero got her wish and created Periwinkle—Blue's next-door neighbor cat.

6. SYLVESTER

One of the most popular animated cats of all time, Sylvester is adored for all his imperfections. From his speech impediment (performed brilliantly by voice character impressionist Mel Blanc) to his highly elaborate, yet always bungled, schemes to eat Tweety, Sylvester reigns supreme in every cat lover's heart.

7. TOM

Created by cartoon gods William Hanna, Joseph Barbera, and Fred Quimby in 1939, Tom made his animated debut in the short film, "Puss Gets the Boot," and was a huge success. The speechless feline won seven Oscars and even served his country in World Wars I and II, when Hollywood producers sent movies overseas to relieve American soldiers from the strains of war. The slapstick exchanges between Tom and Jerry, who were similar in popularity to the Three Stooges, made Tom the cat icon he is today.

8. TONY THE TIGER

In 1952 Kellogg Company ran a contest, letting the American public choose one of three new mascots for their Frosted Flakes cereal: Katy the Kangaroo, Elmo the Elephant, and Tony the Tiger. While Katy and Tony ran neck and neck in the initial voting, Tony won out and became the official spokescat in 1953. Since then, Tony, whose voice was originally recorded by Thurl Ravenscroft (also famous for singing "You're a Mean One, Mr. Grinch), can be seen and heard in over forty-two countries. Kellogg says the animated cat that we see in commercials stands six feet, six inches tall with a muscular build, serving as a role model to kids everywhere. Eat right, grow strong. In the 1990s Tony was part of a campaign using real kids in various sports to promote exercise and better nutrition. He's gr-r-reat!!

9. CATDOG

Nickelodeon's wildly popular cartoon show, CatDog, features an animal that is a cat on one end and a dog on the other. However did such an idea develop in creator Peter Hannon's mind? Well, however it came about, kids love it! Nickelodeon describes the "hip" animal: "Cat and Dog have been sharing quarters (hindquarters, that is) since they were born, which hasn't been easy since they're as different as, well, cats and dogs. Dog loves rock 'n roll, Cat doesn't. Dog lives to chase garbage trucks, Cat REALLLLY doesn't. But believe it or not, they're the best of friends and they really stick together—they don't have any choice!"

10. SAGWA

In the early 1990s cat lover Amy Tan learned her beloved Siamese cat only had a month to live. At the age of seventeen, Sagwa had lived a full life with Tan and was dearly loved, but had become weakened with illness in her old age. Grief stricken that she would soon lose her dear friend, Tan had a dream about the adventures of a young Siamese. The next morning she wrote about her dreams, and in 1994 the first Sagwa book was born. Sagwa herself would be the first to hear the story; she lived another four years to the ripe old age of twenty-one.

In the book, Sagwa, the middle child in the extended cat family, has many adventures and lots of fun. Her grandparents, Yeh-Yeh and Nai-Nai, are wonderful storytellers, teaching their young kittens (and the audience) about traditions and customs. The Public Broadcast System (PBS) now airs the cartoon, entertaining children of all ages around the world.

BONUS ANIMATED CAT:

In 1926 A. A. Milne's classic *Winnie the Pooh* was released but it was not until Walt Disney purchased the movie rights in 1961, five years after Milne's death, that Tigger truly became a star. Did you know that Tigger appeared in only four of Milne's original stories, all in "The House At Pooh Corner"?

Most Popular Fictional Cats

Whether appearing in murder mysteries or in popular nursery rhymes, cats have entertained us through the pages of fictional works for centuries. These quirky, delightful, mysterious creatures make for excellent characters as they teach us about ourselves and the world around us. While there are too many fictional cats to count, here are some of the most beloved:

1. *THE CAT IN THE HAT*

Who doesn't know *The Cat in the Hat*? Created by Dr. Seuss in 1957, this mischievous cat with a magical hat and whimsical ways delights two bored children and millions of fans around the world. The most improbable, unimaginable things occur in the fantastic, funny, fast-paced, whirlwind way that is unique to *The Cat in the Hat*. And for cat lovers around the world, the behavior of this cat, who shows up from seemingly nowhere to give just an hour of his time in the most engaging, entertaining manner, is the essence of every cat. Millions of copies of this book have been read, and in 2003 comedian Mike Myers brought *The Cat in the Hat* to life in a movie version of Dr. Seuss's wonderful story.

2. **"THE CAT THAT WALKED HIMSELF"**

While the Dog, the Horse, and the Cow had all established themselves with the new species of humans, the Cat was a holdout, not wanting to give up its independence or last piece of wilderness. After some time, the Cat appeared at the cave of the humans and announced, "I am not a friend, and I am not a servant. I am the Cat who walks by himself and I wish to come into your cave." From this, the relationship between cats and humans began.

This engaging story of the cat, written by Rudyard Kipling and published in 1902, portrays the cat as it has lived throughout history.

3. THE CHESHIRE CAT

In 1865 Lewis Carroll published the children's classic *Alice's Adventures in Wonderland*. While the story was about the adventures of a young girl, the Cheshire Cat became a favorite character among readers. It is believed the term Cheshire dates back to a particular brand of cheese that was often molded in the shape of grinning cats. By the early 1800s the expression "grinning like a Cheshire cat" was common, and Carroll had fun with the expressions of the day. What made this character so popular was it's oh-so-catlike mannerisms. When Alice first reprimands the cat for disappearing so suddenly, he begs her pardon and vanishes slowly, "beginning with the end of the tail, and ending with the grin, which remained some time after the rest of it had gone."

4. WHITTINGTON'S CAT

The story of author Dick Whittington and his cat, which was adapted into a play in 1605 (and has since been lost), told of a poor young man who walked to London with his faithful sidekick—a cat. The duo had many adventures, as the cat brought his master good luck. While the real Whittington was wealthy, the poor-boy-goes-to-London-to-find-fortune makes for a good story, especially with a cat.

5. THE RUM TUM TUGGER

In 1939 cat lover T. S. Eliot created the book *Old Possum's Book of Practical Cats*, as part satirical tribute to his era and part ode to his beloved cats. Of the character the Rum Tum Tugger, Eliot writes:

"The Rum Tum Tugger is a Curious Cat:
If you offer him a pheasant he would rather have a grouse.
If you put him in a house he would much prefer a flat,
If you put him in a flat then he'd rather have a house.
If you set him on a mouse then he only wants a rat,
If you set him on a rat then he'd rather chase a mouse.
Yes the Rum Tum Tugger is a Curious Cat—
　And there isn't any call for me to shout it:
　　For he will do
　　　As he does do
　　　　And there's no doing anything about it!

For many, this verse begs another question. Was this the inspiration for Dr. Seuss's *Green Eggs and Ham* (the third best-selling book in the English language)?

The Broadway production *Cats* was based on Eliot's book. With music by Andrew Lloyd Webber, it went on to become the longest running musical in London and New York and has received worldwide acclaim.

6. PUSS IN BOOTS

In 1697 French writer Charles Perrault depicted this legendary cat in his *Contes du temps passé*, a story that remains popular even today. Upon his master's death, Puss learns that he has been willed to a surviving son who plans on eating him and using his fur as a muff. Desperate to save his own hide, he promises to bring fortune to his new master and so begin the adventures of Puss in Boots—required gear for a seventeenth century super hero.

7. THE TALE OF TOM KITTEN

"Once upon a time there were three little kittens, and their names were Mittens, Tom Kitten and Moppett." Tom Kitten, a Beatrix Potter creation, quickly became a beloved character, following in the footsteps of Peter Rabbit. Potter introduced this character in *The Tale of Tom Kitten* in 1907, four years after her book *The Tailor of Gloucester*, which featured the feline character Simpkin, and two years preceding *Ginger and Pickles*, which featured a cat named Ginger. But few cat characters of Potter's, or any other author for that matter, were as dear to the public as Tom Kitten.

8. PUSSYCAT

In 1878 author Edward Lear, famous for his silly but insightful poems, introduced an unlikely love affair between an owl and a pussycat. Modeling Pussycat after his own cat, Foss, Lear sent his fictitious feline on a poetic adventure that remains just as silly today. "And they danced by the light of the moon!"

9. THE CAT WHO . . .

In the brilliant detective series by Lilian Jackson Braun, two Siamese cats by the names of Yum Yum and Koko use logic and reason to fight crime as only two felines could. After her beloved Koko was killed in a fall from her apartment, Braun dedicated this series to her cat. Her first cat-sleuthing book, *The Cat Who Could Read Backwards* appeared in 1966. The best-selling author has more than three dozen *The Cat Who* . . . books in print around the world, and her cat-adoring public continues to place her books on the *New York Times* bestseller list.

10. TCHAIKOVSKY'S CATS

Who would have ever guessed that Tchaikovsky's production of his ballet *Sleeping Beauty*, based on Charles Perrault's children stories, originally featured cats as main characters? First performed in St. Petersburg in 1890, Tchaikovsky's rendition of *Sleeping Beauty* included Puss in Boots and White Cat. One of the main highlights of the ballet is a scene in which White Cat enters in a wedding procession, and Puss in Boots, who is smitten with her, begins to court her. Although the ballet received mixed reviews at first, it was Tchaikovsky's first major success in ballet composition, set the standard for what is now called "classical ballet," and is one of the most beloved ballets of all time.

The Legend of Catwoman

Perhaps one of the most exciting characters—more so for some than others—is Catwoman. Sexy, mysterious, dangerous, and exotic. What's not to love? Throughout the 1900s there have been many "cat women" to entertain and intrigue us, from fictional felines and super heroes to actual lion and tiger tamers.

1. THE FIRST CATWOMAN

In the 1920s a woman named Mabel Stark became famous in her trademark tights, white bodysuit, and a dangerous act with tigers. No one had ever seen such a performance! Stark's act outlived a number of marriages, divorces, and scandals and her 1938 autobiography, *Hold That Tiger*, until she was mauled by her tiger Rajah. While she survived the attack, she did not perform again. As an elderly woman, she said she once wished Rajah had killed her—that was the way she wanted to die. It has been long speculated that Stark served as the role model for the supervillain Catwoman in the Batman series.

2. THE CATWOMAN IN MYTHOLOGY

Long before Batman had to fight Catwoman or before Mabel Stark and her tigers, there were legends connecting cats and women. In one Greek myth, there is a man whose cat is so

woman, so he could marry
e, overhears his wish and
han marries her at once.
vely bride sees a mouse.
she springs from the bed
ole. The man is so ap-
e the cat a cat again. A

.ield published "Curse of the Catwoman," a
_...orous and disturbing poem about "that woman you meet and fall in love with [who] is of that strange Transylvanian people with an affinity for cats." Field compares a man's liaison with a woman to a relationship with a cat—one in which you must expect scratches and, sometimes, violent actions. However much the cat's reputation has evolved since the Middle Ages, it will always be linked with mystery, danger, and fear.

4. THE TIGER LADY

When Jocelyne Wildenstein discovered her billionaire husband was having an affair, she turned to plastic surgery and regained her husband's attention—for a while. But when her husband began to see other women again, Wildenstein tried something so radical, she was sure it would save her marriage: she endured more plastic surgery to make herself look like her husband's exotic cats. While she now looks like a real-life catwoman, her plan to win her husband back failed. Wildenstein has filed for a $50,000,000 trust and $2,400,000 a year in alimony.

Photos of Wildenstein's dramatic transformation from housewife to catwoman can be found on the Internet.

4. BATMAN'S CATWOMAN

In 1940 Catwoman, the alter ego of Selina Kyle, appeared in Batman's comic number 600 as a costumed jewel thief making Batman fans everywhere smitten. As the story goes, Selina Kyle, left on death's door, was brought back to life by alley cats, who gave her the powers and personality of a cat. The Catwoman character acted as both a nemesis and a possible love interest for Batman. As is typical of the cat, when she was expected to be bad, she was good; when she was expected to be good, she was bad. Her moves were unpredictable and suspenseful. While she was a solitary figure, she could also communicate with other cats and often included them in her crimes. Alone or with others, Catwoman—like the feline—was simultaneously self-reliant and demanding, aloof and demonstrative, comforting and frightening. In other words, Catwoman was a perfect cat.

5. THE CHARACTER

Also known as the Princess of Plunder, Feline Fatale, and Feline Felon, Catwoman quickly became a sex symbol— risky business for the comic book industry. But by the 1950s, new storylines and movies emerged depicting scantily clad (by the days' standard), mysterious women in search of a mate. Not to be outdone by their own creation, DC Comics began to intensify the sexual friction between Batman and Catwoman.

6. PRIME TIME CATWOMAN

On January 12, 1966, Catwoman appeared on the popular *Batman* television series and wowed audiences around the world. Wearing her skintight black leather outfit, actress Julie Newmar became an overnight sensation. The statuesque, curvaceous beauty became a pin-up and was singly responsible for male college students everywhere skipping classes in hopes of a glimpse of the feline fatale. Although she only appeared in six *Batman* episodes, she remains the all-time popular Catwoman.

7. THE STAND-IN

The sexual chemistry between Batman and Julie Newmar's Catwoman was tremendous, but at the height of Ms. New-

mar's career as the feline tease, she suddenly became un-
available. Rumors swirled that network executives were
worried about the actress's oozing sex appeal. And in her
place came the black actress Eartha Kitt, a safe bet because
sexual attraction between black and white actors was believed unlikely in 1968. While Kitt didn't have the curves or
sexual prowess of Newmar, she did have the best growly cat
voice of any Catwoman. After Kitt came actress Lee Meri-
wether, a white girl-next-door who could also keep sexual
content to a minimum.

8. BATMAN RETURNS

In 1992 *Batman Returns* hit the movie theaters and a new
Catwoman wowed the audiences. Actress Michelle Pfeiffer,
wearing a black leather outfit tighter than any Julie Newmar
ever dreamed of wearing, burst on the scene, snapping a
whip and purring to a whole new level. To prepare for the
movie, Pfeiffer spent hours and hours just learning how to
use a whip properly. It's hard work to learn to act like a cat.

9. CATWOMAN OF THE NEW MILLENNIUM

A new, different Catwoman, named Patience Philips, was
created for the movies in 2004 and was intended to be
played by kittenish actress Ashley Judd. But a conflicting
schedule forced Judd to bow out, allowing actress Halle
Berry to step in. Granted catlike powers, this new Catwoman
is more agile, more powerful, more mysterious, and sexier
than ever.

10. THE CAT'S MEOW

Of all the good guys, of all the crime-fighting heroes there
are to pick from, *Hero* magazine reported that Catwoman
ranked in the top twenty-five best and all-time loved comic
heroes. Hero? Hold on, a new Catwoman is coming around
the corner. Created by comic book writer Ed Brubaker, the
number one cat burglar decided to use her power for good
and help the helpless and downtrodden of Gotham City. In
the new age of girl power, why not? It's a cat's prerogative to
change her mind.

The Real Cat Woman

In 1987 former schoolteacher and entrepreneur Kay Mc-Elroy saw an ad in a local newspaper advertising the sale of a six-month-old cougar for $1,000. She had never seen a cougar before, so she decided to meet the cat. What she found was a shadow of a cougar—malnourished and living in horrific conditions. She knew she had to act. Today, Mc-Elroy is the founder and president of the Cedarhill Animal Sanctuary, one of the best animal sanctuaries in the world. As one of the world's foremost activists for animal rights, McElroy shares some of her joys and experiences in working with cats.

1. **ZACK**

When McElroy first laid eyes on the cougar, the big cat was chained up in a small pen with pus coming out of old wounds and cement sores (caused by living in concrete-only cells) all over his body. Zack was just skin and bones, and the animal lover knew she had to save him. Temporarily out of work and furnishing a brand new house, she offered a tractor in exchange for the cat because she couldn't pay $1,000 that she didn't have. The man initially refused, but two weeks later he pulled up to her house ready to make the trade—a cat for a tractor.

"Now what?" she wondered. She spent the next two

weeks calling zoos, but no one could or would take the cat. "It was pretty clear I would have to build a pen or have him put to sleep." And so she built the pen and promptly entered the world of exotic animals. Today, a very happy sixteen-year-old Zack lives in Cedarhill.

2. BABY

One morning in 1993, McElroy got a phone call from a group of animal activists hoping to save a lioness named Baby. They told her the story of a couple living in Biloxi, Mississippi, who had purchased a lion cub and paraded around the neighborhood with their new pride and joy. Neighbors, however, were less than joyful. The lioness was ill cared for, and one night, as she was waiting hungrily to be fed scraps, she jumped up and bit the owner's wife. As punishment, the lion's feet were bound, and she was dragged outside to be beaten.

Using the legal system to free the lion, McElroy provided evidence that the animal was a danger to the two small children who also lived in the house. It seemed an open-and-shut case as the couple was presented with a choice: either the children go or the cat does. But to everyone's surprise, the couple gave up the children, sending them off as wards of the state. The story made the national news and, concerned for his cat, the owner hid her with a vet, who promptly called McElroy.

The story of Baby is bittersweet. Because big cats are extremely inbred they often have serious medical problems; Baby was no exception. In 1994 Baby was put to sleep in McElroy's arms.

3. SPARKLES AND BIG AL

Declawed and defanged, Sparkles was a rare Chinese spotted leopard, who used to star in commercials and print ads. When not in front of the camera, Sparkles lived with several other big cats in an underground bunker. But on December 24, 1989, his breeder's wife was killed in a car accident and he lost the desire and resources to care for all of his cats. McElroy was called for help, but she had to pass a test before she could take Sparkles. If she could walk with Sparkles out into a nearby pasture, past the cows and back to the barn, she could have the cat. "Well, I came back with cowdung all over me but I took that cat!" And with Sparkles came a tiger named Big Al.

At Cedarhill, the cats walked on grass for the first time, played with toys, and lived in living quarters nearly quadruple the size of their old bunker. In 2003 Sparkles died at the age of thirty-two, and Big Al, at the age of sixteen, suffers from deteriorating arthritis.

4. GUNTHER AND SHAM

In 1992 McElroy went to the airport to pick up a cougar named Sham, who had been flown in from the Idaho Falls zoo. On her way there, she passed an old milk truck that now housed a lion under a billboard that read: "See the lion roar for 25 cents." Stopping to check things out, she found that the lion's owner made the cat roar by jabbing him with a stick. McElroy tried to convince the owner that Gunther the lion would be happier with her, but the owner was uncertain. It was not until the man committed suicide that McElroy got the cat, who was left to her by the owner. To this day, she says, Gunther blames her for the loss of his owner—however horribly he was treated, the cat remains loyal.

She also discovered that Sham, the cougar she picked up from the airport that day, was deaf. He lived to be nineteen years old.

5. KC

Also in 1992, while visiting her mother in Oklahoma, McElroy learned of a cougar named KC who had been left abandoned after his owner was arrested for dealing drugs. The cat had been left in an enclosed pen with no water, no food, and no shelter in ten-degree weather. The former owners had taken a weed-eater to his face and body and left him for dead. McElroy convinced a local vet to come out to examine the cat, who was obviously in dire need of medical attention, while she untied him from his pen—dangerous business. This former schoolteacher from Los Angeles's Watts District was no stranger to challenges. With food in her hand, she baited the cat, saying, "Come on, boy, let's get the hell out of here!" KC jumped up on the truck and off they went—headed to a new home some five hundred miles away.

6. CAESAR

In 1994 McElroy traveled to Huntsville, Alabama, to check up on two cougars who had been left alone after their owner had been arrested. When she arrived, she found that the female cat had tried to jump a fence but ended up hanging herself on the chain to which she had been fastened. The male, named Caesar, had been left in a darkened room with no sunlight and no water, and was fed two dead chickens only once a week. Caesar had lived this way for three months, slowly losing his mind. Although McElroy has had Caesar in Cedarhill for ten years, he continues to hiss at her. "But I say that's better than when I first brought him here and he hid for months. When he hisses at me I say, 'Hey, that's better than no greeting at all.'"

7. THE DOMESTICS

Initially, only three or four small cats wandered into Cedarhill and stayed. But when McElroy worked on the board of an animal shelter, she continued to bring home cats on death row, unable to accept euthanasia. Then in 1987, because the board was not forthcoming about the actual number of animals being put to sleep or where the bodies were being dumped, she could no longer stay on as a member. Today, she has over 150 domesticated cats in need of love, shelter, and food—which McElroy and her staff try to provide.

8. LITTLE STEVIE WONDER

To care for the animals and keep a staff on hand, Cedarhill requires approximately $30,000 per month. The care of one ex-

otic cat alone costs $1,000 a month
medical bills and the cost of feedi
cat. There are days when McElroy
going to make it to the month's end.
her domestic, Little Stevie Wonder. Although
deaf, McElroy says she's learned more from this ca
other living creature on earth. "He's taught me acceptan
of life. He doesn't feel sorry for himself and accepts what's
been dealt to him." Often when all the caregivers have gone
home, McElroy goes out to her domestics and lets them
climb all over her. "It soothes my soul and I think, 'You can't
fail.'"

9. RACHEL

Born in 1992, Rachel was taken from her mother when she
was just a few days old. The Bengal/Siberian tiger was bot-
tle-fed and hand-raised, but because of her young mother's
growth developmental problem, Rachel suffered from severe
calcium deficiency. She had to have her baby teeth surgi-
cally removed as they rotted in place and caused draining
cysts rather than falling out naturally. Today, she lives with
Kimba, a neutered Siberian tiger, who was rescued from the
pet trade.

10. FRIDAY

Friday is a lioness who was dropped off at a veterinarian's
office in Lawrence, Kansas, on a Friday morning in 1991. At
four months old, she was in a coma, weighing less than seven
pounds and suffering from abrasions on her head. She had
been fed small amounts of goat milk to keep her small—a
plan devised to sell her as a "miniature lioness." While two
of her siblings eventually died of starvation, Friday was sta-
bilized after two months of round-the-clock care. Today, Friday weighs over five hundred pounds and enjoys her life at
Cedarhill.

For more information about the remarkable Kay McElroy
and her beautiful cats, log on to www.cedrhill.org and perhaps you can help a cat!

Cedarhill Animal Sanctuary

Rachel reclines in a pool in her new home.

Famous Cat Artists

Artist/photographers Heather Busch and Burton Silver published a beautiful book entitled *Why Cats Paint* (Ten Speed Press, California, 1994), an in-depth analysis of cat artistry. For decades, biologists have made claims that the markings of a cat are not simply random scratches, but are "aesthetically motivated" pieces of art relating to their own particular territory. Perhaps you have a feline artist in your own home. Do all cats paint? Are some breeds more likely to paint than others? How do you know if your cat will paint? For more information about the nature of feline artists, visit www.monpa.com/wcp/faq.html. Following are some of the best artists or artistic duos of the feline world.

1. WONG WONG AND LU LU

Italian artist Lu Lu, a seal lynx, was already an established painter when he met Wong Wong, a small Havana brown. Lu Lu had been working on his painting, *Mural in White*, when Wong Wong strolled over and added to the painting. While this first encounter did not go well—Wong Wong ended up covered in white paint—the two began collaborating, creating over a dozen works, including the infamous *Wonglu*, which sold at an auction in 1993 for $19,000.

2. PEPPER AND VENUS

New York artist Pepper began his career in 1981. His initial effort, moisturizing cream on a vanity mirror, lacked clear form. As he grew more bold, experimenting with cosmetics and whatever creams he could get his paws on, his owner realized he had a gift and supplied him with acrylic paints and paper. Almost all of Pepper's first acrylic works were a reflection of himself, as he would stare into a mirror for hours before creating. In 1987 Pepper broke out of his traditional works and began painting his housemate, a silver tabby named Venus. While they would often fight—really—their creations were unique. Although Venus would often drift off, falling asleep, Pepper remained focused. Venus was his guiding light. In 1988 Pepper held the first showing of his works— and the first ever all-cat exhibit—and was clearly on his way to becoming one of the greatest feline painters of all time. But in 1991, after Venus became crippled with arthritis, Pepper stopped painting.

3. TIGER

Perhaps German artist Tiger is the most temperamental of all the well-known cat artists. Known to destroy his work as soon as he finishes it, Tiger uses bold colors, often in long strokes across the canvas. It is believed that Tiger intends to "save" his work by tearing it apart with his own claws before anyone else can get their paws on it. A few pieces, such as *Eclectic Currents* in 1992, have been saved in a private collection, thanks to claw-proof canvases—which tend to upset Tiger for several months after the completion of a painting.

4. MISTY

As both a fine artist and a performance artist, Misty is well-known in Canada, which she calls home. Misty's works have no evident boundaries. She is known to paint off the canvas and onto the wall, moving out as far or high as her artistic instincts take her. There have been instances when she simply cannot reach high enough, even when jumping, and she will meow loudly until she is given a stool. In 1993 her painting, *Interring the Terrier*, which has been interpreted as depicting a headless dog being stuffed into a red armchair by two frogs and a sardine, sold for $21,000.

5.   MINNIE MONET MANET

Known for her vigorous strokes and lightning speed swats at the canvas, French artist Minnie becomes so entranced with her work that she barely takes the time to look at it until it is complete. So popular is Minnie Monet Manet that one of the kittens was sold in Japan for $20,000, where an art-loving cat-owner no doubt hopes talent runs in the family.

6.   SMOKEY

Keenly aware of his gorgeous setting, this artist from New Zealand insisted on working outside, where he was able to paint from live subjects, including his family's fifteen-year-old ram. That piece, titled *Serious Ramification*, sold for $6,000, although not without controversy. When it was revealed that the McGillicuddy Gallery purchased the painting with public funds scandal erupted—and Smokey wanted no part. He liked to work alone, secluded in the rear of the garden, where he was free to roam, investigate, and return to his work undisturbed. Choosing different places in which to paint, he let his owner know where to leave his art supplies by "flamboyantly" marking the precise spot with urine.

7.   CHARLIE

Van Gogh and Picasso, both brilliant artists, suffered prepubescent claustrophobic traumas, leading many to believe that inner turmoil and suffering made them so expressive and creative. It is understandable then that Australian cat artist Charlie, who was unintentionally shut in a refrigerator for five hours, suddenly became quite expressive upon his release. He chooses to paint on the refrigerator, perhaps in an effort to redesign the place of his trauma or to make it look better. He recognizes the need to have the refrigerator in the house; after all that is where his food is kept. But maybe he is making some kind of expression against the icebox? Regardless of his precise reason, authors Busch and Silver note that by using the refrigerator as his canvas, "he is able to gain power over it, which must surely be why he paints it."

8. **BOOTSIE**

Bootsie knows pain. In one short week, his family moved, and he was neutered, boarded, and got his tail caught in a heater unit. And he was attacked by a dog. So, when the native of San Francisco was introduced to cat painting as a way to relieve his stress, he was receptive. A good thing, too. Within his first four years after turning professional, Bootsie had five exhibitions and earned over $75,000. In 1993 he won the Zampa d'Oro (Golden Paw) award at the Esposizione dell'Arte Felino in Milan.

9. **GINGER**

British artist Ginger wasn't always an artist. In fact, her owners had to teach her how to paint, by dipping her paws into the wet sand of her litter box, then marking the wall to let her see the magic her paws could work. She must have liked what she saw because soon thereafter she began using acrylics on canvas, walls, and windows. Ginger often became so enamored with her work—which looks like paw marks across the canvas—she would rub against the still-wet paint, many times losing the art forever.

10. **MATTISA**

Perhaps the best known cat painter, a small ginger tabby named Mattisa, lived in the late 1880s. She was the star attraction in Mrs. Broadmoore's show at the Chatsworth Gardens, which was billed to be the most emphatically, the most phenomenally, the most prodigious, the most extraordinary traveling exhibition in the world, and toted a cat who offered "compelling sketches occasioned by deft movements of the paw." Mrs. Broadmore, actually a large man disguised as a ditzy upper-class matron, was a pioneer in his own right, realizing Mattissa's great talent. As the poster promised, audiences were amazed by the cats "pawtraits."

World Record Cats

In 1951 Sir Hugh Beaver, a managing director of the Guinness Brewery, began a fact-finding agency in London that would ultimately create and publish the *Guinness Book of World Records*. Since the first publication of this one-of-a-kind book in 1955, there has been a growing public interest in record-setting around the world. Cat lovers were quick to join the search for information about the most exotic, the most unusual, and the most beloved breeds. The following record-breaking cats are the most popular Guinness cats:

1. LONGEST CAT

On November 11, 1997, a large white cat from Scotland named Snowbie claimed the title of world's longest cat, measuring 40.8 inches from his nose to the tip of his tail. At the age of four, this cat stood thirteen inches tall. However, in 2002 the world record was taken from Snowbie by Verismo Leonetti Reserve Red. Known as Leo to his friends and family, the Maine coon measured forty-eight inches with feet so large his paws fit snuggly into a child's size two shoe.

2. LONGEST CAT WHISKERS

A three-year-old black and white domestic longhair broke the *Guinness Book* record for longest whiskers in Burlington, Iowa, with the confirmed measurement of 5.5 inch-long whiskers. But in July 2004 Mingo, a Maine coon who lives in Turku, Finland, measured in with 6.8-inch whiskers.

3. MOST KITTENS

This title was earned by a cat who should have been spayed long before she made her way into the record books after giving birth to 420 kittens. Dusty, may she rest—really rest—in peace lived and bred in Bonham, Texas, delivering her last litter on June 12, 1952.

4. BIGGEST LITTER

While she didn't have 420 kittens, Tarawood Antigone of England did have the largest known single litter. On August 7, 1970, the brown Burmese gave birth to nineteen—one female, fourteen males, and four stillborn. The father was Siamese.

5. MOST TOES

In Bonfield, Ontario, Canada, an orange tabby named Jake holds the record of having the most toes. Confirmed by a team of veterinarians, each of the seven toes (on each foot) have their own pads and claws. The record was previously held by Mickey, also an orange tabby, from Deep River, New York, who had twenty-seven toes.

6. GREATEST CLIMB

In 1950 a kitten who followed mountain climbers in Switzerland was left behind. Deciding to continue the climb alone, the kitten followed their footsteps, reaching an altitude of 12,556 feet. He continued on and was spotted the next morning by a second set of climbers. The persistent kitty continued on until, on the third day, he reached the summit at 14,780 feet and shared a meal with a stunned climbing party. The world quickly learned of this amazing cat upon his return, and he came to be known as the Matterhorn Cat.

7. OLDEST CAT

Spike, an orange and white tabby from Dorset, United Kingdom, has garnered much publicity as the oldest cat. Remarkably, he survived a rottweiler attack at the age of nineteen, and lived to the ripe old age of thirty-one. But it is Granpa, a thirty-four-year-old tabby, who is Guinness's confirmed oldest cat. One year prior to his death on April 1, 1998, Granpa posed as a centerfold for *Cat Fancy* magazine.

As of 2004 Guinness recognizes Kataleena Lady of Victoria, Australia, as the oldest living cat, born on March 11, 1977.

8. MOST EXPENSIVE WEDDING

In September 1996 two rare diamond-eyed cats named Phet and Ploy were married in matching pink outfits in Thailand in what is known to be the biggest animal wedding of all time. The cost of the wedding to Phet's owner, Wichan Jaratarcha, was $16,241, topped by a dowry of $23,202. However, with more than five hundred guests in attendance, the cats raked in over $60,000 in cash and wedding presents. Phet arrived at the wedding in a Rolls Royce, while Ploy made his entrance by way of helicopter. A parrot stood in as best man and an iguana served as maid of honor.

After the wedding, however, Phet and Ploy went to separate households to live. In Thailand, Phet and Ploy, who were both born with a rare type of glaucoma called "diamond eye" are believed to be symbols of God and are highly valued.

9. LONGEST FALL

Imagine falling from a sixteenth-floor balcony and living to meow about it. That's exactly what happened to Andy, who belonged to then–Florida Senator Ken Myer in the 1970s. Andy still holds the record for the longest nonfatal fall in feline history.

10. SMALLEST CAT

Until July 2004 the honor of smallest cat went to a male Himalayan named Tinker Toy, who was only two inches tall and seven inches long. Today, a two-year-old cat named Mr. Peebles is the world's smallest cat, according to Guinness. Veterinarian Dr. Donna Sassman confirmed Mr. Peebles has a genetic defect that restricts him to a weight of only three pounds.

Pussycat, Pussycat, Where Have You Been?

While many cat owners debate whether to let their cat out the front door, other cats have been traveling around the world. The adventures of these cats have inspired books and tested the spirit of the cat—the natural wanderer.

1. THE CAT WHO COVERED THE WORLD

Henrietta traveled the world with her owner, *New York Times* foreign correspondent Christopher S. Wren, and his family, crisscrossing the globe on adventures so grand that Wren penned a book, *The Cat Who Covered the World: The Adventures of Henrietta and Her Foreign Correspondent*. The feline befriended Nobel laureate Andrei Sakharov in Russia and once disrupted a diplomatic dinner by offering a mouse to the guest of honor. Henrietta also got lost in Egypt for several weeks, but just when her frantic family had finally given up hope of her survival, she found her way back home, having survived on food scraps along the Nile River. She traveled to China, Canada, France, Italy, Portugal, Japan, and South Africa. In her twilight years in South Africa, Henrietta fought against apartheid guard dogs. With tens of thousands of miles travel under her belt, Henrietta charmed the world over with her adventuresome, curious, always friendly demeanor for seventeen years.

2. THE CAT WHO WENT TO PARIS AND ABROAD

Publisher and screenwriter Peter Gethers was a confirmed cat hater. But when he was given a six-week-old Scottish Fold named Norton, everything changed. As Gethers walked around New York with the floppy-eared kitten tucked in his coat pocket, he began to develop a real attachment to Norton. Gethers went on to write a bestselling book, *The Cat Who Went to Paris*, and its sequel, *A Cat Abroad*, about his adventures with Norton throughout Europe. When Gethers and his cat returned to the United States, Norton found himself on the A-list of celebrities, appearing on national talk shows (with Gethers), staying in only the finest of hotels, and receiving fan mail from both humans and felines all over the world. In 2002 Gethers penned the final, poignant chapter in his trilogy of true stories about his adventures with his beloved Norton, who was with him for almost twenty years, *The Cat Who'll Live Forever: The Final Adventures of Norton, the Perfect Cat, and His Imperfect Human*. What else would you expect when an ailurophobe spends a little time with a floppy-eared Scottish Fold?

3. SUKI OF THE NILE

When American businessman Paul Novak and his wife, Glenda, moved their family to Kuwait, they had no idea how their lives would change. Their daughter, Cristina, had begged for a cat, and so, when Glenda went to the market one day and found a half-starved Siamese inside a birdcage in a small flower shop, she bought the kitten for her daughter's seventh birthday. Named Suki, the Siamese quickly became a jet-setter in the feline world, traveling from Kuwait to the United Arab Emirates, Tunisia, Algeria, Egypt, Holland, Germany, France, and the United States. She had her own passport (with photo and full name—Suki June Novak); flew first-class in her own seat; stayed in the finest hotels, with special litter boxes always provided by hotel staff; and dined on the finest cuisine, served on silver platters and fine crys-

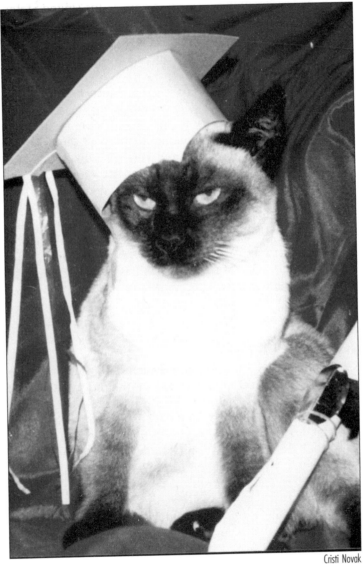

Cristi Novak

Suki graduates and earns her spot in the high school yearbook.

tal. When the Novak family moved back to the United States so that Cristina and her brother, Paul, could finish high school, Suki went to high school parties, wearing Cabbage Patch doll dresses and gel in her fur, and she even had her photograph in the high school yearbook, complete with cap and gown. She was Cristina's best friend for eighteen years.

4. SPREADING THE WORD

For Yeti, a lynx, work is never done. As the most-traveled ambassador for the International Society of Endangered Cats (ISEC), Yeti's job is to educate people about the threat of extinction posed on exotic cats by humans. While Yeti appears to be just another pretty face, he helps the ISEC in its dedication to the conservation of wildcats and their ever-diminishing habitats, traveling across the globe to raise public awareness about wildcats.

For more information about this worthy cause and Yeti, visit www.isec.org.

5. TRIM THE CAT

In 1802–1803 Captain Matthew Flinders, with his best cat, Trim, and crew, became the first captain to sail around Australia. Trim was a black and white cat with great sea legs, able to climb the ship's ropes and riggings as easily as he would climb trees. He sailed around Tasmania and Bass with Flinders as well, spending his days catching rats and taking catnaps in the captain's quarters. Trim escaped death many times, surviving falling overboard, being shipwrecked, and eventually, being captured by the French. When Captain Flinders and crew docked at the island of Mauritius, unaware that the British and French were at war, they were promptly imprisoned. While the captain sat in his jail cell, Trim wandered off, never to be seen again. Heartbroken, Captain Flinders requested pen and paper and wrote a children's story immortalizing his adventurous cat.

6. TODAY'S TRIM

In 1995 the *Windeward Bound*, a beautifully crafted brigantine, was built in Hobart, Australia, for a reenactment of

Captain Flinders's voyage in 2002–2003. The voyage was designed as an educational and environmental exploration of Australia's coastline with a seasoned crew that included Trim the cat. Just like his predecessor, the new Trim is a black and white cat who loves the sea. You can visit www .windbound.com to see pictures of Trim in action or send the seafaring cat a personal note at sailing@windbound.com.

7. TRAVELING CIRCUS CATS

The Catman website claims Dominique LeFort to be the greatest domestic cat trainer in the world. Dominique and his wondrous cats have appeared in national publications and televised events, leaving audiences astounded as these seemingly everyday cats leap through rings of fire, perform tricks, and listen to their trainer's every command. "Welcome to the Best Cat Show on Earth!" For more information about Dominique and his cats, visit www.catmankeywest .com

8. MY CAT SPIT MCGEE

Writer and journalist Willie Morris (author of *My Dog Skip*) is a great cat lover—now. Like author Peter Gethers, he used to hate cats. But when Morris married a cat lover named Jo-Anne, he was forced to change his ways. For Christmas one year, the Morrises were given a stray kitten named Rivers Applewhite. Willie Morris was not too pleased with this gift until Rivers gave birth to a trouble-prone kitten named Spit. Spit was nearly strangled by his own birth sac but, yelling "live, boy, live!" the author saved him. Willie Morris saved Spit's life again when the kitten was just a week old. Spit and his littermates were infested with fleas, and Willie pulled Spit through (sadly, none of his siblings survived). A bond formed between the two as Spit and Morris traveled together, visiting places of the author's past. In fact, Morris believes that Spit was his dog Skip reincarnated.

9. CHEYENNE, THE TRAVELIN' CAT

April Fools' Day 2004 did not start off well for Florida resident Pamela Edwards. She had been forced to put her cat of nineteen years to sleep due to health complications. At work that day she received a phone call. "We found your cat," came a voice on the other end of the line. Because it was April Fools' Day, Edwards thought it was a joke—a cruel joke. But she quickly realized the other person was talking about her cat, Cheyenne, who had disappeared seven years before. Cheyenne, who had lived with Edwards in Florida, was found in San Francisco, California, where she was taken to an animal shelter. Rescue workers at the shelter discovered a microchip imbedded in Cheyenne's skin and were able to locate Edwards.

"We thought she had been eaten by an alligator," explained Edwards, who lives near a canal that serves as home to many reptiles. No one knows just how Cheyenne made it across the country. With the help of the *Ellen DeGeneres Show* and *Animal Planet*, Edwards and her daughter were able to fly across the United States to reunite with Cheyenne. Once there, Pamela Edwards and Cheyenne appeared on both television shows, including an *Ellen DeGeneres* segment, "Cheyenne, the Travelin' Cat." DeGeneres displayed a series of pictures of Cheyenne, asking viewers to write in and share any information they may have about the cat's travels. Although Cheyenne's not talking, the comedienne hopes to retrace the feline's footsteps.

10. THE TRAVELING CAT

Some cats (like Samuel Tinker) are naturally good traveling companions, while others have anxiety attacks at the mere sight of a suitcase. Cleveland Amory, author of *The Cat Who Came for Christmas*, says friends warned him against taking his cat traveling with him because "cats rank as fellow travelers on long trips somewhere above alligators and orangutans." Amory admits that cats aren't always the best of companions while traveling, but he took his cats all the same. Still, he reminds us that the simple luxury of a hotel room is often missed by the feline, for whom the room is "uncharted wilderness, around any corner of which lurked dangers which would put to shame a Chamber of Horrors in a wax museum on Halloween."

Should you decide to travel with your feline friend, check out www.PetTravel.com, www.PetPlace.com, and www.furr-angels.com/travelingpet.htm.

Cat Astrology

Everyday all over the world, people check their daily horoscopes to learn how their days will play out. Will I find true love? Will I get that raise? Win the lottery? Hopeful that the planets and the stars are properly aligned, we also study our astrological signs to learn more about why we do what we do. Geminis are the volatile twins, Scorpio has the temper, Aquarius is the flower child through all ages, and Aries, while bullheaded, often plays the peacemaker. And to feed our obsession with the stars (and our felines) further cat enthusiast/author Michael Zullo published *Cat Astrology: The Complete Guide to Feline Horoscopes* (Tribune Publishing, Orlando, 1983). Now we know everything we need to know about our felines—including when to stay out of their way!

1. ARIES (MARCH 21–APRIL 20)

The Aries cat is energetic, ready to pounce. This cat is impatient, playful, friendly, and often combative. A social kitty, the Aries cat needs lots of affection and does not enjoy being left alone, but if you have to work, he'll forgive you if you give him lots of love when you get home. Aries love having their heads scratched vigorously and are quite physical in demonstrating their enjoyment. And watch out—they may not be willing to wait for you to get the food from the can into the dish before they attack.

2. **TAURUS (APRIL 21–MAY 21)**

Homebodies at heart, these cats like a routine. Feeding, sleeping, and loving schedules should be fairly predictable—particularly the feeding schedule. Because this cat tends to put on more weight than others, be careful of his medical needs. Generally a laid-back cat, he can spend hours watching fish swim around in a bowl or leaves blowing outside a window. Serenity is what the Taurus cat seeks, and he will fight like a wild tiger if forced to ride in a car or take a bath.

3. **GEMINI (MAY 22–JUNE 21)**

This cat will make you the maddest, but he will also make you laugh the most. High-spirited, mischievous, and clever, the Gemini cat loves to be the center of attention. Darting wildly through the house, this cat will cause you to trip, but he'll give you kisses later as an apology. If left alone for too long, the Gemini cat will likely shred your favorite houseplant or ruin the blinds. She needs a lot of affection and physical attention—and learning a few ground rules wouldn't hurt either.

4. **CANCER (JUNE 22–JULY 23)**

Moody, affectionate, and sensitive, the Cancer cat is one you will have to learn to read. He needs lots of hugs, but be sure not to hug him for too long. Play with him, but don't play too hard. Only the Cancer cat knows the rules of his game. He'll follow you all over the house and be your best friend, and then he'll suddenly disappear for a stint—needing some extra alone time. This cat has a creative spirit, enjoying activities such as swiping at foggy bathroom mirrors; he may be the perfect cat painter.

5. **LEO (JULY 24–AUGUST 23)**

Leo the Lion rules all other animals and, in the mind of the Leo cat, so does the domestic feline. This cat can be proud, self-centered, and the star of the show. Vanity is his name; he loves to be groomed and fussed over. The Leo cat is, in general, a well-behaved cat, but if he's ignored for too long a period, he will punish you. The world, after all, is centered on the Leo.

6. VIRGO (AUGUST 24–SEPTEMBER 23)

Cautious and aloof, this cat does not like surprises. Everything that comes into the Virgo cat's domain is thoroughly inspected and questioned, as are you after returning home from work or a party. Don't even think about petting someone else's cat before coming home; the Virgo cat will not tolerate being second best. And while he is perfectly content to be left alone in the house, he does have certain demands: dinner must be on time and his food must be good. This finicky feline will turn tail to certain dishes.

7. LIBRA (SEPTEMBER 24–OCTOBER 23)

A Libra kitty believes he's human. If you are thinking about getting a cat for the sake of having a good mouser and little more, you should pass on the Libra cat, who demands more than just being part of the family. This cat IS the family. Happy, vocal, highly social, and loving, this cat likes to visit everyone at all hours of the day and night. Although he's fickle, his affection for you is real. The Libra cat loves to be held, carried around, and talked to.

8. SCORPIO (OCTOBER 24–NOVEMBER 22)

The Scorpio appreciates a regular schedule but won't wait around for you. This cat is extremely demanding, strong-willed, and perfectly content to take matters into his own paws. He eats when he wants and sleeps when he wants. He will stalk, hunt, and chase anything—including your feet first thing in the morning. While unafraid of people and other animals, the Scorpio is not particularly social and prefers to be alone or with his immediate family.

9. SAGITTARIUS (NOVEMBER 23–DECEMBER 21)

Once a kitten, always a kitten. This cat loves to play. In fact, a Sagittarius kitten probably inspired the saying "Curiosity killed the cat." Of all the cats, this one is most prone to untimely deaths—i.e., being hit by a car or caught by a dog. Always getting into something, this kitten lives on the edge and is noted to be the messiest of all the cats. A little bit on the clumsy side, she will knock over your flower vase or spill food all over the floor.

10. CAPRICORN (DECEMBER 22–JANUARY 20)

The Capricorn does not like to hear the word "no" and will pout if told it repeatedly. And while he pouts, he will plot. Persistent, determined, and sneaky when pushed, this cat will do anything that is needed to get what he wants. Still, he loves his people and enjoys long snuggle sessions or simply relaxing on an owner's lap.

OK, so we've got two extra:

11. AQUARIUS (JANUARY 21–FEBRUARY 19)

Typically the Aquarian cat is vibrant, easygoing, and fun-loving, but just when you think you have him figured out, he will do something bizarre. Unpredictable, curious, and frisky, this cat loves to be in the center of a busy room, filled with people and animals. The Aquarian cat enjoys greeting everyone and truly loves a crowd. While he is fun to be around, he is not the easiest cat to train. No, he is not dumb, but he tends to have a very short attention span.

12. PISCES (FEBRUARY 20–MARCH 20)

The Pisces cat operates on Pisces time. This cat can lie in one spot for hours and hours, perfectly content to catnap through the day, only moving when he hears the sound of a can opener or the refrigerator door opening. The consummate lounge cat, the Pisces kitty loves to be held and cuddled for long periods of time, and most likely, you'll get tired of holding him long before he tires of you.

Celebrated Cats

Cats everywhere can rest assured that they continue to be revered and celebrated by people around the world—as they have for thousands of years.

1. THE ANCIENT EGYPTIANS

Aside from the Pyramids, almost nothing of ancient Egyptian culture evokes more awe and mystery than the Egyptians' fascination with cats. Felines were not only the most popular pet in the Egyptian house, but they also gained the status of sacred animals and then the most esteemed as deities, in a way no other creature had.

We know that the cat has been domesticated for at least 9,500 years, and some of the earliest domesticated cats (if not the earliest) were from Egypt. The ancient Egyptians did not distinguish between wild and tame cats in their descriptions of the felines they encountered, but we can assume that cats, whether wild or tame, began to ingratiate themselves to the Egyptians by hunting down the snakes, rats, and mice that depleted food supplies in home and village granaries. Mummified cats and tomb paintings of cats with people on hunting expeditions and as part of family life offer evidence of domestication.

Perhaps the most famous cat goddess in the world is Bastet (who is also known as Bast, Pasch, Ubasti). The

Egyptians loved Bastet so much that she became a household goddess and protector of women, children, and domestic cats. With their popularity and mystique elevated to the status of deities, cats began to appear on objects of everyday life: bracelets, small golden pendants, and amulets for necklaces and rings. By wearing the amulets on their clothing, ordinary people could enjoy the protection of the cat goddess. Ancient Egyptians formed numerous cults and held many celebrations devoted to Bastet, a testament to the cat's importance in their lives. Once a year, around October 31, they threw the festival of Bastet, during which hundreds of thousands of people made pilgrimages to pray to the goddess.

2. **CELTS, CATS, WITCHES, AND HALLOWEEN**

Cats have been closely associated with mystery and religion from the Egyptians to the Norse. But the Celts had a particular fear of cats, believing they were humans who had been changed into feline form by evil powers. They believed the black cat in particular was connected to demonic powers. Rooted in two-thousand-year-old Druidic demon worship, Halloween—which continues to cast its spell on modern peoples—was once called the Feast of Samhain, Lord of the Dead by the Celtic people of pre-Christian Ireland and Scotland, who observed the holiday on November 1. The Feast of Samhain signaled the beginning of the Celtic new year and was a time to give thanks to the sun god for the harvest. But it was also a terrifying night when time stood still and the souls of the dead walked abroad, mingling with the living and playing malicious tricks on them. The Celts thought the sinful souls who died during the year had been turned into forms of animals, specifically cats. Through gifts and sacrifices these souls could be freed to claim a heavenly reward. So the Celts laid out banquet-laden tables to appease the spirits, and when the feast was over villagers donned masks and costumes to represent the souls of the dead and paraded to the outskirts of town to lead the ghosts away. Amid all this superstition, Druid priests offered sacrifices to the sun god: horses (because they were sacred to the sun god), humans (mostly male criminals imprisoned in cages shaped liked animals or giants), and black cats (which were thought to be the friends of witches).

The trick-or-treat ritual of Halloween, which began as costumed children who offered to fast for departed souls in exchange for money or an offering, reenacts these ancient customs, which included decorating with black cats and the belief that a black cat crossing one's path brings bad luck.

3. THE CELEBRATION OF THE LYNX

Like the ancient Egyptians, the early Scandinavians and Norse people revered cats. In the Scandinavian and Norse traditions, the lynx was sacred to the goddess Freyja, and her chariot was sometimes depicted as being drawn by a lynx.

The Greeks believed the lynx could see through solid objects. In fact, the lynx was named for Lynceus, an Argonaut in Greek mythology who could also see objects underground.

In 1603 Italian scholars formed the Academy of Lynxes, dedicated to the search for truth and the fight against superstition. The academy's symbol depicted a lynx tearing Cerberus (the three-headed watchdog who guarded the entrance of Hades) with its claws, implying that knowledge would end darkness and suffering. Galileo was the academy's most famous member.

4. THE PANTHER

The panther has long been associated with people and power, but perhaps its most significant association is with Jesus. The Abodazara, early Jewish commentaries on the scriptures, lists "Panther" as a surname for the family of Joseph and tells how a man was healed "in the name of Jesus ben Panther."

The panther also was associated with the Greek god of

wine, Dionysus, who is sometimes depicted riding a chariot drawn by panthers.

The early natives of North and South America believed the jaguar—especially in the form of a black panther—was endowed with great magic and power. The feline was seen as a symbol for mastery over all dimensions. It was believed that the jaguar ruled the night and controlled the sun. For this reason the Tucano Indians, Aztecs, and Hayans practiced shape-shifting rituals (becoming half-human, half-jaguar) to protect themselves by conjuring the cat's power.

Even Egyptians wore panther tails around their wrists or knotted around their necks to protect and strengthen them in certain rituals. They used these cat tails in a process called "passage through the skin"—the Egyptians' version of shape-shifting to engender themselves with the power of the elusive panther.

5. MIDDLE AGES TO THE MODERN AGE

Cats remain a rich part of history in the small town of Ieper, Belgium. While Ieper was one of the more wealthy regions in the Flemish/Dutch-speaking part of Belgium, its citizens were very much a part of the anti-cat movement of the Middle Ages, during which millions of felines were tortured and murdered throughout Europe out of fear that they spread the plague. Cats were thrown from Ieper's belfry tower into the marketplace, where crowds gathered and chanted death to the cats. The year 1817 is the last recorded date of such cat-oriented spectacles, and in 1955 city officials decided to repent for their ancestors' sins against cats by celebrating the feline. Kattenstoet, a cat spectacular that lasts all weekend and is also known as the Big Cat Parade, is held every three years during the second weekend in May. On the Sunday of Kattenstoet, the traditional cat throw from the city tower continues, with citizens throwing velvet cats to adoring, cheering crowds. (Cats everywhere sigh in relief!) The velvet cats are representative not only of the past but also of Belgium's future. In fact, Kattenstoet has helped to build a strong local tourist economy. Concerts, fireworks, and delicious foods accompany Sunday's daylong, nearly two-mile parade of dancers, floats, and bands. Cat lovers from around the world come to watch. In May 2000 a record breaking eight thousand-plus visitors were in attendance. For more information about the town and the next parade, visit www .ieper.be or e-mail tourisme@ieper.be.

6. CELEBRATING LENT THE NORWEGIAN WAY

Celebrations mark the passage and pulse of time, but they also change with location, religious affiliation, social differences, and individual choice. In Norway, the Shrovetide festival was originally a church celebration that preceded Lent. After the Reformation in 1536, it became more of a secular celebration of the approach of spring and a new working year. Because of its connections with Lent this carnival has never held much significance in Protestant Norway, but it is still celebrated by many Catholics. The Shrovetide festival takes place indoors and involves special celebrations held in nursery schools, during which children dress up and play "knock the cat off the barrel." Norwegian nursery schools borrowed this tradition, involving a wooden barrel filled with sweets and a toy black cat, from the Danish. Standing in a row near the barrel, the children strike it with a wooden stick. The one who succeeds in shattering the barrel is named cat king and wins the cat and a crown to wear.

7. CAT DAY

On April 4, 2004, Taipei City in Taiwan did something extraordinary, considering the Taiwanese still have considerable prejudice against animals and those who raise them. The city—where cat owners have little hope of renting apartments—celebrated Taiwan Cat Day, luring some seven hundred cat lovers out to participate in the opening ceremonies. The holiday was conceived by the Taipei Cat Lovers' Club, which could formally declare Cat Day after two years of planning and debate and a vote involving 1,208 ballots cast. The club's chairman and writer Shin Dai expressed hope that the new holiday would increase awareness of the beauty of cats and also help construct a new ethic for human-animal relations, in a city and country where most cats are strays and are cruelly treated and often killed by intolerant citizens.

Taipei Cat Lovers' Club also hopes to educate the public with evidence from scientific studies of human-animal interaction that illustrates how people and animals benefit one another. Such evidence shows that "animal companion raisers" have a lower incidence of seeking medical help for heart problems, high blood pressure, high cholesterol, or insomnia, and less frequently require pharmacological treatment for such illnesses, even when they do need to seek medical advice. Compared to people without animal companions (according to a 1996 Australian study), those who have cats see the doctor 12 percent less often (and those with dogs, 8 percent less often).

8. **THE FIRST CAT SHOW**

When the first officially recognized cat show was staged at London's Crystal Palace on Thursday, July 13, 1871, no one could be certain how it would be received. While the show's organizer, Harrison Weir, was certain there would be interest, he was nervous all the same. The Crystal Palace was one of London's leading venues at the time, putting Weir and his cats under great scrutiny. Weir had long been distressed with the poor treatment of felines and hoped a cat show would raise public awareness of cat abuse. Because there were no established rules, much less breed distinctions, Weir had no idea how many exhibits would appear or the condition in which they might arrive. The Duke of Sutherland brought his favorite cat—a three-legged British wildcat that behaved "like a mad devil."

On July 14, the reviews were in. According to the *Morning Post*: "The greatest novelty of the day in the way of shows is the show of cats at Crystal Palace. We have had cattle shows, horse shows, dog shows and shows of various other animals more or less domesticated. But this is the first cat show of an extensive and thoroughly organized character the world has ever seen." Success. This would be the beginning of many cat shows to come around the world.

9. CEREMONIAL CATS

Wanli, an emperor of the Ming dynasty, was a famed ailurophile who loved his cats so much that he bestowed upon them the highest honor. In a ceremony meant only for the most brave warriors and honorable members of the ministry and treasury, the emperor gave official ranks to all the cats in his palace, from the lower level servant to the highest official. How this fared among his human servants and officials is unknown, but legend has it that the cats were raised with dignity and lived well. Some, it is said, grew to be bigger than dogs.

10. THE GREATEST HOPE

Esperanza, which means "hope" in Spanish, is the only captive female Iberian lynx of breeding age, one of an estimated 150 lynx left in the entire world and, for many conservationists, the last great hope. The Iberian lynx, also known as the tiger of Europe or the majestic tiger of the Mediterranean jungle, is officially the most endangered big cat in the world. A cat that once roamed the entire Iberian Peninsula and southern France, it now only exists in scattered pockets in southwestern Spain. In 1988 there were an estimated twelve hundred Iberian lynxes. Today, with just 150 remaining, conservationists at the breeding center at Donana National Park near Seville, Spain, are hopeful they can help save the gene pool with a healthy litter from Esperanza and a captive male named Garfio. In a race against time to save this gorgeous lynx, a healthy litter would truly be something for the world to celebrate.

For more information about Esperanza and the Iberian lynx, visit www.soslynx.org.

SOS Lynx at www.soslynx.org

Esperanza—hope for the Iberian lynx.

V
Your Cat's Health
and Behavior

Ways Your Cat Can Improve Your Life

Human-health and animal-health experts have joined efforts to educate people about the benefits of interacting with animals. The medical significance of the bond people have with their pets can no longer be ignored. Your cat may affect everything from the health of your heart to your sense of security. Here are ten ways your kitty can keep you healthy.

1. LONG-TERM CAT CARE

Because of the responsibility that pet owners feel, senior citizens who are cat owners are overall in better condition than those who are not animal owners. Pet care requires people to be more active, more outgoing, and more nurturing, and as a result, pet owners are often more in touch with their own needs.

2. LOWER BLOOD PRESSURE

Pet owners over the age of forty have lower blood pressure and have triglyceride levels 20 percent lower than non–pet owners.

3. NINE LIVES

The frisky new kitten in your life gives you more than just hours of entertainment. A pet owner's love for his cat has power beyond fun and laughter. Indoor pet owners typically need to see the doctor less often than non–pet owners. This is one reason retirement and assisted-living communities have started using the services of animal clubs or shelters to develop a bond between their residents and loving cats.

4. DEPRESSION AND/OR LONELINESS

Cats' purrs and the way they rub against us or weave through our feet heal us. When we are feeling blue, our best friend and confidant is often our cat. For this reason, therapy cats have become very popular for adults and for children stricken with cancer and other life-threatening illnesses, abuse, or neglect. Caregivers who work with the elderly, the sick, or the needy report that contact with animals makes the patients stronger, healthier, and happier, and research studies are beginning to support their observations.

5. LIFESAVER

According to the National Institute of Mental Health, the second cause of death among twenty-somethings, after automobile accidents, is suicide. Those who have considered suicide often report that they were unable to go through with their attempt because of love and concern for their pets. In many instances, sudden changes in a pet owner's routine or requests for help with the care of a pet have helped family members discover that their loved one has been contemplating suicide.

6. ALLERGIES AND ASTHMA

For nearly a century, many moms haven't allowed cats in the house because they believe these pets cause allergies. A recent study from the Allergy and Immunology Department at the Medical College of Georgia in Augusta reports that children who grow up in a house with indoor pets have a reduced risk of developing common allergies and asthma, defying all the blame we've placed on our four-legged friends for making us sniffle and sneeze.

7. DOGS VS. CATS

In a recent study conducted at the Penn State College of Medicine, scientists exposed over eight hundred people with asthma to dog and cat saliva and dander. Throwing our preconceived notions to the wind, the dog saliva and dander triggered the greatest release of nitric oxide in the subjects' lungs and caused the most immune cells to appear in phlegm. While cats do make people sneeze more, dogs cause more severe reactions, including wheezing and coughing.

8. THE LOSS OF A SPOUSE

The loss of a spouse is one of the most traumatic things that can happen in our lives. We know that the health of surviving spouses—particularly senior citizens—often rapidly deteriorates in the wake of a loss. Those with feline companions fare much better than those without, as cats offer their owners comfort, support, a daily routine to keep the mind distracted (or comforted), security, and love.

9. LAUGHTER

We are most at ease when we are alone with our cats. With no one else around, we tend to be more relaxed, talking and playing with our cat. Experts say that while they seem insignificant, the chuckles and giggles our cats elicit from us, while they roll around in toilet paper or bat wildly at a piece of string hanging from the edge of a table, distract us and lighten our moods.

10. HOME SECURITY

Throughout history, cats have patrolled human territories, keeping us safe from vermin and snakes. And in some more remarkable stories, our feline friends have actually stood up against intruders to protect owners and property against harm. Though small in stature, these magnificent animals are proud, fierce, and determined against an enemy; they are undyingly loving and protective of those they love.

Cats of Your Dreams

S weet dreams. Everyone has dreams, and if you're lucky, you dream about cats. Dream interpretation goes back thousands of years when medicine men used dreams to predict the future and learn more about people's hopes and desires. The cat, part of the human family since the ancient Egyptians, offers insights into our families, our professional lives, our levels of happiness, and our hopes when they appear in our dreams. Understanding your cat—even as it appears in your dreams—means a better, healthier relationship with your animal. Dream analysts provide ten interesting interpretations of our cat dreams in *Dreams* by Frank Garfield and Rhondda Stewart-Garfield.

1. THE DOMESTIC CAT

Dreams about the domestic cat generally mean the dreamer must put aside feelings of self-pity and despair and move forward in a positive manner. In the typical domestic dream sequence, cats simply mill around or sit on walls doing nothing more than watching birds fly or cleaning themselves.

2. FIGHTING CATS

Dreams about fighting cats usually signify a dreamer's inner turmoil and conflict. Because of the ferocity with which cats fight, fighting cats may signify the ultimate battle.

3. CIRCLING KITTIES

A dream in which seemingly friendly cats circle around the dreamer is believed to be a very good and powerful sign of the dreamer's spiritual awakening. Good things are in store for one who has such dreams.

4. BLACK CATS

No surprises here. Because the black cat is so heavily shrouded in superstition and witchcraft, a black cat often signifies the dreamer's inability to distinguish between reality and fantasy. The black cat may also represent uncertainty, helplessness, or fear.

5. HISSING CAT

A dream in which a spitting, hissing cat appears suggests that the dreamer feels persecuted and attacked by someone trusted or loved. It may also mean he has feelings of hostility against someone else and would like to act against them.

6. PLAYFUL KITTENS

The scene can vary—cats playing in a field, two kittens rolling around in a playful manner, perhaps batting a butterfly. One who dreams of such happy cats has great feelings of harmony, trust, and happiness. This may be a strong sign for a solid future.

7. THE GROWLING CAT

Whether the growling cat of one's dreams is the ten-pound domestic or the king of the jungle, it signifies inner strength. The dreamer is making a stand for himself or herself in a personal or professional life. A life-altering event may be on the horizon.

8. THE STALKING CAT

The image is vivid—a cat crouched down low in the bushes, eyes glowering as its prey gets closer. The cat—big or small, domestic or wild—twitches slightly, ready to spring. This dream implies that the dreamer is about to embark on a new voyage. Some new challenge is just around the corner, and the dreamer is ready to meet it.

9. A BIG CAT

Dreams of lions, tigers, or leopards (oh, my) capture the essence of the powerful animal, who fears little and knows very few boundaries. These images may come to mind when a person is either facing a personal attack or embarking on an attack of their own.

10. RUNNING SCARED

A dream in which cats—again, big or small—are chasing or stalking the dreamer suggest that he may not like what he sees in himself but he may soon be forced to face his fear of what is inside.

Most Common Behavioral Problems

One of the most difficult aspects of training cats is dealing with their many undesirable behaviors—such as scratching furniture or jumping on counters—which are instinctive to felines. Before you "fix" any one behavior, you must understand why your cat does what he does. (See Recommended Reading for sources on cat behavior.) Learning about the instincts that trigger your cat's behaviors will help you train him, but it is also good to realize that aside from natural impulses the four most common reasons for perceived bad cat behavior are medical problems, boredom, lack of training, and an owner's unrealistic expectations. When cats do not feel well or are not properly trained, they cannot be expected to live by human rules; and therein lies the problem.

1. WHAT'S THAT?

Our cunning cats can often convince us that they do not understand our commands and cannot be trained. You can, however, teach your cat to live by your rules rather than by her own. With a squirt bottle and a firm voice, you can teach your cat almost anything. There are two important elements in cat training. First, you must never hit your pet. The squirt bottle should act as the "punisher." You want your cat to think his punishment comes from the water bottle, not from you, so try not to make eye contact with your cat while squirting him. Second, you must say "No!" and use the squirt bottle at the same time. The verbal command identifies the undesirable behavior and the squirt of water is the consequence of breaking the rule you want to establish. Never use one without the other.

As you progress, you can enhance your cat training by taking advantage of the feline's naturally territorial nature. By limiting the kitty-accessible spaces in your house, you help your cat learn your rules in manageable pieces. Limiting his territory also allows you to prevent damage that might result from the cat's well-known curiosity. As your cat learns the rules, you can increase his territory.

2. **WILD THING!**

Sudden bursts of energy and wild streaks through the house are normal—to a point. By learning more about your cat's breed and behavioral patterns, you may be able to figure out his pattern. Most cats have certain times—usually around midnight—when they get the sudden desire to play. This is normal. Remember, some breeds are naturally more energetic than others. But nonstop wildness is a strong indicator that Fluffy isn't getting enough exercise or attention. By establishing a playtime with a simple ball or a feather duster, you may give your cat the exercise he needs and deepen your bond of friendship. And playtime has a third benefit: it is also an excellent way to teach your cat control—attacking the toy, not you.

3. **BOLTING OUT THE DOOR**

This problem spurs on one of the biggest debates within the cat community. Is it unfair to keep a cat exclusively indoors? While many cat owners answer, yes, it is the will of the cat to run free, a large number of animal behaviorists, trainers, and veterinarians argue that cats who live indoors are safe from contagious diseases, such as feline leukemia and feline infectious peritonitis, and from dogs, cars, and poisons. So strong is the indoor-only debate that many breeders make potential buyers sign a contract stating they will never let their cat outside.

Still, the grass is always greener outside, and cats know it. Always curious, always inquisitive, many cats will try to make their break out the door. Indoor cats often need to be trained to stay inside, and the most effective way to teach your kitty is to create an escape situation. For this you will need a second person, some kind of blockade (such as a net to ensure your cat cannot escape into the yard should he make it past the second person), and a spray bottle. When everything and everyone is in place, open the door so that Fluffy can make his move. As he bolts out the door, yell, "No!" If he continues the escape, have your partner step out, blocking the cat's path, and spray him with the bottle. Escape means getting sprayed!

An additional training technique is to mark a territory in the hall leading to the door. By placing a line tape or rope or even a sticker on the floor, you can create a boundary that kitty should not pass. Each time Fluffy passes over that line, tell him "No!" and give him a squirt.

4. CAT ATTACK

How many times have you been minding you own business, walking down the hall (sometimes on your way to feed your kitten or cat) when you were suddenly ambushed, attacked at the ankles? Because it hurts like the dickens, your first impulse is to hit your animal. But by physically correcting your enthusiastic cat, you may damage the trust between feline and owner. The reality is, if your cat lacks a feline playmate or sufficient toys, he may have no other recourse but to experiment with his hunting instincts on you. First, make sure your cat has ample toys. Should you be attacked anyway, quickly redirect your cat's attention to a toy (after you've climbed down from the chair), and praise your cat when he plays with and attacks the toy.

Sometimes, particularly around smaller children, cats

will attack when they've gotten too much attention. For the most part, they are not interested in rough play with humans, and they certainly don't believe they have to take it. If your cat is temperamental, be sure to give him quiet time along with a reasonable amount of physical contact.

5. JUMPING

Cats love to jump! That's a fact you can't change. The desire to jump will override any positive reinforcement training you might be able to provide, but you can guide your cat as to what is acceptable to jump on and what is off-limits. Booby traps are the best training tools. Cover countertops that should not be jumped upon with aluminum foil or Saran Wrap covered with double-sided sticky tape. The foil and sticky tape work very well to deter the cats—one or two times on these materials and the cat usually learns to stay away. As you train your cat, be sure to provide a few places where he can jump, such as window rests and cat trees. Your kitty will be quite happy if you periodically leave "surprises" in these designated jumping areas!

6. CLAWING

Scratching is as natural to cats as jumping. But do not de-claw your cat! This procedure is extremely painful to cats as it requires that part of their toes be removed along with their claws. A series of training techniques, listed in the next chapter, Facts and Tips about Cat-Scratch Training, can be used to stop your cat from this unpleasant behavior. As you enter the no-scratch training phase, remember that clawing is a perfectly natural and necessary physical response for cats.

7. KITTY LITTER BOX BLUES

Make sure your cat's litter boxes—both the litter and the box itself—are clean. Cats may turn away from the box if they feel it is unclean or has unattractive smells. For young kittens, be sure to repeatedly show them where the box is and encourage them to use it after they have eaten, awakened from a cat nap, or are just finished playing—these are the most common times young cats need to relieve themselves.

Unneutered males and females in season are prone to spray. Because they are so territorial, the mere sight of another cat from the window can trigger the need to mark a territory. Just as you would with a new kitten, you should limit the amount of space your unneutered cat has to one or two rooms with plenty of litter box access until he has proven trustworthy.

8. NO DUMPING ALLOWED!

Many new kitten owners are frustrated to discover their cats using houseplants or darkened closets as litter boxes. When you bring a kitten home, it may be necessary to place several litter boxes around the house. By putting several boxes out for the cat, you eliminate the chances that (1) the kitten will not have enough time to get to the litter box or (2) the young cat will forget where the box is kept. As the kitten grows and becomes more competent, you can slowly reduce the number of litter boxes down to one. If urination and defecation continue with multiple boxes, your kitty (particularly if he's older) may have a medical problem. Urinary infections are common among cats, so the solution could be simple. Discuss your concerns with your vet.

9. NO PLANT IS SAFE

Cats think plants are yummy. But they can also be poisonous. Check with your vet to make sure your plants are cat-safe.

If your plants are non-toxic, you may still have a problem. Cats can spoil your green-thumbed efforts, nibbling on leaves and using the pot as their favorite litter box. Many owners simply hang their plants from the ceiling or put them outside. Out of sight, out of mind. But you can also use aluminum foil and Bitter Apple (a product that can be found in most pet stores) to deter this behavior. Spray Bitter Apple on the leaves to deter nibbling. The taste is so bitter, the cat will leave it alone after one bite, but the leaves will periodi-cally have to be resprayed to keep the bitter taste alive. Alu-minum or double-sided sticky tape should be placed in the potted plant to keep cat paws away from the soil.

10. DOGS AND LITTER BOXES

Because your cat's litter boxes provide a reliable source for snacks—gross as that is—it is extremely difficult to keep dogs away from them. Even the best-trained dog is rewarded each time he visits the box, and each reward will encourage him to come back. Obviously, keeping the boxes clean and using covered boxes can be helpful in preventing the dog's snacking, but these methods are not foolproof. Cats with asthma, for example, cannot use covered litter boxes. Dog trainers agree that putting up barriers is the most effective way to stop dogs from eating cat feces. Try using a cat door to a closed room, such as a laundry room, or a baby gate that only the cat can pass through.

Facts and Tips about Cat-Scratch Training

Perhaps the number one asked question for animal behaviorists, trainers, and veterinarians is, "How can I get my cat to stop scratching my furniture?" The answer: You can't. However, you can redirect *how* and *when* your cats needs to scratch.

1. WHY THEY SCRATCH

As you watch your once beautiful couch slowly succumb to the scratching needs of your cat, it's hard to care *why* your cat does it. You just want him to stop! You've yelled, tossed shoes at him, and feebly attempted to cover the couch with more material, but he's the feline Terminator: He'll be back! Yes, cats will claw out of boredom. Animal behaviorists urge owners to purchase toys—of all shapes, sizes, smells, and textures—to dissuade their cats from destroying furniture. But scratching goes deeper than entertainment. Cats scratch for exercise, to maintain nail health, to sate hunting instincts, to mark territory, and to relieve stress. When cats scratch, they feel the way people feel when they exercise, releasing endorphins that make them happier and healthier. Cats do not scratch out of vengeance or disobedience. They scratch because it is their nature.

2. DECLAWING YOUR CAT

The procedure requires the surgical amputation of the last part of the toe, which has been likened to the amputation of a human finger at the first joint. The skin is stitched up over the exposed joint, and after time, the cat's wounds heal leaving him without claws. Without claws, a cat has a much more difficult time defending himself or climbing. While animal trainers argue that this procedure is unfair to the animal and that cats with claws—small and big—can be trained, many animal activists are less tolerant and have campaigned long and hard to have the procedure, which goes against the nature of the animal, made illegal. Simply stated: declawing your cat is the easy way out, and it's not very nice. This procedure is often at the root of a cat's future problems. Animal shelter workers say that the majority of the indoor cats brought to their shelters for behavioral problems are patients of the declawing procedure who have lost their best means of exercise and stress relief.

3. AMPLE SUPPLIES

Without a designated place to scratch, cats turn to furniture. Put a scratching post as close as possible to the area your cat has been scratching. If he appears to be disinterested in the post, use catnip as an attractor. Rubbing catnip around the base of the post will catch the interest of most cats. The biggest mistake eager owners make is forcibly trying to make the cat scratch by putting paws on the post. This will only make him avoid the post.

4. THE COVER-UP

Once you have introduced the scratching post, cover up the areas that have been under siege with undesirable materials such as double-sided sticky tape or netting. Be sure the tape you use is meant for furniture so that it won't leave a sticky residue on the fabric. Because cats do not like to catch their claws in materials, netting is a perfect cover. Foil and sandpaper are also very effective anti-claw techniques. Meantime, be sure to keep the scratching post as attractive as possible, leaving an occasional treat or toy nearby.

5. SAY IT AIN'T SO

Cats really do hear the word "no," especially if it is accompanied with a spray of water. Each and every time you see your cats clawing something other than their designated posts, yell out and, if handy, give the water bottle a squirt. Shake cans (i.e., a coffee can filled with pennies) and whistles are also effective. Startle your cat each time he tries to scratch your furniture. He will quickly realize that scratching furniture elicits terrible noises and/or water, whereas the scratching posts seems to make everyone happy and sometimes has goodies nearby.

6. WHY MY FAVORITE CHAIR!?

Ever watch how your cat scratches? It is a rhythmic motion: First, a long downward swipe with the left paw; then, the right, stopping only briefly before repeating the process. In fact, your cat is squeezing his own scent onto the fabric of your favorite chair, adding his scent to yours. Yes, it is *because* the chair is your favorite, filled with all your luscious scents that your cat feels the need to claw and scratch at it. For this reason, owners are advised not to be discouraged when the scratching post appears to be less appealing. The next time you set off to do laundry, stop. Pull out your stinkiest, you-smelling shirt and rub it against one side of the post to add your own smell.

7. RISE AND SHINE

Most cats scratch immediately after waking up from a nice catnap. Because this is an instinctual reaction, they may not even be aware of what they are doing. Be watchful. Keep an eye on that sleeping cat. As soon as he wakes, have your water bottle ready. If you have a kitten, gently pick him up and carry him directly to the scratching posts. Many new kitten owners will scratch the post themselves, showing the kitten how to scratch, but remember, you should not try to force a kitten to scratch.

8. FLEX-APPEAL

It does not matter how fancy, how beautiful, or how expensive the new scratching post is if it has a texture the cat does not like. A scratching post is a good investment only if the cat uses it. Sisal-covered or rope materials are quite popular among cats. Cardboard cat posts, while they do not last very long, are also highly entertaining for cats. Cat experts warn owners not to buy posts that match their furniture too closely. You want to ensure that your cat is able to distinguish the difference between his post and the furniture.

9. POSITIVE REINFORCEMENT

One of the appeals of owning a cat is the animal's independence. Unlike dogs, cats are easy to housebreak and maintain. Many animal lovers get cats because they want companionship without all the hassles of training that are part of dog ownership. But at this stage of the game, when you are trying to teach lifelong habits, you should not be impatient. Remember that you hope to have your feline friend for the next twenty-plus years. For the relatively short time you are trying to teach your cat not to scratch your furniture, watch his every move. Every time your cat uses the scratching post, be sure to give lots of positive reinforcement—yummy treats and affection.

10. DOUBLE NEGATIVE

One negative response will only garner a second negative response. Because your cat is only doing what is natural, he will not understand why he is being punished for it. Physically punishing your cat for scratching furniture will not deter him as you hope. Instead of chasing or hitting your cat, use positive reinforcements, and remember that the time you put in now will last for years and years to come.

Facts You May Not Know about Your Kitty

Why does your cat do what he does? Cats never cease to amaze. Physically, the cat is superior in all ways, from the design of their feet and claws to their amazing balance and agility to their hunting senses and keen eyesight. Mentally, they are survivalists. Although they are creatures of habit and prefer a routine, they are not easily upset and will find food and shelter easily enough if lost or abandoned. As we learn more about these animals, we realize how perfect the species is, and we better understand how to live with them.

1. CAT WHISKERS

Whiskers on the chin of a cat are unnecessary as cats do not root around for food or prey. However, the whiskers on their cheeks provide a sense of balance and serve as short-range radar to keep the cat from bumping into unexpected pieces of furniture or unnoticed outdoor obstacles. A scientist at four years old, this author cut all the whiskers off the family cat. For her safety, the outdoor cat lived indoors for several weeks, while her whiskers grew back. During that time, she had numerous collisions with furniture, doorways, and residents of the household because she could not judge distances without her natural sensing system.

2. WHO'S YOUR DADDY?

A cat's litter can have more than one father, which may explain why many litters throw a varied combination of color and hair textures among the kittens.

3. SNAKE BITE

Cats are effective snake hunters—another reason they were worshipped in Egyptian times. With their lightening fast strikes and tremendous patience, they can literally worry a snake until it is worn out and has little fight.

4. THE FIVE SENSES

As for their taste, cats possess five senses: bitter, sour, sweet, salt, and water. Interestingly, laboratory experiments indicate that cats have a difficult time distinguishing the taste of sugar.

5. ONE COOL CAT

Always the creative creature, cats have their own kind of air conditioning system. As they lick the top coat of their fur, they deposit a fine layer of saliva that evaporates and acts as a cooling system during hotter months.

6. CAT TALK

Cats' language is more varied and sophisticated than most animals lovers give them credit for. In fact, studies have shown that cats use five vowels, nine consonants, two diphthongs, and one triphthong when they speak to us. Maybe we should have a cat-English dictionary.

7. THE FLEHMEN RESPONSE

The Flehmen response is a cat's open-mouthed grimace reaction to certain odors. Cats use what is called the vomeronasal organ, a small organ located in the front of the roof of the mouth that is connected by nerves to a part of the brain that controls sexual behavior. Scientists believe that the Flehmen response increases the flow of smell to the vomeronasal organ, which in turn sends information (about the smell) to the brain—this reaction is more frequent when a female cat is in season.

8. THE TOUCH

Zoologists agree that of all the mammals in the animal kingdom, cats have the most delicate sense of touch.

9. BLACK OR BROWN

Black Persian kittens are born brown.

10. LEFT OR RIGHT

Felines are ambidextrous.

Cat Tails

While many animal lovers can read the mood of a dog based on its tail activity, they don't realize that cats offer far more mood indicators with the positioning and movement of their tails. If you learn to read cat tails, you can better assess the mood of your feline friend.

1.   THE GREETING

If your cat walks toward you, his tail held erect with a slight sway, he is offering a friendly, affectionate greeting. He is relaxed, focusing only on you.

2.   THE CURIOUS HELLO

If your cat greets you with an erect tail slightly bent at the tip he has some concerns about what you are doing or what is going on around you, but otherwise he is pleased to see you. This greeting may also mean he is very happy to see you because he wants something—dinner, and you're late!

3.   WHAT'S NEW, PUSSYCAT?

With his tail raised slightly and softly curved, your cat has become interested in something around him—perhaps a bird, a new toy, or a blowing leaf. Whatever it is, he is in a good mood, feeling curious yet peaceful.

4. **LIFE IS GOOD**

As your cat looks out the window or lounges on a chair, her tail is hanging loosely toward the ground with a curve up toward the tip. With nary a care in the world, this cat is quite content and might easily be contemplating a good, long nap.

5. **THE WAG**

Perhaps the most misinterpreted is the erect tail wagging back and forth. For years, this movement has been perceived to indicate that a cat is angry. In truth, it is the sign of a frustrated or conflicted cat. A cat's tail will flick back and forth when the feline has to deal with, for example, a desire to go outside only to discover it is raining or a hunger for a mouse trapped behind a glass the cat cannot get through.

6. **PUFF KITTY**

Violent swishing (or wagging) back and forth with a fat, puffed-out tail, usually combined with a tensed body and possibly hissing, is a true indicator of anger. This is a sign of an agitated cat ready to hold his ground. Another indicator of agression is an erect, puffed-out tail. This tail should be taken seriously.

7. **FEARFUL FELINE**

When your cat is feeling threatened or fearful, he may drop his tail into a lowered position, hair fluffed out. This is not to be confused with the tail's hunting or stalking position—lowered and stiff with a twitch at the end.

8. **ON THE DEFENSE**

Whereas the angry cat holds her tail straight out, as a flag of warning, the defensive cat holds her tail in an arch, stiff and bristled.

9. **CAT SUBMISSION**

Whether a cat loses a fight with another cat or suddenly finds himself standing on the examining table at the vet, he will let you know he has accepted defeat with a tail fully tucked between his legs and pulled tightly down against his hind quarters.

10. 'TIS THE SEASON

A tail held to one side often indicates a female cat is in heat. A tail held erect and shaking or quivering is a sign that a male cat is marking his territory. Not only are cat motions and positions mood indicators to humans, they are strong signals for fellow felines, as well. Interestingly, the erect, tail-quivering motion can also be a form of greeting to owners upon their arrival home. Within the territorial concept, they are welcoming the human back to their home.

Top Tricks for a Super Kitty

Dogs come when they are called. Cats take a message and get back to you later. Ever hear that one? Animal lovers always delight in the notion of a cat doing tricks, especially since cats aren't prone to performing. We like to think of our cats as independent and sometimes defiant. That is what makes cats cats. But the reality is cats are healthiest when they are exercised and well cared for. And exercise and care go beyond chasing mice and being petted. When you work with your cat and require special skills from him, you are mentally and physically challenging him and rewarding him with praise and affection. While generally the feline facade is "I von to be alooone," most cats enjoy learning new tricks. Here are ten of the most popular and common kitty tricks you can try with your pet.

1. COME, KITTY

"You stupid cat! Get over here! Man, I can't believe you shredded this couch! Argh!!! Get over here." Guess what? Fluffy's not coming. The neighbor cat heard you, and he's not coming either. If you want your cat to come, only call him when you are speaking in a happy, upbeat tone. Always call him by name ("Fluffy, come!") and have a reward on hand. Trainers advise that you start by using this command at mealtime, so that the cat will associate his or her name with a good meal. Once the cat comes consistently when called to mealtime, try calling to him away from the mealtime. While the average dog will come for hugs and pats, your feline will want to see what goodies you have. Be prepared before you call, and he will learn to come consistently.

Sound cues can be effectively used as well. Many cat treats come in small cylinder containers that make great thumping sounds when shaken. Once he's heard it a few times, your cat will come running at the sound. Cats in show business are cued by all kinds of sounds from bells to whistles to clapping. You can choose your own sound cues.

2. SIT

Once your kitty learns to come, it is easy to teach the sit command. Again, armed with the best yummies possible, hold the treat in front of you as you call to your feline. When he comes, tell him "Good boy!" and then ask him to sit. The first several times he may not understand what you are asking. Bend down as though you are going to reward him (for coming) and hold the treat just above his head so that he must rock back on his haunches to see it more clearly. Continue to repeat the command: "Sit." "Good, sit. Sit. Good boy, good sit." As soon as he sits, praise him again and offer the treat. In no time, he will learn to sit when waiting for his goody.

3. BEGGING KITTY

Yes, even the regal cat is willing to beg for a good treat. Once your cat has proven confident with the come and sit commands, you can move on to a new trick. While he is in the seated position, raise the treat a little higher and behind his head. Because the two of you have done the sit command many times, he will be quite sure he will get the treat; he will rear back to keep his reward in view. And being a graceful feline, he will have no trouble balancing himself upright.

You may use any command name you want for this trick, as long as it is different from "sit." "Up" and "beg" are common choices. As soon as he rears back into a begging position, reward him with his treat, saying, "Good beg, good boy. Good beg."

4. **ROLLOVER**

Once your kitty has come and is seated in front of you, show him the treat. Say, "Rollover," and arch the treat over his head from his left (your right) to his right shoulder, dropping your hand toward the floor on his right side. You will have to give this command many times before your cat truly understands what you are asking, so be patient. Your cat may try to nibble or swat at the treat but you should continue the motion, saying the command over and over again. "Rollover." Keep the treat over but close to his head so that as he turns to try to look at the treat, he will naturally fall over, rolling to one side. As soon as he rolls over, reward him and repeat the command words again and again, praising him mightily. Teaching this trick can be tedious and certainly requires patience, but you and your cat should always have fun during the training process. The minute this trick becomes frustrating or boring, your cat will lose interest.

5. **STAY**

To dog trainers, this command is the most critical. In fact, basic obedience is a joke unless a dog has a strong hold on the stay command. Learning to stay has saved many animals' lives. There is no reason why a cat cannot learn the command as well.

Once you have called your cat and commanded him to sit, put your left hand up, palm facing your cat, and tell him to "stay." Because he knows you are holding a treat in your right hand, he may want to come forward to retrieve it. He's thinking, "Hey, I came!" So, it is important that you only ask him to stay for a few seconds. This trick cannot be accomplished in just a few lessons. Each time he comes and sits, command him to stay a little longer. But be warned: if you ask him to stay for too long, too quickly, he will become frustrated and give up on the command altogether. During the first week, you should only expect him to hold a stay for ten seconds. During week two, command him to stay for fifteen seconds. Increase the hold at similar increments during weeks three and four and so on. If your cat holds a thirty second stay on Monday, do not expect him to stay for a minute on Friday; that is too big a leap.

Each time you ask your cat to stay, be sure to show him the hand motion and repeat the command over and over again. "Stay, stay . . . good boy. Good sit, good stay." Using your key words over and over again, you are giving your cat cues that he really will listen to. He will learn to watch the hand command and listen to the verbal command as well.

6. HOW DO YOU DO

Okay, dogs may shake hands—well, paw-to-hand—but cats are far more polite. Because cats naturally use their paws for everything, this trick is fairly easy. After you have called to your cat and had him sit, ask him, "How do you do?" Touch the treat to your cat's paw, repeating the command again. As he lifts his paw against the treat, catch your hand under his paw and pump a fake handshake. "Good 'How do you do.' Good boy. How do you do." Repeat this command over and over again. As you practice this routine, your cat will reach a point where he will simply lift the paw high into the air for you to touch and shake before he gets his treat.

7. SPIN

Teaching a cat to chase his tail or simply spin in a circle is always fun for cat owners. The spin is also one of the easier tricks to teach a cat. Again, as soon as your cat has come to you when called, show him the treat. Move in a circular motion just above his reach, and say, "Spin!" Make an effort to have your cat follow the treat in a circle, making sure the circle is not too tight. As you begin, make a big looping path with the treat, so your cat has plenty of room to move. When he understands the command and becomes more confident with the trick, he will be able to make a tight, quick spinning turn before you praise him ("Good spin. Spin. Good spin.") and reward him with a treat.

8. FETCH

If you have an open space for training, you can teach your kitty cat to fetch. While some cat owners have had success with this trick without the use of treats, others have had to use a treat to keep their cats interested. Whether your cat performs for food or praise, this is wonderful exercise and a great bonding experience for you and your feline, who will, after several rounds of fetching, see you as part of the hunt. And isn't the big hunt what life is all about?

A wadded up piece of paper, a favorite small toy, or a bottle cap are perfect for this game. Once you have your cat's attention, throw the object across the room and down the hall. As soon as he is off and running, praise him highly. "Good boy, go get it!" or "Good boy, fetch it!" Once he has the object, call him back. Call him by name and repeat the "fetch" or "get it" command until he returns to you. Again, many owners have a treat on hand to ensure the cat returns with his prize rather than running off to keep it for himself. And remember, practice makes perfect.

9. SPEAK

This trick is not for every cat. Because some cats are naturally more vocal than others, this request is more reasonable for a Siamese than for other, quieter, breeds. Still, attentive owners may be able to teach the speak trick to any cat. Again, patience, patience, patience. Each time you hear your cat speak, tell him, "Good speak! Good boy, good speak!" and as quickly as possible, offer a treat.

10. JUMPING THROUGH HOOPS

Another kid favorite! As soon as you have called your cat and had him sit, tell him to stay. Holding a Hoola-Hoop in your left hand and a treat in your right, encourage your sitting cat to jump through the hoop. Initially, he might simply step through the hoop. That's fine. As he begins to learn the routine—again, remember that this is a drill you will have to perform many times before he begins to feel confident with the command—you may raise the hoop slightly, causing him to jump rather than step though the hoop.

BONUS RESOURCE:

For more information about cat training, check out Karen Pryor's *Getting Started: Clicker Training for Cats*, a popular new method for teaching basic obedience. Or check Pryor's Web site at www.clickertraining.com.

Tips for
Effective Training

B ottom line: Training and tricks should be fun. But owners often get swept up in the idea of how the trick should be performed, which can take away all the fun of training as well as the animal's desire to learn. Here are some tips for how to ensure quality—and fun—training time. And remember, an old cat *can* learn new tricks.

1. **PATIENCE IS A VIRTURE**

It might take your cat two times to learn a trick or it might take sixty-four times before he finally understands and accepts it. Losing your patience will only slow down or completely ruin an experience that should be very gratifying for both cat and owner.

2. **CONSISTENCY IS KEY**

Once you have called your cat and asked him to, for example, roll over, do not give up and hand him the treat before he manages the trick. Your cat will learn only if you are consistent in your training techniques. Cats are very intelligent; they will work around the trick if they think they can get the treat without meeting your request. So only give your cat a treat if he does what you have asked. Also, be sure that you always have a treat on hand to reward your cat.

3. SPEAK UP!

Be sure to use verbal and hand cues that your cat can understand. Your cat cannot read your mind; he will not know you want him to sit or stay or roll over unless you tell him clearly and consistently. Always give him the command verbally and, when needed, give a hand cue as well. This will help the learning process and enhance the way the two of you communicate.

4. MOVE SLOWLY

Don't rush things. Whether you are working on the length of time your cat can stay or how high he can jump, do not rush the learning process. It is very easy for a cat to become frustrated and give up if you ask too much too quickly.

5. PRAISE

Use a very enthusiastic and upbeat voice while training. Your encouraging tone will tell your cat that this is fun and that you are excited about doing something with him. Your tone also serves as a great reassuring tool to your cat as he tries to learn new tricks.

6. BUILDING THE FOUNDATION

Do not bombard your cat with multiple tricks. Teaching too much, too quickly will only confuse and frustrate him. In fairness to your cat, teach him only one trick at a time and do not move on to another until he has grasped the trick and its commands. Start with come and sit—because most tricks begin with these basic commands—and move from there.

7. TRAINING TOOLS

Be sure you have gathered all of the supplies you need for training before you begin. If you call your kitty and then have to go in search of fetching toys, hoops, and treats, he will lose interest, and he might not be so eager to come the next time. Because treats are a huge part of training cats, have plenty on hand. However, do not give your cat so many treats in one setting that you risk upsetting his stomach or weight gain.

8. TRAINING TIME

One way to ensure you do not give too many treats or frustrate your feline pupil is to limit the amount of time you spend training. The typical basic obedience lesson for a dog lasts twenty to thirty minutes. Cats will never last this long. Each training session with your cat should last not more than five minutes. Daily five-minute training sessions will ensure a smart, fun cat who is eager to learn with you.

9. YOUR CAT'S MOOD

Just because you are in the mood to train does not necessarily mean your cat is in the mood. Forcing a cat to perform tricks is as productive as playing with superglue—it might even land you in the emergency room. Choose a time when your cat is feeling affectionate and ready to work. Do not choose a time close to feeding or naptime; this will only agitate him. Find a time that he is usually affectionate and looking for praise and attention.

10. WHERE AND WHEN TO TRAIN

Finally, train in a place that is conducive to learning. Most cats are more comfortable working in the main living area or kitchen. Find a time when the house is quiet and your cat is most receptive to working. If your house is full of rambunctious children or you start training too close to dinner time, your cat will be too distracted to learn. Foot traffic, outside noises, or other animals can all be major distractions for your cat as well. As the two of you are learning new tricks, it is also important that your cat feel he has all of your attention.

Most Common Dangers to Your Cat in Your Home

E very day, cats visit emergency rooms because they have ingested or climbed into something harmful. To us, these items—whether useful appliances or miscellaneous objects—appear completely harmless, but to the curious cat they can be (and often are) deadly. Before you let your cat roam freely, be sure you've kitty-proofed your home.

1. HOUSEPLANTS

Plants can be a great temptation for cats. Cat owners may ask, "How do I stop my cat from chewing up my plants?" (See the chapter on "Most Common Behavioral Problems") and "Why does my cat chew my plants?" As discussed earlier, boredom is one reason that cats eat houseplants. Animal experts also think that cats may crave the partially digested plant matter found in the bellies of their prey. Whatever the reason they eat them, one thing is clear: plants can be hazardous to indoor cats. Learn more about the plants you have in your home before leaving your cat alone with the green temptations. For a partial list of dangerous plants, see the next chapter, "Most Toxic Plants for Cats."

2. CABLES AND WIRES

You may have never noticed the loose cable to the television, but you can be sure your kitten will. Every year, hundreds of cats die from electrocution while playing with and biting exposed cables and wires. If you simply cover the exposed wires, your inquisitive cat won't give them a second glance. Remember that even though you can't see the wiring hidden under your bed or couch, your kitten may be playing with it while you are sleeping or at work. Be sure to check all outlets and secure all loose wires.

3. STRINGS 'N' THINGS

Balls of yarn, ribbons, rubber bands, dangling cords or beads, stockings, and Christmas tinsel can be the most entertaining toys a kitten has ever had. But they can also be deadly. All too often, enthusiastic cats are strangled by their own toys. If you've ever watched a cat wrap himself up in a ball of yarn, you know how wild felines can get with their playthings. If you are not home to detangle your cat, however, he may succumb to panic and choke himself.

More often than they choke themselves, play-happy cats strangle their intestines by eating up strings 'n' things. Tinsel and stockings can actually act as saws, severing intestines and killing the animal.

4. WHAT'S FOR DINNER?

Ever curious, cats always want to see what is happening around the house. Counter jumpers may learn about the stove the hard (and extremely painful) way. Counter hazards also include cutting knives, griddle irons, and coffee makers. See "Most Common Behavior Problems" to learn how to train your cat not to jump on the counters.

5. LAUNDRY DAY

The author of this book once tossed some clothing in the dryer, slammed the door shut, and pushed heat dry, not knowing her tomcat was inside. Returning to the laundry room shortly after starting the dryer, this careless laundress heard an unusual thumping sound that couldn't possibly be towels. She opened the dryer to discover her cat—very warm and dizzy but otherwise alright. While this story had a happy ending, every year many cats accidentally caught in the dryer are not discovered until it is too late. Dark and warm, the dryer is very appealing to cats, and often this appliance sits just low enough that few people look inside before throwing in laundry. Always be sure to keep the door to your dryer closed, and always check the dryer before throwing things inside. It only takes a moment for you to turn your back on an empty but warm dryer for Fluffy to jump in.

6. HEARTHS AND HEAT

It seems natural that a cat would avoid a fire blazing in the fireplace, doesn't it? Why on earth would your feline get into such a death trap? But as ashes float up around the fire and smoke swirls around, your curious kitten may creep closer and closer to the flames. Be sure to install a fire guard across the opening to your fireplace, using fasteners at both the sides and bottom of the grate.

7. KITTEN IN A CUPBOARD

Just as the dryer and fireplace need to be closed to kittens, so does the medicine cabinet. Rolling bottles with clanking and rattling pills are fun to play with and can provide hours of entertainment—until a lid is finally knocked or gnawed off. Painkillers meant for humans, including low dosages of aspirin and acetaminophen (the active ingredient in Tylenol), are lethal to cats. Make sure your medicines are locked up tight. If your cat is in pain, be sure to call your vet before handing out painkillers.

8. BALCONIES AND WINDOWS

Cat lovers always want to be sure their indoor cats can see the great outdoors. Many well-meaning owners allow cats to peer out windows and balconies from high in the sky, sure that their cats have enough sense not to jump out. But sometimes emotion can get the best of even the smartest cat. A low-flying bird or butterfly may prompt a cat to reach out and make a hopeful swipe, only to lose his balance. Or, an overconfident cat may become used to leaning against a screen only to have it give way. Be sure to fully cat-proof your windows and balconies so that there is no way your cat can fall, lean, or jump out.

9. **WRINKLE-FREE**

Most people who iron or use a curling iron walk away from these appliances while they warm up, multitasking as most mornings demand. To the curious cat, irons are interesting because they have strings (what we know to be electrical cords) that hang down. In only a few seconds, a cat can pull a hot iron down and burn himself. Cat-proof everything!

10. **BAG IT**

Polythene bags are fun, fun, fun to play in. This, of course, is the cat's perspective. But it is all too easy for enthusiastic cats to roll around and suffocate in plastic bags. Today many people keep and recycle plastic bags. If you are a recycler, be sure to keep your plastic bags out of paws' way.

*BONUS DANGERS:

Do not overlook the garage. The garage is always an interesting place to investigate, but it holds many dangers for the kitty, from antifreeze and gasoline to cleaning supplies, mouse traps, and fertilizers. The number one danger to the garage-loving kitty is the car itself. While thousands of cats are killed every year when crossing the street, an alarming number of cats are killed in their own garages, having crept up into a warm engine block and fallen asleep. An unknowing owner may start his car and inadvertently kill his cat. The solution: Know where your kitty is, and give your horn a little toot before starting the car.

Most Toxic Plants for Cats

W hat could be more natural than a cat playing with and nibbling on plants? But this natural instinct can be lethal. The ASPCA/National Animal Poison Control Center has identified a long list of plants that pose a danger to your feline friend. Before you begin working on your yard or bring houseplants into your home, speak to your local nursery and veterinarian about plants and cats, and check out the ASPCA/National Animal Poison Control Center at www .aspca.org or call (888) 426-4435.

The following is a list of plants that cause cats abdominal pain, seizures, and convulsions possibly followed by coma and death.

1. Azalea

2. Belladonna

3. Black Locust, Castor Bean

4. Jasmine

5. Lily of the Valley, Oleander

6. Morning Glory

7. Periwinkle

8. Rhubarb

9. St.-John's-Wort

10. Yew

The following garden plants may cause your cat to vomit, have diarrhea, have difficulty breathing, and be disoriented.

1. Baby's Breath

2. Branching Ivy

3. Caladium, Skunk Cabbage

4. Daffodil

5. Daphne, Honeysuckle

6. English Holly

7. Geranium

8. Indian Rubber Plant

9. Mother-in-Law's Tongue

10. Mistletoe

There are also a wide variety of houseplants that pose a threat to your cat's health.

1. Aloe Vera

2. Asparagus Fern

3. Caladium*

4. Devil's Ivy*

*In extreme cases, these plants may cause seizures and even death.

5.   Elephant Ears*

6.   Jerusalem Cherry

7.   Oleander

8.   Philodendron

9.   Poinsettia

10. Weeping Fig

Growing a Garden
for Your Cat

You know you have (or wish you had) a green thumb, but did you know that Fluffy also loves gardens? To avoid a turf war with your cat, you need to accommodate his fondness for plants.

1. MINE AND YOURS GARDENS

Cat lovers and cat haters alike complain about feline invasions into their gardens—digging up plants and doing even more unpleasant things such as using the garden as a personal litter box. By creating a special garden for your cat, you provide a pet paradise that offers hours of joy for the cat and keeps your garden free of felines. Mark your garden off limits with deterrents such as mothballs on the soil and Bitter Apple spray on the leaves. Your space will be respected if your cat has an alternative.

2. MARKING THE BOUNDARIES

Although mothballs and Bitter Apple will help to distinguish your garden from the cat's, physical borders, including rows of bricks, rocks, or garden edging tiles, provide a visual boundary that your cat can see and respect. Be sure that your cat's garden is removed from your garden. It can be one foot or fifty feet away, depending on the amount of space you have.

3. **CHOOSE WISELY**

Choose a spot that will be enjoyable to your cat. Your pet will not be pleased with a shady patch of land behind the shed. Instead pick a place where plants will get plenty of sunshine, where your cat can enjoy the scenery, and where you can keep an eye on him.

4. **THE BED**

The centerpiece to your cat's garden can be a catnip bed. (Yes, you can grow your own catnip.) The catmint, a summer perennial with lavender-blue flowers and minty-grey leaves, is a beautiful plant that your cat can enjoy—both visually and nutritionally. Surrounding the catmint, you might consider summer-long blooms such as French lavender, or the butterfly-attracting butterfly bush—a wonderful source of entertainment for the cats and a lovely sight outside your window. You may plant a number of herbs around the catmint and lavender to add to the fragrance and greenery, truly making this a garden cats will love.

5. **BUILD IT AND THE CAT WILL COME**

Ah, all the sweet-smelling greenery will only lead to one thing—the cat will ruin it all. Not necessarily so. You can add longevity to the cat garden's life by constructing a safety box around the catmint, which will protect the base of the plant from being destroyed while allowing your cat to nibble on the higher leaves and branch tips.

Build a box around the base of the catmint with garden edging tiles, bricks, or large stone, leaving enough room for plant growth. Using chicken wire or a stronger wire mesh, create a net over the plant. You may also consider covering the plant with a box spring, which is strong enough to support the weight of a twenty-pound cat who has crawled atop to chew the catnip. These wire structures allow sunlight and water through to feed the plant, while keeping cat paws from digging up its roots. They also make nice beds for cats to sit on, while enjoying their new garden.

6. MAKE A LIST, CHECK IT TWICE

Before planting the new garden, check with both a nursery and your veterinarian to be sure you understand what you are planting. You want to ensure that the plants you choose are in no way harmful or toxic to animals. Not everyone who works at a nursery necessarily knows which plants are cat-unfriendly, so be sure to double-check with your vet.

7. THE HERBS

Feline favorites are thyme, sage, parsley, chickweed, lawn grass, colt's foot grass, and cereal grass. Mmm, mmm, good.

8. BUILD IT AND OTHERS WILL COME

Be prepared for other cats to come to the garden as well. This can be a real medical concern as other cats can carry disease and infection, contaminating your new garden and putting your cat in danger. Some owners build wire-mesh tent frames around their gardens, allowing otherwise indoor cats to enjoy the space while keeping strays out. Such wire structures prevent disease from being carried into the garden as well as possible cat fights.

Tethering your cat outdoors may seem an appealing option, but remember that your cat can tangle himself up, or worse, fall victim to a dog or coyote, if chained in your yard. Tethering is not recommended.

9. THE HEALTH FACTOR

Allowing your cat fresh air, greenery, and the feeling of one-ness with nature may be among the healthiest things you can do for your cat. For this reason, some owners have added more natural items to their indoor cat's enclosed garden. Lawn services will usually provide downed large tree limbs for free (although you must be willing to pick them up), or you may be lucky enough to find an appropriate branch on your own. Tree limbs serve as natural scratching posts and bring tremendous joy to your cat.

10. NEXT BEST THING

A screened-in porch or balcony can be the next best thing to a garden paradise. Even an area inside the house can be turned into a jungle for your cat. Again, you can create a cat paradise with tree limbs, anchored in such a way that the cat can climb, perch, scratch, and lie on the branches, or with the more common carpeted cat tree. Supplement your cats indoor playground with rye grass in flat trays or planters, to create a grassy area, as well as other potted plants. Thyme, parsley, sage, and catnip, among other aromatic herbs, can be added to enhance the garden feel. By providing a green room, you will likely lengthen your cat's life and save the lives of your houseplants!

Most Serious Cat Illnesses

M any cat owners believe cats make better pets because they are low maintenance. You will often hear owners and non-owners say cats can take care of themselves. While it is true that felines are independent and strong animals, they also have medical concerns that need to be addressed. Yes, cats have allergies; owners who smoke can trigger asthma in their beloved pets; and outdoor cats face all kinds of diseases. If treated for their ailments, cats can live long and healthy lives. If they go untreated or neglected, cats will be miserable. Remember, the nine lives myth is just that—a myth.

1. UPPER RESPIRATORY INFECTIONS (URIs)

At the onset, a URI seems very similar to the common cold. Your cat may experience sneezing, runny nose, watery eyes, decreased appetite, lack of energy, and possibly, fever. However, an upper respiratory infection can prove deadly for a cat. Airborne viruses such as feline viral rhinotracheitis (FVR) and feline calicivirus (FCV) are highly contagious. Viral infections may be transmitted to cats through contact with other cats, shared objects (such as grooming tools or food bowls), and humans. It is important not to handle cats you do not know, so that you avoid unwittingly exposing your own cat to infection. With regular checkups and vaccinations, your cat has a far better chance of warding off these common infections.

2. FELINE PANLEUKOPENIA (FP)

Most commonly known as feline distemper, this disease is highly contagious and may be transmitted through other infected cats, clothing, shared tools (including pet carriers or cages at a boarding facility), and humans who have a pet or have held another infected cat. This disease strikes suddenly against cats that have not been vaccinated. Symptoms include diarrhea, vomiting of bile, extreme pain, and fatigue.

3. FELINE LEUKEMIA VIRUS (FeLV)

Feline leukemia is an infectious virus that can be transmitted through the saliva, urine, and feces of other infected cats. While there is no link between human and feline leukemia, both are fatal. FeLV strikes quickly, causing diarrhea, vomiting, difficulty breathing, fatigue, and fever. Although a vaccine was created in the 1980s, this virus continues to plaque feral and outdoor cats that are in constant contact with other cats.

4. FELINE INFECTIOUS PERITONITIS (FIP)

Feline infectious peritonitis is a swift-moving, deadly disease that causes diarrhea, vomiting, fatigue, and loss of appetite. The good news is that single-cat homes that make annual visits to the veterinarian are at minimal risk for contracting the disease. FIP can wreak havoc upon a multi-cat home. While doctors know that a virus known as coronavirus causes FIP, they are not sure which of the several strains of coronavirus is responsible for the disease. To date, there is no effective treatment for FIP. Veterinarians suggest the best way to prevent FIP is to keep cats indoors and away from strays.

5. FELINE IMMUNODEFICIENCY VIRUS (FIV)

This disease is the counterpart to human immunodeficiency virus (HIV). Like HIV carriers, cats infected with FIV suffer weakened immune systems, making them more susceptible to other diseases such as cancer and viral infections. This disease cannot be passed from felines to humans, but it is fatal to cats. The good news is that FIV-positive cats can live for months and years after diagnosis, as long as their illness is treated aggressively. The best insurance against FIV is to keep your cat indoors and away from unknown or untested cats.

6. FELINE LOWER URINARY TRACT DISEASE (FLUTD)

Also known as feline urologic syndrome (FUS), FLUTD describes all lower urinary tract infections that affect cats, including kidney disease, bladder stones, cystitis (the infection or inflammation of the bladder), and urinary blockage. FLUTD afflicts approximately 40 percent of domestic cats (the statistics are unknown on strays and feral cats), with effects ranging from mild discomfort to extreme pain and the need for emergency medical assistance.

In mild cases, a cat's bladder becomes infected, causing him to frequent the litter box more than usual. You might notice that your pet is suddenly missing the box or unable to control his bladder, sure signs that he needs to see the vet. In more extreme cases, symptoms include decreased appetite, vomiting, weight loss, fatigue, bloody urine, and severe abdominal discomfort. FLUTD may cause a blockage in the urethra (the tube connected to the bladder that takes urine out of the bladder), which will cause frequent trips to the litter box with little result. Because an infected cat has difficulty making bowel movements, many owners may mistake this symptom for constipation. Do not hesitate to take your cat to the vet when you notice any of the above behavior. If untreated, FLUTD can cause kidney damage and result in death.

7. TUMORS

While some tumors are linked to feline leukemia, many tumors cannot be explained. Sometimes, tumors are simply deposits of fat. Other times, they are malignant or cancerous. A cat's body will reject, or push out, a foreign growth—regardless of the reason it developed—creating a noticeable lump. Often, owners are uncertain if a lump warrants a mad dash to the vet. When in doubt, have your cat examined by a professional.

8. HEART DISEASE

Although very few cats suffer from heart attacks, they do suffer from heart disease, primarily hypertrophic cardiomyopathy (the most common feline heart problem). Although heart disease takes several weeks to develop into a serious condition, many symptoms—fatigue and poor appetite—are recognizable early on. Coughing, gasping for air, and in the case of some cats, leg weakness caused by blood clots are symptoms that develop as the disease progresses. If this chronic disorder is caught early enough, cats may be treated successfully.

9. ALLERGIES

Cat allergies are more common than you think. Pollen, dust, grass, plants, and even food can trigger allergic reactions that make your cat miserable. Symptoms may include watery eyes, restlessness, irritability, hot spots (i.e., irritated patches of skin), weight loss, vomiting, and diarrhea—all of which can be controlled by regular visits to the veterinarian.

10. ASTHMA

Asthma is a type of allergic bronchitis that constricts a cat's airways, making him wheeze and cough. While environmental allergens such as ragweed and pollen can cause a cat's asthma attack, in-home allergens can also pose a problem. Perfume, dusty litter boxes, and smoking are common triggers of feline asthma. The good news is that this disease can be treated. Regular visits to the veterinarian and an observant owner can keep an asthmatic cat living and breathing comfortably. Unfortunately, asthma is not a temporary condition but rather a disease that will return if medication is discontinued.

You, Your Cat, and Baby Makes Three

E very year thousands of cats are abandoned because expectant parents believe cats and babies cannot live together. In fact, most cats are extremely nurturing and loving to human babies, if they are properly introduced to the new family member. But in light of centuries of myths, such as a cat will steal your baby's breath or a cat will be extremely jealous of your newborn, it is easy to understand how apprehensive new parents might question whether having a cat is best for the baby.

1. THE NEW FAMILY MEMBER

Many families report that while their baby was in utero, their cat was extremely loving and always wanting to lie next to or on top of Momma's growing belly. As soon as the baby came home, however, the cat's behavior changed. Actually, it is almost always the new parents' behavior that will change when baby comes home. A cat will feed on his owners' anxious, sleep-deprived, excited, and nervous symptoms, and while he may not understand that all the tension ties directly to the new bundle of joy, he does understand that something is very different. And change is upsetting to most cats.

2. THE JEALOUSY MYTH

No, your cat is not jealous of the new baby, only confused by the change in his owners' behavior. Suddenly, you are pushing him away and knocking him off of furniture he once had access to. As soon as you learn you are pregnant and begin bringing in baby furniture, new rules need to be established. Being a naturally curious animal, your cat will want to investigate the crib, changing table, and new toys. If you have determined these to be off limits, train your cat to stay away from them as you would train him to stay away from certain countertops and plants. (See "Most Common Behavioral Problems.")

In *Lady and the Tramp* Tramp enlightens Lady about life after a new baby's arrival: "When the baby moves in, the dog moves out!" With some special attention, assure your cat early on that you will not leave him out in the cold, and be sure to make time to love your cat after the baby comes.

3. BABY'S ROOM

Should you decide you want the baby's room entirely cat-free, you can train your cat to stay out. Because cats always want to go where they are prohibited, you may have to invest in deterrents that are more high-tech than foil and spray bottles. Most pet suppliers offer a variety of products for intensive cat training, such as motion detectors, sound alarms, and scent deterrents. You may also want to consult one of the animal behaviorists in "Why Does My Cat Do That?" for additional information and training techniques.

4. GETTING TO KNOW YOU, GETTING TO KNOW ALL ABOUT YOU

Beyond teaching your cat furniture manners, you should also introduce baby toys and baby sounds before the newborn arrives. Ask a friend or relative to record a baby crying and play the recording for your cat randomly throughout the day. As good as it may be for you to get used to the new sound—it's always a shocker at 2 A.M.—it will be even better for your cat, who will eventually get used to the recording and then find the real thing less unsettling.

Smells are equally important. Let your cat get used to the smells of powders, diapers, lotions, and wipes. As he investigates these smells, be sure to love and praise your cat.

He should regard every baby accoutrement as a positive addition to his home.

Remember, cats are very territorial animals. You are bringing new things into *his* home, so you best make happy, pleasant introductions.

5. **THE ROUTINE**

Establish a routine and try to stick with it. Of course, you don't know exactly when the baby is coming, but if you have arranged to have a caregiver come into the house for the cat while you and your significant other are away at the hospital, be sure your cat has met this person more than once and that, despite your hospital visit, feeding schedules will remain regular. And carry this routine over after baby's arrival. This will reassure your cat that everything is OK and that he has nothing to be concerned about. Again, cats do not appreciate change—especially when it affects their routine.

6. **THE CONCERNS**

We have all heard that having a cat in the house can cause children to develop severe allergies, even asthma. In the August 28, 2002, issue of the *Journal of the American Medical Association*, a new study reported that children exposed to cats at a very early age build up antibodies that make them less likely to be allergic to felines as they grow up.

7. **SHARING THE JOY**

Child experts suggest that new parents buy presents—however small—for older siblings as more and more gifts for the newborn come into the house. Offering a new doll or stuffed animal to the older children will reassure them that the new baby is not loved any more than they. Animals also need this reassurance. As new baby things come into the home, do not neglect your cat. A new ball or stuffed mouse will remind him that he is loved and cared for.

8. **HERE COMES BABY**

Okay, so the baby is on the way, and you are rushing (or hobbling) out the door. Before you leave, lay out some clothing that you have recently worn along with some of the baby's clothing on or near the cat's favorite sleeping places. The smells will give the cat a sense of both security that you are nearby and familiarity when the strange new baby comes home.

9.   WHEN FRIENDS COME CALLING

When friends and family come calling to see the new beautiful bundle of joy, many owners shut their animals up in a separate room. Often, this is for the pets' own good, preventing them from escaping out the door, getting stepped on, or annoying a non-cat lover (go figure). Your cat, however, may think he is no longer wanted. Be sure to ask your cat-loving guests to say hello to the cat. Also bring out some of the cat goodies you may have bought while baby shopping. More important, allow some time for your cat to enjoy the new baby along with everyone else. Rather than exclude Fluffy, include him in the festivities as a member of your family. The paybacks are huge. Your happy, included cat will prove to be a great feline friend again and again to you and your baby.

10.   THE INTRODUCTION

As you hold the swaddled baby, let your cat sniff him or her from head to toe. Your cat will love the baby's smells as much as you do. Your cat may show immediate interest, but don't worry if he initially snubs you and the baby. If you get the brush off, continue with his schedule as normal, offering your cat affection when the baby is down and anytime he is willing to speak to you. Time will win him over.

If your cat is instantly interested, take advantage of his curiosity, letting him rub against you as you hold the baby (when you are seated) and smell the baby. Be aware of your baby's hands as the child grows. Accidental hair pulling or eye poking may turn your sweet, naturally inquisitive kitty into a skittish cat around small children. Be sure to read the next chapter, "Golden Rules for Children and Cats."

Golden Rules for Children and Cats

Cats are soft, cuddly, and very much fun to tease and torment. While there are some cats that are willing to take whatever punishment a small child can dish out, more are apt to strike back, leaving a nice scratch along your child's arm or, worse, face. You can't always be on hand to watch the cat, so it is all the more important to teach your child how to treat animals.

1. **OWNER OF THE CAT**

Children should never be left to discipline or train a cat, even if the cat belongs to a child. Because the signals from and reasoning skills of small children are unpredictable, the messages they send can be confusing and unfair to an animal, causing frustration and sometimes hostility on the part of the cat. For the safety of everyone involved, make sure your children understand that discipline and training are not their responsibilities.

2. **TEASING**

Never, under any circumstances, should a child be allowed to tease a cat. Playing with the cat under adult supervision is one thing and should be encouraged to build a bond between a child and the cat, but pulling toys away from and throwing things on or around the cat are altogether different. Be sure your child is always supervised while playing with your cat.

3. **ROUGHHOUSING**

Even the most patient of cats will tolerate only so much roughhousing. Again, children should always be supervised while playing with a cat. A child who has just been bitten or scratched may be completely perplexed about why they were attacked. "We were having fun!" they say. But pulling tails and hair are not a cat's idea of a good time.

4. **DINNERTIME**

Never let your child play with the cat's food. Never in the history of cats have cats let others play with their food. They offer food as gifts or may play with live soon-to-be-food themselves, but they are not fond of sharing in food play. Your child needs to be taught to leave the cat alone during dinnertime.

5. **POTTY TIME**

Although it may seem obvious, it is important to remind children that they should never play in or around the kitty litter box. The litter box should be completely off-limits to your child, especially when the cat is using it. In addition to the potential health hazards to children of inhaling litter fumes or playing in the litter, there is the issue of kitty privacy. Often adults will allow their child to watch the kitty use the potty, but cats are very private about these matters and really don't appreciate an audience. If possible, place the litter box in an out-of-the-way place where your child doesn't see or even think about it.

6. **CATNAPS**

Catnaps are sacred. Children need to learn from the start that a cat should never be disturbed while sleeping, both to prevent the possibility of an annoyed cat lashing out when rudely awakened and to instill respect and a sense of boundaries in the child. Rules should be in place to ensure that a child understands when the family feline should not be touched.

7. **SICK OR INJURED CATS**

The rules for sleeping kitties also apply to sick and injured kitties. Toddlers and young children need to understand that even the sweetest cat in the world will scratch and bite when she is hurt or feeling badly.

8. **NO MAN'S LAND**

Cats have their retreats. They withdraw to dark, warm places—under the bed or the couch, behind the big chair, or behind boxes—when they are nervous, anxious, or crabby, or just want to be alone. It is important to teach your child to never stick a hand or face under or in something in search of kitty.

9. **NO MEANS NO**

For adults, a hissing cat is a scary thing that we take very seriously. But for many children, a cat's hiss is a challenge. It's funny, even a little exciting. While the cat is saying, "I've had enough. Go away!" children will continue to poke and prod. You cannot punish a cat for lashing out against a child when the cat has tried everything he can think of, including hissing a warning for ten minutes, to get away from the child. The child, not the cat, needs to be chastised for pursuing and provoking the feline. Your pet will not understand being punished and will only grow more agitated by the child, whereas the child can learn quickly when to leave kitty alone.

10. **FRIENDS FOREVER**

Guidelines understood by both child and cat create room for an incredible bond to form. As soon as your cat believes he can spend time with your child without being hurt, he will come around more often, rubbing against legs and sleeping with his new buddy. Your cat will become more trusting and confident about his role in the family, and your child will learn to become a more gentle, empathetic, generous person in life. By setting strict pet rules for your child, you are creating a win-win situation for everyone.

Questions to Ask a Breeder

You've decided on the breed you want and are very excited about getting your brand new kitten. Please do remember that animal shelters have absolutely wonderful, beautiful cats and kittens in need of good homes. But if you are hard-set on a certain breed, you need to consider a few things before you rush into buying your new kitten. Here is a list of ten important questions to ask the breeder to learn more about not only the kind of cat you have chosen but also, more important, the kind of breeder from whom you are buying your pet.

1. HOW LONG HAS THE BREEDER BEEN INVOLVED WITH THIS BREED?

Be wary of breeders who are selling their first litter of kittens. Although they may be nice people, they don't necessarily know what they are doing. Ask if they have worked with other breeds as well. While it is common for well-known, well-established breeders to invest in two or three different breeds, someone who is only involved with the "it" breeds—the popular breeds—is likely only in the business for the money. Beware. Look for a breeder with experience.

2. WHAT'S THE DOWNSIDE TO THIS BREED?

All good breeders can provide a long list of the congenital defects of their breeds. If they know what they are doing and have been paying attention to their kittens, they are well aware of the problems specific to their cats and aren't afraid to share that information with you in the interest of raising strong, healthy kittens. Know this: Every breed has problems. Just like people, cats aren't perfect. You should be wary of anyone who says otherwise.

3. WHAT ARE YOUR LONG-TERM PLANS FOR YOUR CATS?

Good breeders will be personally invested in better health and nutrition for their cats. It is a good sign if they can tell you that their cats are tested or screened for any problems common to the breed.

4. WHERE ARE THE FELINE PARENTS?

Meeting both parents allows you to see their condition and overall physique, as well as how they behave. Aggressive or unruly parents may raise a red flag.

More important, you should see how the owners interact with the parents. Good breeders will be able to tell you honestly the pros and cons of their adult cats. They will want you to know, for example, that the mother is not good with children or can be antisocial. Because they want to make sure that you are happy with your kitten and that your kitten is happy with you, they should not be giving you the hard sell. Good breeders should be most concerned with finding great homes for their kittens.

5. WHAT'S IN A NAME?

Breeders should also be able to show you a solid family history—the pedigree—and respond convincingly to any questions you have about the pedigree. They should explain who is who on the family tree and what the titles mean. Do not be afraid to ask.

6. WHERE DO THE KITTENS LIVE AND SLEEP?

Often when owners-to-be arrive, the kittens are outside, frolicking and looking cute, but it is important to see where and how the kittens live most of their lives. Many kittens are kept in crates or in the basement—which means they are probably lacking socialization and proper care. This is not what you want. When you ask this question, you want to hear words like, "everywhere!"

7.   ARE THESE SHOW CATS?

There is a difference between show cats and pets. Just because your kitten has a stunning pedigree does not make him show material. Something as minor as an overbite or a poor coat can be a very big deal in the show ring. It is important that you know the kittens have been evaluated and that you understand the quality of cat you are considering. A good breeder will not try to sell you a pet at a show-quality price.

8.   WHAT ARE YOUR GUARANTEES?

Reputable breeders will guarantee the cat—essentially the pedigree—they are selling you and will be willing to guarantee the health and quality of their kittens. Get these guarantees in writing. Remember the story of Suki, the Siamese in the chapter "Pussycat, Pussycat, Where Have You Been?" Almost fifteen years after she was sold, in a different country, in an airplane, Suki's breeder recognized her as a cat from his line. Quality breeders will take such pride in their cats that they will know them anywhere. Literally. And good breeders are proud of their names and their reputations.

9.   DO YOU HAVE REFERENCES?

This is the one question most owners are too embarrassed to ask. It seems rude. In truth, reputable breeders want and expect you to ask. They are proud of their kittens and like to build their reputations, especially by word of mouth. Before you agree to buy a kitten, ask for references and check them out. Guarantees and pedigrees are one thing, but talking to owners is the best way to know what you're buying.

10. **WHEN CAN I TAKE MY KITTEN HOME?**

Veterinarians, animal behaviorists, and trainers never like to see kittens leave their mother before the age of eight to ten weeks. Although a breeder might tell you a kitten is ready at six weeks, those extra two to four weeks of socialization with his mother and the junior tribe are vital. A breeder who would let kittens go before they are six weeks old may not be making a good decision, and this should raise a red flag for you.

Signs That This Is not a Cat-Friendly Breeder

When choosing a kitten, you learn a lot by both asking breeders thoughtful questions and by observing the breeders and their felines. Here are ten things for which you want to watch.

1. BACKYARD BREEDERS

The term "backyard breeders" identifies people who know very little about their breed except that they like them and think they are pretty. The problem with backyard breeders is that they don't have enough knowledge to ensure good breeding. If your breeder lacks knowledge about the breed, its origins, and its problems, you need to look elsewhere.

2. THOROUGH ANSWERS

Again, all breeders should be able to speak openly and knowledgeably about the problems common to their specific breeds. What congenital defects do they have? What diseases are most common in the breed? You should arrive at the breeder's with some basic information, gleaned from the Internet or the library, about your breed of choice. Also bring a list of medical questions. Your breeder should be able to answer these questions and more.

3. **nO DEFECTS**

A breeder who insists that there is nothing wrong with the breed should set off a serious warning signal in your head. Good breeders will want you to be aware of all the potential problems your cat may face so that you will learn how to handle any problems.

4. **INVOLVEMENT In THE CAT COMMUNITY**

Today's top breeders are extremely busy people. They are involved in various clubs and shows because they know that the more they are involved in the cat community, the more knowledgeable they will become. Additionally, showing their cats is the best way to earn titles and championships. So, be wary of a breeder who is not doing anything except breeding cats.

The quality of a breeder's involvement in the cat community is also a validation of his credentials. Ask for a list of clubs your breeder is involved in and call those organizations.

5. **ABSENT PARENTS**

Unbelievably, some "breeders" do not wish to have people meet the parents of the litter in question. This is a red flag. You want and need to see how the parent cats look and act before purchasing their kittens.

6. **DOCUMENTATION**

Simply put, if you are paying the "asking rate" for a specific breed, you need to see the proper paperwork (registration forms and pedigrees) for the cat. You have a right to receive documentation that matches the quality claimed for the kitten you are buying.

7. **SOCIALIZATION**

You do not want kittens that have lived in virtual isolation. Behavioral problems such as aggression, extreme shyness, and nervousness all stem from lack of proper socialization.

You want a kitten that is well socialized and not afraid of anything new or anything loud. Also, remember that your kitten-to-be learns how to stalk and hunt prey from his mother, who will make him the mouser you've always wanted.

8. REFERRALS

If you've gathered the nerve to ask for referrals, be sure you get them. Too many times owners report they were promised referrals, but because they didn't insist on them, they never received them. Insist! You need to find out who you are dealing with because your kitten-to-be can't tell you.

9. THE EARLY SEND OFF

This is another issue that is important enough to repeat. New owners become so excited about their new kitten, they often forget about what is best for the animal. Any breeder who is willing to sell a kitten under the age of eight weeks is likely a breeder-for-profit-only. The ideal age for sale is eight to ten weeks—no sooner.

10. QUESTIONS

Just as you are asking questions of and about the breeders you visit, they should be asking questions of you. Good breeders want to know that their kittens are going to good homes; they want to know about you and your intentions for your new cat. They will ask about your home, your family life, your daily routine, exercise and play routines, and what, when, and where you will feed the kitten. If a breeder doesn't ask, be concerned. Many breeders today will also require that you sign a letter of promise not to declaw the cat you buy from them.

Questions to Ask Yourself before Getting a Cat

If you have not yet picked out a cat—and even if you already have—there are some important issues you need to consider and discuss with your family. Too often people choose a breed because of the way it looks and do not consider how (or when) a cat of that breed—or any cat for that matter—will fit into their lifestyles. Here are ten questions you need to ask yourself before getting a cat.

1. ARE YOU READY FOR A CAT?

Every day, all over the United States, unwanted cats appear in animal shelters because they simply don't fit into the family plan anymore. People get cats for a variety of reasons. While it may seem like a good idea at one time to get a cat, you may soon realize that you don't have enough time for a kitten, particularly a rambunctious and trouble-making kitten. People who have never owned an animal before are always surprised at how much time, effort, and yes, money is involved. Pet ownership should not be a passing phase but a lifelong commitment.

2. IS IMAGE EVERYTHING?

Is your cat a status symbol? Are you looking for that beautiful Persian in the Fancy Feast commercial? Or worse, are

301

you smitten with the idea of having a wildcat—maybe a bob-cat or some other large exotic cat? Today, more tigers live in cages than in the wild, and sadly, a huge number of these caged cats are living in homemade bunkers. Not only is it exceedingly dangerous to keep wildcats caged, it is inhumane and unnatural.

3. DO YOU HAVE ALLERGIES?

Although we now know that cats may actually help fight allergies, cat hair can agitate allergy sufferers enough to cause sneezing, watering eyes, sore throats, and coughing. Before you bring a cat into your life, perhaps you should visit a friend with a cat and handle the pet for a while to see how you will react. How much do you really want a cat? Are you willing to take allergy medication or shots? Talk to your vet before choosing a breed, and remember that you hope to have this cat for years and years. Before you bring a cat into your home, make sure the new living arrangement will be fair to both of you.

4. WILL A NEW CAT GET ALONG WITH YOUR CHILDREN?

You have a rough-and-tumble three-year-old. Do you really think getting a cat is a good idea? Take a hard look at the children who are living in your house and those who come to visit frequently (e.g., nieces and nephews). Hyperactive, loud, and rough children may not do well with a cat. Also consider the kind of breed you want. Some breeds of cats are better suited for children than others. Speak to breeders, animal trainers, and vets before making the final decision.

5. WILL A NEW CAT GET ALONG WITH THE OTHER ANIMAL IN THE HOUSE?

You have a cat that despises other cats, or your dog is a known cat hater. Perhaps throwing in a brand new, wildly happy kitten isn't the best idea. You may want to bring home a new kitten for your other cat, who seems bored and lonely, but before you add to the mix, speak with your vet and a trainer. Many experts advise against getting a rambunctious kitten as a "pet" to entertain an older cat. You want to be sure everyone is going to be happy.

But what if you are considering getting two kittens at the same time? Is having two kittens double the trouble? Unlike puppies, two kittens may be less trouble, as they will entertain each other for hours, playing and rolling around on the floor.

6. **WILL THE NEW CAT REQUIRE A LOT OF GROOMING?**

Owning cats that require heavy grooming involves two things: time and (possibly) money. The Persian and the Ragdoll require daily grooming. Outdoor cats may need professional grooming about every eight weeks to remove heavy matting and tangles. The Turkish Van, the Birman, and the Siberian may require grooming two to three times a week. The Scottish Fold needs constant grooming for its ears.

Susan dee Cohen

Two littermates are as easy to raise as one,
and they will entertain each other for years.

Speaking to a breeder and veterinarian before deciding on a breed can help you determine the amount of grooming (and time) required for your cat.

7. WILL YOU GET AN INDOOR OR AN OUTDOOR CAT?

Which will your cat be? Of course, you want your kitty to be happy. When you see her looking longingly out the window and racing for the door every time it opens, you may be really tempted to let her run free. After all, she's a cat; she's supposed to chase and climb and explore.

Before you decide to let her experience nature firsthand, however, you need to consider the less pleasant aspects of life for the outdoor cat. There are the dogs—even in neighborhoods with leash laws—and coyotes that are on the constant prowl for cats, and other cats may even pose a greater threat than these animals. Territorial creatures, cats claim their own areas; an unsuspecting cat that wanders into the territory of a bad cat may be attacked. Neighbors must also be considered. Think about asking them before you allow your cat to walk over their cars and use their flower beds as a litter box. Sometimes speaking to a neighbor first can ease any tension that might develop.

8. CAN YOU AFFORD A CAT?

Providing that you have a healthy cat, you can reasonably expect to make two veterinarian visits per year. Add to veterinarian trips the cost of quality cat food, treats, toys, a leash and collar, grooming, and the occasional need for boarding or petsitting. This does not include the cost of the actual cat should you decide to purchase a cat with excellent pedigree. The cost question must be answered honestly for the sake of both you and your pet. By avoiding veterinarian bills, you could expose your cat to all kinds of risks, including heartworms. Quality cat food will prolong your cat's life, making him healthier and happier. Bottom line: You must be willing to accept the costs of having a healthy and happy cat.

9. WHAT IF YOU GET A KITTEN AS A GIFT?

Receiving a cute, rolly-polly kitten as a holiday gift makes for a difficult situation. If the kitten does not fit into your life, how do you return it? Animal behaviorists have the answer: Find the kitten a new home. It is better to find the kitten a loving, welcoming home than have the kitten become attached to you before you give him away. It is also better to wound the gift-giver's ego slightly than to raise an unhappy cat.

10. SHOULD YOU GIVE A KITTEN AS A GIFT?

Keeping in mind the preceding point, be sure that you really know the intended recipient wants and can properly care for a cat before making a commitment to buy. And be sure the breed and temperament of the cat will work with the new owner's lifestyle before bringing the two together.

Moving with Your Cat

oving can be one of the most stressful times in your life, not to mention your very territorial pet's life. This is a time when many cats, confused by all the disruption, packing, and foot traffic, run away or are lost. But moving can also be a happy, stress-free period for your cat. Following are some tips to help ensure a safe and happy move for you both.

1. PACKING THE HOUSE

As the process of moving begins, be sure to keep your cat's routine as normal as possible. He will see boxes moving about and will certainly feel your stress elevate, but by keeping his feeding, napping, bird-watching, and play schedules the same, he will feel more secure.

A moving family's most common mistake is ignoring the cat. After all, when so much is going on, it's hard to keep up with him and his needs. If your feline feels ignored, however, he will simply find entertainment or attention somewhere else—right out the back door—or he will become destructive out of nervousness. Also because doors are left open for long periods during this time, unsupervised cats are more likely to take themselves for a walk. And be careful not to inadvertently pack your cat *inside* boxes or moving crates! To pre-

306

vent these mishaps, try to pay more—not less—attention to your cat as moving day approaches.

2. PACKING THE SUITCASE

Again, keep your cat's routine as normal as possible. Many cats recognize the sight of a suitcase as the sign they will be boarded, and as a result, cats often associate a suitcase with great anxiety. If this is true for your cat, pack while he is outside or in the other room.

3. TRAVELING BY CAR

If traveling by car, be sure to pack a cat-friendly car. Have food, water, and toys easily accessible. Be prepared for a breakdown. Should you be stranded on the side of the highway, be sure your cat has an ample supply of water and a properly fitting collar and leash or, better, a comfy carrying case. Even if you never have your cat wear a collar, have a travel collar in case of an emergency. To eliminate the possibility of your cat running away while making a roadside potty stop, you may consider packing the litter box in the car (at the far end of the car) so that your cat can relieve himself when necessary (although this is not recommended for people with asthma or sensitive noses). Most animal trainers suggest crating your cat for the duration of the trip—for his safety and yours.

Finding a hotel on the road may be difficult. *Vacationing with Your Pet* by Eileen Barish (Pet Friendly Publications, at 800-638-3637 is an excellent resource for all the hotels and motels in the United States that accept dogs and cats.

4. CARSICKNESS

While many cats do very well when traveling by car, some get carsick. Be sure not to feed or water your cat just before going on a long trip. Give him plenty of time to go to the bathroom before loading him into the car.

If you know carsickness is a problem for your cat, practicing the big move well before the actual date can help.

Begin with short, relatively easy trips, slowly lengthening the travel time so that your cat can adjust to longer and longer trips. A stomach-calming medication or tranquilizer may help. Speak with your vet about these options.

5. TRAVELING BY PLANE

As soon as you know you are flying, be sure to contact the airline about their animal policies. Every airline has different policies about animals, including sizes and breeds. Depending on your cat's size and breed, you may or may not be able to carry him on board. Again, be sure to practice crate training with your cat. Drive around the neighborhood or take short trips to the pet store or the bank to get your cat used to spending time in the crate and to being shuffled around. This will help him considerably on the plane.

You might have to check your cat in cargo. If this is the case, you will want to travel in mild weather, as cargo sections are not heated or air-conditioned. Also, consider how long your cat might be on the tarmac. Crate training is imperative if your cat is flying as cargo. You will want him to be as comfortable as possible. Introducing your cat to his crate just three minutes before boarding is unfair to Fluffy. Be sure to practice getting in and out of a crate, make sure your crate is the right size (your cat should be able to stand up and do a full circle inside), and give Fluffy lots of love and attention to reassure him that you're not abandoning him before he boards. Also, be sure to check and recheck the bolts or fasteners on the carrier crate. Proper identification of your cat and any special medical needs must be displayed on the outside of the crate, as well as on his collar. Anyone see *Homeward Bound II*?

6. MEDICAL RECORDS

Traveling with medical records is a must. Do not wait until you have moved to your new city or town to send for your cat's records. Plan in advance. As soon as you know you are moving, discuss the move with your vet and ask for recommendations for a veterinarian in the new city. If you can, be sure to have a veterinarian contact in your new city before you move, so you have someone to contact should something happen when you move in. With records on hand, you will be ready for the first doctor visit.

7. BE PREPARED FOR A DIFFERENT PERSONALITY

While traveling, discourage strangers from playing with your cat at rest stops and from getting kissy-wissy in his face. Many travelers have asked, "Is it my imagination or is my cat depressed?" It is possible that your travel-weary cat has become irritable, depressed, and/or confused. Although it is difficult to keep his schedule the same while you are on the road, you should try to feed him at the same time every day and continue to give him nice play sessions at the end of the day. By keeping his tummy on schedule and giving him regular exercise, he will be a happier traveler.

8. COMFORT TOYS

Security blankets, favorite toys, and treats are very important. As he watches you pack up your worldly possessions, your cat needs to know that his belongings are going along as well. For added security during a drive or flight, give him an old, worn shirt of yours that he can snuggle up to for additional comfort.

9. UNPACKING IN THE NEW HOME

Unpacking is even more dangerous for your kitty than the initial packing. While he was confused by all the boxes and suitcases at his old house, the environment was still familiar to him. In his new home and new town, everything is strange, new, exciting—and dangerous. He might bolt from fear or strike out on an adventure only to become lost. Be sure, as movers are walking in and out of the house, there is no way for your cat to escape. And no matter how tired you are that first night in your new home, take the time to slowly introduce your cat to his unfamiliar surroundings—room by room. Many experts suggest confining your cat to one room for the duration of the unpacking process. Each night, when the house is secured, you can let him out to investigate on his own and become more familiar with his new home. If he is an indoor/outdoor cat and tolerates a leash, snap one on and take him for a walk in his new neighborhood. However, be sure not to rush this familiarization process. Let him become comfortable and more confident with his new home. Too early an introduction to the great outdoors may be the last time you see your feline friend.

10. **THE NEW ENVIRONMENT**

Learn all about the new environment as quickly as you can. Many cities and towns have their own leash and cat laws. Learn about the other neighborhood animals and, most important, who your neighbors are. Be aware that there are many people out there who are ailurophobes and may do awful things to cats.

VI
Looking For Help

Top Feline Organizations

Throughout the ages, cats have helped, healed, and entertained us. They've saved our lives and warmed our hearts. But we simply do not give our feline friends enough credit, often thinking of them as lazy animals that prefer finding the perfect spot for a catnap over rescuing us from danger. But throughout history, cats have come to our rescue and remained wonderful companions. This gives us all the more reason to admire those people who have dedicated their lives to saving cats and to help those organizations that keep cats alive and healthy. Perhaps you will find an organization in which you would like to become involved through volunteer work or sponsorship.

1. **HUMANE SOCIETY OF THE UNITED STATES**

The Humane Society of the United States has a wonderful website designed to help the entire family learn more about animals, including how to care for and train them.

www.hsus.org
2100 L St. NW
Washington, DC 20037
(202) 452-1100

2. **AMERICAN VETERINARY MEDICAL FOUNDATION**

This organization is dedicated to helping veterinarians heal animals. The AVMF provides nearly $1 million to animal research, animal disaster relief, and financial assistance for veterinarians.

> www.avmf.org
> 1931 N. Meacham Rd., Ste. 1
> Schaumburg, IL 60173
> (800) 248-2862 ext. 6689
> info@avmf.org

3. **DELTA SOCIETY**

This is a human-animal health connection that offers information on therapy animals and all the health benefits cats and dogs have to offer. It is a great resource for information about animals.

> www.deltasociety.org
> 875 124th Ave. NE, Ste. 101
> Bellevue, WA 98005
> info@deltasociety.org

4. **MORRIS ANIMAL FOUNDATION**

This foundation was established in 1948 to provide support for students pursuing higher education in the field of animal health, including those who have gone on to get their doctorates in veterinarian medicine.

> www.morrisanimalfoundation.org
> 45 Inverness Drive E
> Englewood, CO 80112
> (800) 243-2345

5. **DORIS DAY ANIMAL LEAGUE**

This nonprofit organization focuses on the humane treatment of animals. The league offers information about health, medical issues, animals in the news, and the humane treatment of animals around the world.

> www.ddal.org
> 227 Massachusetts Ave. NE, Ste. 100

Washington, DC 20002
(202) 546-1761
info@ddal.org

6. FRIENDS OF ANIMALS

This nonprofit was established in 1957 to protect animals
from cruelty, abuse, and neglect around the globe.

www.friendsofanimals.org
777 Post Rd., Ste. 205
Darien, CT 06820
(203) 656-1522

7. CEDARHILL ANIMAL SANCTUARY

This organization is dedicated to improving the quality of life
for exotic and domestic cats—many of whom have been
abused or neglected. To learn more about Cedarhill, refer to
the chapter titled "The Real Cat Woman."

www.cedrhill.org
144 Sanctuary Loop
Caledonia, MS 39740

8. BEST FRIENDS ANIMAL SOCIETY

This national nonprofit organization monitors animal issues
in its monthly magazine. It is the nation's largest sanctuary
for neglected and abused animals.

www.bestfriends.org
5001 Angel Canyon Rd.
Kanab, UT 84741
(435) 644-2001

9. AMERICAN HUMANE ASSOCIATION

Dedicated to the prevention of cruelty to both animals and
children, the AHA provides information, referrals, and disaster relief.

www.americanhumane.org
Animal Services
63 Inverness Drive E
Englewood, CO 80112
(303) 792-5333

10. PETS ARE WONDERFUL SUPPORT

PAWS is a nonprofit organization that serves the needs of disabled pet owners. It offers comprehensive services designed to enable clients to keep their animal companions.

www.pawssf.org
1121 Mission St.
San Francisco, CA 94103
(415) 241-1460
info@pawssf.org

*BONUS ORGANIZATION:

Following the 2004 tsunami, images of starving and abandoned animals (some left tethered to posts and trees) raised the question, "How can I help?" Three organizations offer an answer:

World Society for the Protection of Animals
www.wspa.org.uk

International Fund for Animal Welfare
www.ifaw.org

Society for the Protection of Animals Abroad
www.spana.org

Rescue Shelters

Cats, the most popular pets in the United States and United Kingdom, are also the most euthanized animals in the world. Until pet owners become educated and dedicated to the responsibilities of spaying and neutering, this problem will persist. Fortunately, however, there are a number of no-kill organizations committed to finding homes for felines.

1. SAVE OUR STRAYS

This association has created a list of no-kill shelters in Canada and in the United States, so that residents can contact their closest humane shelter for assistance.

www.saveourstrays.com

2. ASSISSI ANIMAL FOUNDATION

This shelter provides lifetime care for pets whose owners die or can no longer care for them. It also acts as a no-kill shelter and provides animal-assisted therapy.

www.assisi.org
P.O. Box 143
Crystal Lake, IL 60039-0143
(815) 455-9411
info@assisi.org

3. BEST FRIENDS ANIMAL SOCIETY

This is a refuge for abused and abandoned animals that spearheads the nationwide No More Homeless Pets campaign.

> www.bestfriends.org
> 5001 Angel Canyon Rd.
> Kanab, UT 84741
> (435) 644-2001
> info@bestfriends.org

4. CAT CARE SOCIETY

This society operates a cage-free, non-euthanizing shelter for homeless and abused cats.

> www.catcaresociety.org
> 5787 W. 6th Ave.
> Lakewood, CO 80214
> (303) 239-9680

5. COLCHESTER CAT RESCUE

This shelter, which began as a one-woman rescue effort and is now a successful charity, is a strong advocate for unity in the humane community outside London. It offers spacious feral enclosures, lavish gardens, and large pens with grass.

> www.colchestercatrescue.org.uk
> "Lyndhurst," Bromley Rd.
> Ardleigh
> Colchester, Essex CO7 7SF
> 01206 864284
> mail@colchestercatrescue.org.uk

6. FRIENDS OF ANIMALS

This shelter is committed to the protection of all animals, wild and domestic. It subsidizes a spay/neuter program through local vets.

> www.friendsofanimals.org
> 777 Post Rd., Ste. 205

Darien, CT 06820
(203) 656-1522

7. MERRIMACK RIVER FELINE RESCUE SOCIETY

A nationally recognized, nonprofit volunteer organization, this shelter supports the health and welfare of feral and domestic cats by promoting proactive, humane, no-kill programs.

www.mrfrs.org
63 Elm St.
Salisbury, MA 01952
(978) 462-0760

8. SYLVESTER FOUNDATION ANIMAL RESCUE

This nonprofit, no-kill sanctuary provides a peaceful environment for all residents. There is no time limit on pet stay.

www.sylvesteranimals.com
305 Hahani St., #160
Kailua, HI 96734
(808) 259-0064

9. STEVENSON COMPANION ANIMAL LIFE-CARE CENTER

Texas A&M University's College of Veterinary Medicine established a long-term pet care organization for animals whose owners have died or can no longer care for them. The center provides a nice home with couches and carpeting, and offers care by medical students.

www.cvm.tamu.edu/petcare
(979) 845-1188

10. VOLUNTEERS FOR INTERVALLEY ANIMALS

In 1981 this nonprofit, no-kill shelter initiated a program of humane activities, including rescues and adoptions.

www.viva-animal-shelter.org
P.O. Box 896
Lompoc, CA 93438
(805) 735-6741

Why Does My Cat Do That? Web Resources

W hy does your cat tear up upholstery, knock over trash cans, or bite your toes while you sleep? How can you stop your cat from attacking other cats or knocking the phone off the hook? Your Aunt Betty might have the solution, but more often than not, the problem won't be resolved until you understand why you cat does what he does. Asking a certified, trained animal behaviorist is the best way to establish harmony among you, your cat, and your furniture.

1. www.animalbehavior.org

2. www.petbehaviorproblems.com

3. www.petbehaviorsolutions.com

4. www.avma.org

5. www.apbc.org.uk

6. www.healthypet.com

7. www.naturalholistic.com

8. www.familyanimal.com

9. www.winnfelinehealth.org

10. www.feralcats.com

Top Veterinary Groups

Just as it is vital to understand your cat's behavior, it is important to get the most up-to-date medical information and advice possible for him. The following is a top-ten list of veterinary groups committed to medical research, animal wellness, and animal behavior for both owner and pet.

1. **AMERICAN VETERINARY MEDICAL ASSOCIATION**

www.avma.org

2. **CANADIAN VETERINARY MEDICAL ASSOCIATION**

www.cvma-acmv.org

3. **AMERICAN ANIMAL HOSPITAL ASSOCIATION**

www.aahanet.org

4. **AMERICAN COLLEGE OF VETERINARY INTERNAL MEDICINE**

www.acvim.org

5. **ORTHOPEDIC FOUNDATION FOR ANIMALS**

www.offa.org

6. **PENNHIP**

www.pennhip.org

7. **CORNELL FELINE HEALTH CENTER**

www.vet.cornell.edu/fhc

8. **VETERINARIAN BOTANICAL MEDICINE ASSOCIATION**

www.vbma.org

9. **SPAY/USA**

www.spayusa.org

10. **TEXAS A&M UNIVERSITY**

www.cvm.tamu.edu

Cat Magazines and Resources

How can cat lovers around the world see pictures of cats playing pianos, riding horses, or surfing? How can they learn about Ice Breaker, who was named Most Talented Cat in North America by *Cat Fancy* magazine for his surfing talents? This champion seal lynx snow bengal wows crowds in the show ring and on the boogie board. (For more information about Ice Breaker or his breed, contact Jackie Essa by e-mail, satinwoodbengals@aol.com, or mail, 99273 Seaspray Place, Boca Raton, FL 22428.) Thanks to cat-loving magazines and associations, we may learn more about our cats, quality breed characteristics, and show guidelines. Support your love of cats or learn more about your favorite breed by contacting the following resources.

1. **AMERICAN ASSOCIATION OF CAT ENTHUSIASTS**

www.aaceinc.org
P.O. Box 213
Pine Brook, NJ 07058
(973) 335-6717

2. **AMERICAN CAT FANCIERS ASSOCIATION**

www.acfacat.com
P.O. Box 1949

Tuesday Marie Essa

Ice Breaker, the surfing cat.

Nixa, MO 65714
(417) 725-1530

3. ANIMAL FAIR MAGAZINE

www.animalfair.com
545 8th Ave., Ste. 401
New York, NY 10018
(212) 629-0392
info@animalfair.com

4. CANADIAN CAT ASSOCIATION

www.cca-afc.com
289 Rutherford Rd. S, Unit 18
Brampton, ON L6W 3R9
Canada

(905) 459-1481
office@cca-afc.com

5. CAT FANCIERS' ASSOCIATION

www.cfainc.org
P.O. Box 1005
Manasquan, NJ 08736-0805
(732) 528-9797

6. CAT FANCY MAGAZINE

www.catfancy.com
P.O. Box 6050
Mission Viejo, CA 92690-6050
(949) 855-8822

7. CATS AND KITTENS

www.catsandkittens.com
7-L Dundas Cir.
Greensboro, NC 27407
(336) 292-4047
info@petpublishing.com

8. CATS USA

www.catsusa.com

9. FEDERATION INTERNATIONALE FELINE

www.fifeweb.org
Little Dene, Lenham Heath
Maidstone, Kent ME17 2BS
United Kingdom
+44 (0)1622 850913
general-secretary@fifeweb.org

10. INTERNATIONAL CAT ASSOCIATION

www.tica.org
P. O. Box 2684
Harlingen, TX 78551
(956) 428-8046

Pet Suppliers

Looking for that something special for your feline friend? You can find the most unusual or difficult-to-find cat products online. Whether you are buying a gift for a fellow cat lover or for a pet of your own, these are the websites to check out.

1. www.drsfostersmith.com

2. www.cherrybrook.com

3. www.jbpet.com

4. www.petco.com

5. www.petsmart.com

6. www.pet-dog-cat-supply-store.com

7. www.lovethatcat.com

8. www.catconnection.net

9. www.7thheavencatfurniture.com

10. www.petdirect.com.au

Spas for Cats

When your cat has had a stressful week and just needs to get away, relax, and stretch his claws, a cat haven is just a click away. Following are some of the most plush, exotic catteries around.

1. THE CAT'S MEOW

Featured in *Cats Magazine* and on a variety of news programs, including CBS, you have to see this beautiful cat spa to believe it. With majestic settings and plenty of room to run and play, this is a cat's paradise.

> www.catsmeowinn.com
> RR #2
> Maberly, ON K0H 2B0
> Canada
> (613) 268-2004

2. CAT HOTEL

Plush private condos, in-room cable television, and twenty-four-hour room service make this the perfect getaway for your stressed-out, overworked cat. But before you decide that just any resort will do, check out the 240-square-foot Enchanted Forest online. Yes, the Cat Hotel is proud to present the Enchanted Forest room, featuring five natural cedar tree trunks recycled from a Utah forest fire and specially treated for cats. With padded perches, subtle lighting, and exotic atmosphere, your cat may never want to go home again!

www.home.earthlink.net/~cathotel
1807 W. Magnolia Blvd.
Burbank, CA 91506
(818) 845-0222
cathotel@earthlink.net

3. ATWOOD'S PET RESORT

Going on vacation but can't take Fluffy? Let him go on vacation, too. With a gift boutique, a daycare and boarding facility with planned playtime activities, and a pet taxi service, your cat will be living large at the Pet Resort. Services also include a worldwide pet travel agency.

www.petresort.com
2040 S. 142nd
SeaTac, WA 98168
(206) 241-0880

4. BROADLANDS CATTERY

This resort, located on five acres of beautiful Lincolnshire Wolds property, treats cats like kings and queens. With grooming, training, boarding, and plenty of wildlife to enjoy, the Broadlands Cattery offers a relaxing setting for cats of all ages.

www.broadlands-cattery.co.uk
Searby Top
Barnetby, Lincolnshire, DN38 6BL
United Kingdom
01652 629029

5. OLDE TOWNE PET RESORT

Your cat can expect spa treatments, salon services, snacks, daily housekeeping, and lots of love at the Olde Towne Pet

Resort, which offers hotel suites for your pets. With scenic views and play facilities, this is a one-of-a-kind cat spa. When they're not watching birds from strategically placed bird feeders, your cats can watch television programs preselected for feline enjoyment. Featured in *Newsweek* and *National Geographic* magazines, this resort is a haven for only the finest of felines.

www.oldetownepetresort.com
8101 Alban Rd.
Springfield, VA 22150
(703) 455-9000

6. CAT CONNECTION

This award-winning facility provides music, videos, and human interaction for your cats' entertainment and TLC. At the Cat Connection, cats can spend their days watching fish, birds, and mice or playing in a brightly furnished playroom, complete with catwalks and toys. The Cat Connection even offers flight transportation and delivery services.

www.catconnection.net
14233 Inwood Rd.
Dallas, TX 75244
(866) 386-MEOW

7. HANROB PET CARE CENTRE

Your cat can live large Down Under at the Hanrob hotel for cats. This luxury hotel offers sunny rooms with large windows, hammocks with artificial fur coverings, and soothing music. While staying at the Hanrob, your cat will exercise in the cat gym with scratching posts, stairs, toys, catnip balls, and human playmates.

www.hanrob.com.au
Lot 927, Princes Hwy.
Heathcote, NSW 2233
Australia
(02) 9520 6633

8. **ANIMAL RESORTS, INC.**

As the highest rated kennel in the Washington, D.C., area, Animal Resorts, Inc. does not "tolerate" fleas and has never had a single documented case of kennel cough. With a special upstairs cattery, this resort offers cats comfort and cleanliness.

> www.alexandriacitywebsite.com/AnimalResorts.htm
> 3208 Colvin St.
> Alexandria, VA 22314
> (703) 823-3647
> animalresorts@aol.com

9. **THE CAT'S PYJAMAS**

Also known as the Hotel for Pampered Felines, this resort offers cage-free living. With a playground, group play, satellite television, music, and airport pickup service, the Cat's Pyjamas is more like recess than boarding. Your cat may never miss you.

> www.pinkballoon.com/catspyjamas
> Toronto, Ontario
> (416) 876-MEOW

10. **ACADEMY OF CANINE BEHAVIOR**

Don't let the name fool you. This cattery has heated and air conditioned condos, a luxurious playroom, and animal behaviorists on hand to work with your troubled kitty. Set in lovely Bothell, Washington, the academy offers your feline all the creature comforts.

> www.aocb.com/cat_boarding.htm
> 4705 240th SE
> Bothell, WA 98041
> (425) 486-9567

Recommended Reading

Busch, Heather and Burton Silver. *Why Cats Paint: A Theory of Feline Aesthetics*. Berkeley, Calif.: Ten Speed Press, 1994.

Moore, Arden. *50 Simple Ways to Pamper Your Cat*. Pownal, Vt.: Storey Books, 2000.

Morris, Desmond. *Catwatching: Why Cats Purr and Everything Else You Ever Wanted to Know*. New York: Crown Publishing, 1986.

Pollard, Michael. *The Encyclopedia of the Cat*. New York: Barnes & Noble, 2002.

Spadafori, Gina and Paul D. Pion. *Cats for Dummies*. Foster City, Calif.: IDG Books, 2000.

Taylor, David. *You and Your Cat: A Complete Guide to the Health, Care, and Behavior of Cats*. New York: Alfred A. Knopf, 1986.

Index

About the Author

Award-winning writer Alexandra Powe Allred is the author of *Dogs' Most Wanted*™ and *Teaching Basic Obedience: Train the Owner, Train the Dog*, in addition to a variety of sports books (*Atta Girl! A Celebration of Women in Sport*). Powe Allred has been training animals (and their families) for more than twenty years and is the proud owner of a variety of animals, including dogs, horses, and goats. But it is her cats, Sooner and Benson, who run the farm. Powe Allred resides in Midlothian, Texas, with her husband, Robb, her three children, and her animals.